BRISTOL'S AUSTRALIAN PIONEER

The Story of Robert Bush and his
Bishop's Knoll WW1 Hospital

Chris Stephens

Bristol Books CIC, 1 Lyons Court, Long Ashton Business Park,
Yanley Lane, Long Ashton, Bristol BS41 9LB

Bristol's Australian Pioneer,
written and researched by Chris Stephens

Edited by Clive Burlton

Published by Bristol Books 2016

ISBN: 978-1-909446-06-9

Design: Joe Burt (joe@wildsparkdesign.com)

Printed by: Hobbs the Printers Ltd

A CIP record for this book is available from the British Library

MIX
Paper from
responsible sources
FSC® C020438
FSC
www.fsc.org

Bristol Books CIC is a not-for-profit Community Interest Company that publishes important and untold stories about lives, communities, places and events that have significance and interest in Bristol and the surrounding area.

ABOUT THE AUTHOR

Chris Stephens was born in 1942 and educated in London at Dulwich College and Guys Hospital Dental School. When he retired from academic dentistry in 2002, he was able to spend more time undertaking charitable work for the Woodland Trust and the Dry Stone Walling Association of Great Britain of which he had been Deputy Chairman. In 2002 he founded the SW England Branch of the Association.

His interest in local history arose through helping to rebuild the dry stone walls of Dolebury Warren Wood in Somerset owned by the Woodland Trust and this led to the publication of a book on the life of its flamboyant 18th century owner, the Reverend Dr Sedgwick Whalley. This second book came about in a similar way and again concerns the life a former owner of a property now in the care of the Woodland Trust. Chris is an Emeritus Professor of the University of Bristol and was awarded the OBE for services to dental education in 1999. He is an Honorary life member of the both the British and European Orthodontic Societies and a Fellow of the British Dental Association.

ABOUT THE WOODLAND TRUST

Ancient woods have been around for many centuries - long enough to develop into ecosystems that are rich, complex and irreplaceable. Over time humanity has nibbled away at the wildwood and only 2% of the UK is now covered with ancient woodland.

The Woodland Trust is the UK's largest woodland conservation charity. Founded in 1972, it was first to stand against the spiralling threats to our precious woods and trees, and remains at the forefront of the fight to protect, restore and create woodland.

Woods like Bishop's Knoll have important and fascinating histories. For example Joyden's Wood in Kent has Anglo-Saxon earthworks; Great Church Wood in Surrey contains a prehistoric field system and in the heart of Moat Wood in Sussex there is a medieval moat. In fact, nearly every piece of woodland is likely to contain something from the past.

If you love woods or are interested in their history, by joining the Woodland Trust you'll be directly helping to protect them, our wildlife and our heritage.

Visit woodlandtrust.org.uk/join

The Woodland Trust is a charity registered in England and Wales no.294344 and in Scotland no. SC038885.

TO TESSA AND JUNE

June Bush and Tessa Kerry granddaughters of Robert Edwin Bush
with his Knight of the Order of St John of Jerusalem medals.

Then none were for the party;
Then all were for the State;
Then the great man helped the poor,
And the poor man loved the great:

Thomas Macaulay *Lays of ancient Rome*, Horatius 32

ACKNOWLEDGEMENTS

Many people have been of great and generous assistance in the construction of this account. First I should mention Tessa Kerry and her cousin June Bush who allowed me access to family documents in their possession. David Collins gave me assistance in completing the family history of the Bush family. Then I must thank Roger Gibbons, Archivist of the Gloucestershire County Cricket Club and Professor Tony Barker of the University of Australia who has made a study of the early days of cricket there. The Australian War Memorial and its excellent website have been extremely useful and I must particularly thank Diana Rutherford Curator, Military Heraldry and Technology section for her diligent work on my specific questions.

The J.S Battye Library of Western Australia, the staff of the Bristol Record Office, and Dawn Dyer of the Bristol Reference Library have all been a valuable source of information and assistance as have Julie Doherty of the Avon Wildlife Trust, Jenny Weeks of the Stoke Bishop Local History Group, Dr C.S Knighton, the Archivist of Clifton College, Charles Booth of the University of the West of England and Nurse Margaret Slade. Finally there is Bev Knott, leader of the Friends of Bishop's Knoll Wood, without whom this account would never have been written.

INTRODUCTION

THOSE OF US old enough to do so, will remember the great reluctance, if not blank refusal, of our grandfathers and great uncles to talk about their experiences in the Great War. It is difficult in these days of full media coverage to understand why, but the British public had been largely protected from the horrors of mechanised warfare and those who had experienced it had no common ground to discuss them. Further, many of those who were fortunate enough to have returned unscathed were mentally scarred and many felt guilty that they had survived. It is clear though that while soldiers would not talk to civilians about the War, they clearly did amongst themselves while recovering in Bishop's Knoll hospital.

One can only marvel at the energy, strength of character and cheerfulness of all concerned, both patients and staff, as well as the generosity of Mr and Mrs Bush and of the people of Bristol who supported the voluntary First World War hospitals in the years before the Welfare State.

It is my good fortune that Robert Edwin Bush was a keen photographer from an early age and may indeed have been a member of the Bristol and West of England Photographic Society which was formed in 1856. As a result there is an unusually large number of photographs available to bring his story, and that of the hospital to life. Many of these are contained in two large scrapbooks now deposited with the Bristol Reference Library.

While a great deal has been written about the carnage and sacrifice of the First World War, less has been said about the fortitude and the unity of purpose of the troops and general population. It is hoped that this account covers both, if only in a small way.

CHAPTER 1

A BRIEF HISTORY OF BISHOP'S KNOLL

After the time of the Norman Conquest much of the land north of Bristol belonged to Geoffrey de Montbray the Bishop of Coutances in France. He was more knight than prelate and had been at the Battle of Hastings where he exhorted the Normans to victory. At William's coronation it was he, as one of two bishops, who called upon the congregation in Westminster Abbey to acclaim their duke as king.[1] De Montbray's reward was a mighty fief scattered over twelve English counties. Some years later Wulfstan, Bishop of Worcester, who outlived de Monbray and who was the only English-born bishop to retain his diocese for any significant time after the Conquest, recovered some of these lands for the see of Worcester. Wulstan then rebuilt the church of Westbury (on Trym), making it dependent on the cathedral monastery of Worcester.[2]

Two hundred years later, Bishop Godfrey Giffard (1268-1302) created a deer park within this holding north-west of Bristol known as the "wood of Snede", seemingly without the permission of the King. There seems to have been no royal retribution for this, perhaps because Henry III was engaged in the baronial wars at this time and died the following year. In May 1580 after the dissolution of the monasteries, the Manors of Clifton, Westbury, Snede Park and Henbury were sold by Henry VIII to Sir Ralph Sadleir for 1000 marks.[3] Ralph, a former secretary to Thomas Cromwell, was in high favour at this time and in accordance with Henry's Will, was one of the council of twelve appointed to assist the sixteen executors to whom was entrusted the government of the kingdom after his death and the guardianship of the young King Edward VI.

In September 1547 at the Battle of Pinkie Cleugh, Sadleir showed great bravery in assisting the Earl of Hertford in repelling the Scots and was made knight banneret on the field, a position above a knight and next to a baron.[4] Shortly afterwards he was granted the Manor of Stoke Bishop and the Blaise Castle estates for his services by the young Edward VI. Sadleir later served Elizabeth as the custodian of Mary Queen of Scots at Fotheringay Castle. By the time he died in 1587, the year of her execution, he was known as the richest commoner in England.

After his death his lands in Clifton stayed in the Sadleir family until they were sold by his grandson in 1659 to Joseph Jackson, a wealthy merchant, who had been both Sheriff and Mayor of Bristol as well as Master of the Society of Merchant Venturers.[5] When the last of the Jacksons died in 1811 the Sneyd Park estate passed to the Martin family.[6] By this time Rudder describes what had been parkland as long since turned into farms.[7] Bristol was now a fast growing city and a descendant, James Martin, wished to realise the estate's potential as prime development land. However legal restrictions in the Jackson Will prevented the break up of the Sneyd Park Estate and required a private members bill to set these aside – the Martin's Estate Act – passed in 1853. In April 1855 William Baker a builder of Canon's Marsh Bristol,[8] who had been a powerful influence in promoting the Act, purchased part of the Sneyd Park Estate from James Martin in order to build "superior residences" on this picturesque site.[9] This he carried out over the next 30 years.

The building of the Knoll (later known as Bishop's Knoll)

One report says the house was completed by 1870 and was first occupied by the builder,[10] but a detail above the windows on the front of the house contains the letters "HB" and "1861" suggesting it was completed much earlier. HB are thought to be the initials of the builder's wife Hester Baker.

When William died in March 1870 the house was put up for auction and on April 14th 1870 was sold to Peter Dowling Prankerd (Prankard). It was then described as having 14 bedrooms, central heating, a 42 foot billiard room and a tower room with a rooftop belvedere. The Bishop's Knoll Lodge today bears a stone plaque high up on its north gable carrying the inscription "PDP 1876" which suggests that the Lodge was built for its new owner.

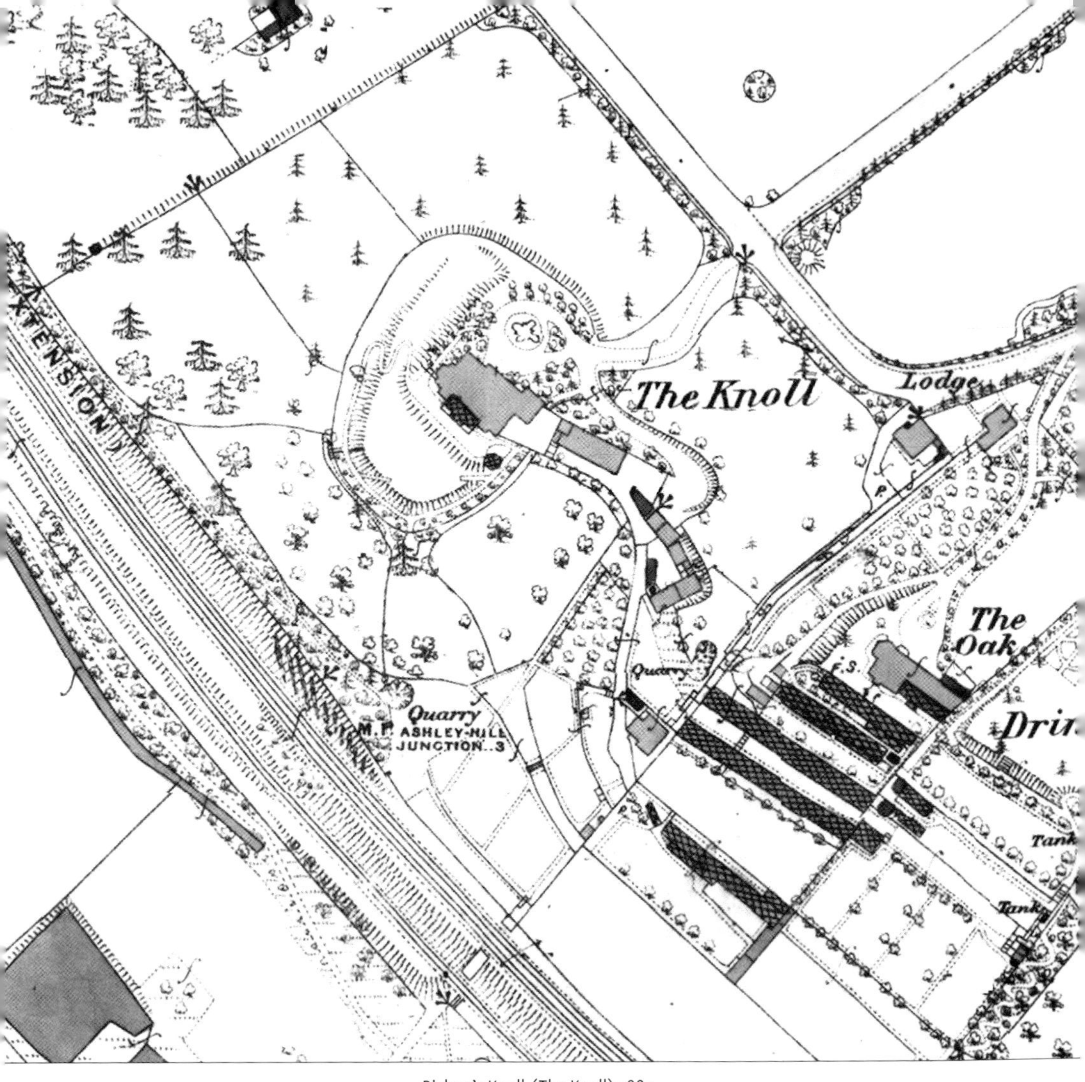

Bishop's Knoll (The Knoll) 1880.

Prankerd was born in Langport, Somerset but emigrated to Adelaide South Australia in 1839 where he became a successful Land Agent. He and his wife Lucy Amelia returned to England in 1872, soon after the birth of their son Percy J Prankerd (1870- 1908). [11,12]

Peter Dowling Prankerd died aged 83 in 1902 and probate was given to his two sons of whom one, Percy John Prankerd, had been a contemporary of Robert Edwin Bush at Clifton College. Percy Prankerd had left Bristol in 1877 to go to Oxford and by 1902 was a barrister living in London, but he died in Tonbridge Wells only six years later in 1908.[13] It was around this time that the house and its garden were bought by Robert Edwin Bush who then lived there until his death in 1939.

Bishop's Knoll from the North East before WW1.

Bishop's Knoll from the NW before WW1.

CHAPTER 2

ROBERT EDWIN BUSH AND HIS FAMILY

THE BUSH FAMILY can trace its ancestry back for nearly 1000 years and has been prominent in Gloucestershire for more than four hundred years. Paul Bushe was consecrated as the first Bishop of Bristol by Henry VIII at Hampton Court on June 25, 1542.[14] His tomb is still located in the north choir aisle of the Cathedral. In 1763 his descendant George Bush (1729-1801) went into partnership with William Elton, trading mainly in sugar and rum and so began a dynasty of Bristol merchants. Two generations later Robert Bush (1762-1829) became Master of the powerful Society of Merchant Venturers. He was by then a very wealthy and prominent merchant who in 1793 also started manufacturing pewter for a lucrative export trade, mainly to America.[15] In later life he bought Clifton Hill House, now a University Hall of Residence, where he died.[16] His Will at this time records him as holding shares in both the Bristol Iron Works and Bristol Docks Companies.[17] His second son (Robert 1809-1877) became a regular army officer who would see service in Tasmania. In 1843 while still serving there Robert married Emily Adria Griffith. Her

Major Robert Bush when a member of Clifton College Council (1860-1877).

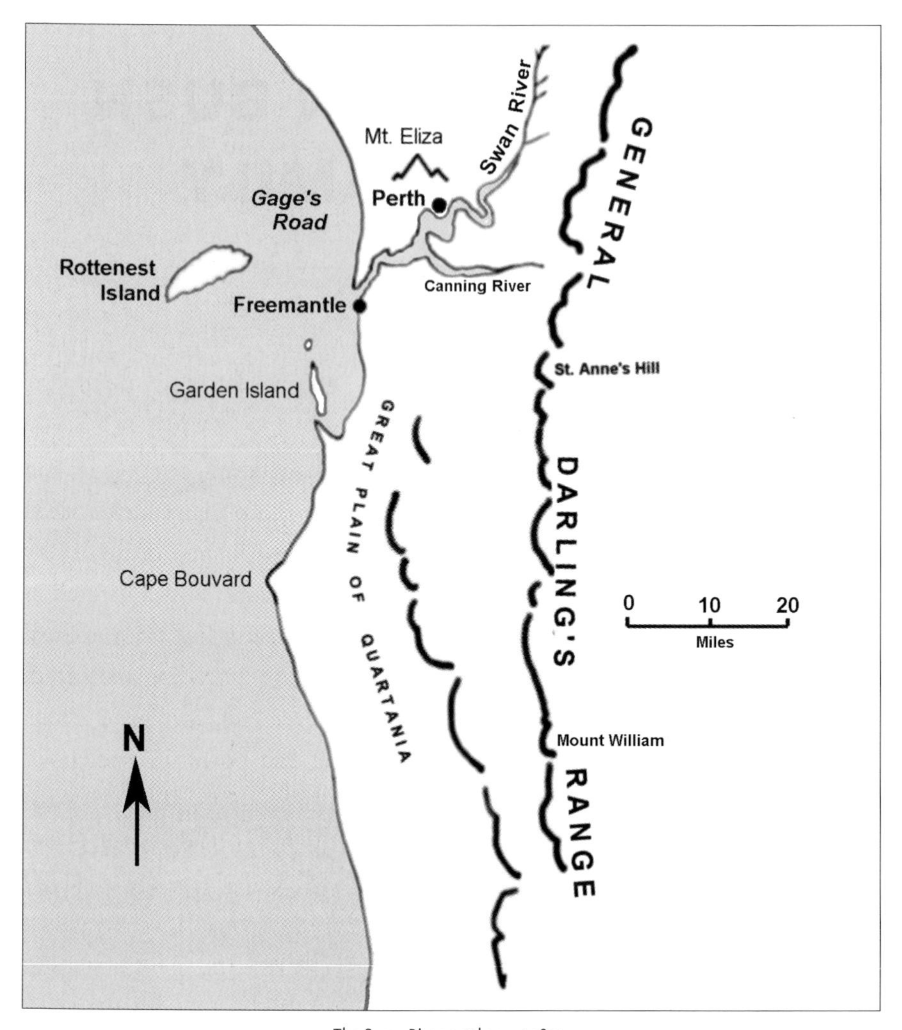

The Swan River settlement 1831.

father was his commanding officer, Lieutenant Colonel Griffith of the 96th Regiment of Foot, whose family came from Cheshunt in Hertfordshire.[18]

Robert and Emily would have six sons and five daughters. Their first son Henry Frederick was born in Tasmania in 1845. Robert then moved to Australia where he commanded a detachment of the 96th Regiment of Foot guarding the Swan River settlement. This outpost of the Empire had been established as a British colony in 1829 and in 1832 became the state of Western Australia, here Alfred (1847) and Mary Ann (1848) were born. The regiment then moved to

In the centre the Bush Warehouse in the 1920s.

Bengal where James Arthur (1850) was born.[19]

In 1851 Robert aged 42 retired from the army and returned to England with his wife, daughter and three sons. Perhaps this was because his eldest son aged six years was now approaching school age. The family lived first in Weston super Mare and then moved to Bristol.

At the annual meeting of the Bristol Anchor Society in 1858,[20] Mr Francis Henry FitzHardinge Berkeley, one of Bristol's two MPs, expressed his concern at Britain's unpreparedness for foreign invasion and contended that the youth of the country should be trained to bear arms.[21] This rapidly became a national movement and on May 12, 1859 the War Office sanctioned the formation of Volunteer Corps throughout the UK.[22] The following week the Bristol Volunteer Rifle Corps was formally established with the Mayor Mr J. Pool as Honorary Colonel. The Earl of Ducie, Lord Lieutenant of the County, declined to become its Lt Colonel, and so the retired Major Robert Bush senior was commissioned as its commanding officer.[23] The 1st (City of Bristol) Battalion comprised 10 companies of Volunteers and Robert served as its energetic Lt Colonel until 1865.[24,25] By 1871 the National Census records that his eldest son Henry was a volunteer Ensign in the force as well as a warehouse keeper, presumably in the family firm of merchants now based in Princes Street.

By 1871 Robert and his family were living in Clifton where they remained for the next 10 years. In the census of that year Robert is recorded as being

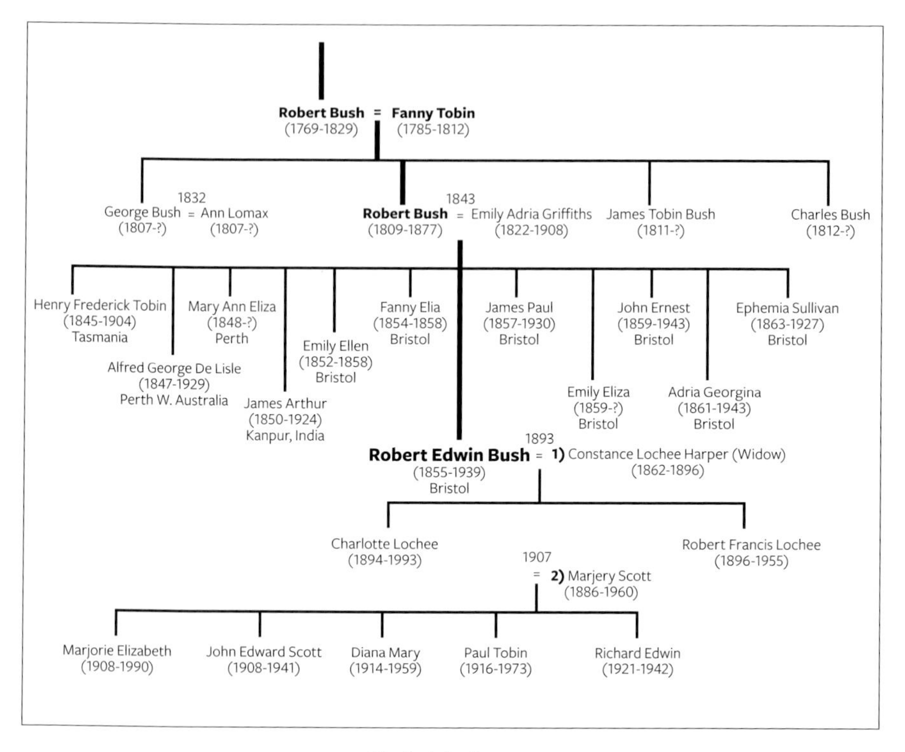

The Bush family tree.

a retired Major *and landowner* but by the time of his death in 1877 he also is described as warehouseman. It is clear that by this time he was part owner of Messrs Acraman, Bush, Castle and Company whose impressive warehouse in Princes Street Bristol, built in 1831,[26] now accommodates the Arnolfini Gallery.[27] In 1905 the ownership of the firm passed from their father to Robert's two sons James Bush and (Alfred) George De Lisle Bush. The company of J and R Bush Ltd. finally ceased trading in the 1960s.

Robert Edwin Bush (1855-1939)

Robert Edwin, the subject of this book, was born on October 11, 1855 in Redland Bristol.[28] Ten years later he entered Clifton College, the year in which his eldest brother Alfred George De Lisle Bush left. His elder brother James Arthur was already a pupil there and they would later be joined by their brothers James Paul Bush, who would go on to study medicine and become a surgeon at the Bristol Royal Infirmary, and John Ernest who would join the

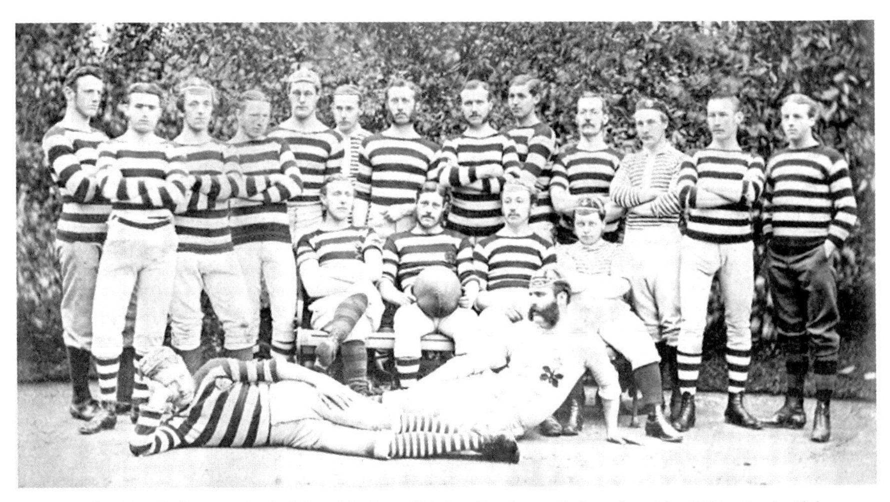

In the 1875-1876 season both Robert Edwin and his brother James Arthur played for Clifton Rugby Club (James Arthur also played for the Southern England team which explains his England shirt).

army and rise to the rank of Brigadier General. Their attendance at Clifton was hardly surprising since their father had joined the new College's Council in September 1860 shortly after its foundation,[29] and would remain on it until his death in 1877.[30,31]

All four Bush boys played rugby for their school and for the newly formed Clifton Rugby Club.[32] It is noteworthy that in the first match between the Club and the College held on 12th December 1874, James Arthur Bush played for the club, while his younger brother Robert Edwin played for the College! [33]

Alfred George, James Arthur and Robert Edwin also played cricket for their school and Robert and Alfred both captained the first XI. Robert Edwin Bush was one the school's most successful captains (1874-5). He scored 116 against Liverpool Blue Coat School in 1874 and 111 against Sherborne the following year and figured in Lillywhite's Annual as the best public schoolboy cricketer of the year.[34,35]

Robert Edwin Bush
County Cricket Statistics

Right handed bat / occasional wicket keeper

1st Class Matches played	17
Runs scored	221
Batting average	9.60
Hundreds/fifties	None
Highest score	42
Balls bowled	None
Catches /stumpings	6/0

Robert Edwin Bush and his friend Tom Lodge. The photographer Marcus Guttenberg had practised as a daguerreotypist in Hungary and moved to Bristol in 1871, six years before Bush left for Australia.

Robert Edwin left Clifton College in July 1875 but was by then already playing county cricket for Gloucestershire, many of whose early matches between August 1874 and June 1877 were played on the College ground. It is interesting to surmise that during one of these county matches Bush would have been observed by the young Douglas, later Field Marshal Lord Haig (1861-1928).[36] In the Gloucestershire County side Bush played alongside the greatest cricketer of all time – W.G. Grace.[37,38] Archibald Powell writing in the Bristol Evening World in 1933 recorded that Mr Bush "...never reproduced his brilliant school form, although 'W. G.' several times opened the innings with him by way of encouragement".[39]

Robert's elder brother James Arthur Bush, was the wicket keeper for Gloucestershire at this time and was W.G. Grace's best man when Grace married in October 1873. James toured in Australia later that year with "W. G. Grace's XI" which trip also served as the Graces' honeymoon![40]

Australian Adventures

One of Robert's closest friends at Clifton was Thomas Soutter Lodge from Highgate London who was two years his senior.[41] On leaving school Thomas had gone to Norfolk to learn farming. They obviously kept in touch as it was on Bush's suggestion that the two decided to try their luck in Western Australia. His parents still had contacts there and had provided Robert Edwin with introductions to a number of settlers.[42]

In late November 1877, only four months after his father died,[43] Robert

This was not the ship Robert sailed in but a replacement of the same name and design, built in 1887 after the original ship was wrecked shortly after Bush's arrival in Australia.

Edwin and his companion set out for Australia. They and the other 10 first class passengers and 85 emigrants sailed from Gravesend on December 15, 1877 on board the 658 ton barque *Lady Elizabeth*, with its crew of 20 captained by Thomas Scott.

Bush kept a detailed journal of his voyage which included a daily record of the ship's position, daily temperatures and barometric pressure.[44] His entries show him to be an observant, well informed and sensitive young man.

> Dec. 30. (off Madeira). Did a lot of reading today at Milton, read several books of Paradise Lost, and as I came across pieces I had learnt for old Brown I began to think of dear old Clifton and all its associations, how one does think at sea. No service today as it was too rough. A very beautiful sunset, the water is now a deep dark blue, can now really be called the "deep blue sea". A little cold, we have had today a heavy sea, tacked several times today. Fresh breeze and fine weather.

> Dec. 31. The last day of another year, a year full of events for me, how all the incidents of the past twelve months rush on one. A dead calm not a breath of

wind. Looked over my photos, this I always do on great days, Sundays etc. Tom and self ate some plum pudding, out of his hat box, where we kept it under lock and key only one knife between us, like two greedy schoolboys, it's first class. We drank Emmie's and John's health in some sherry, the first we have opened, that's not bad at all. We sang after dinner, and also on deck after tea, very jolly. After doing some writing went up on deck about 11 p.m. where we (Mrs Paine, Mrs Jubb and the Doctor) had a rare spree, dancing, tug of war, and other jokes. All the rest of the people were asleep, and at 12 midnight, I rang the old year out, and the new year in, on the ship's bell. I don't think the Captain liked it.

Jan. 17. Had my usual bath at 6 a.m. – breakfast in bed. I got up about noon, on hearing look out cry "Homeward bound on the weather bow." We signalled her, but as we had no book of signals, we could not tell her we wanted to send letters. Fancy a decent ship not having such a book, she was only about two and a half miles away. I finished the book Toffie Lodge gave me "Five years of penal servitude" a very amusing and instructive book. It has been pretty warm today, but I have not felt it in the slightest degree too warm for me as yet. Mrs King and Mrs Jubb both continue to be ill every day. A slight shower this evening. Tom Lodge has been fishing for two days, and has caught nothing.

Jan. 24. Fine day, during which we had several very heavy squalls. We are now out of the tropics again, having been nineteen days in them, during which time I have been greatly surprised by not experiencing hotter weather than we have done. The grub is still very bad, Tom Lodge will starve when our private stock runs out. What a pity it is one cannot put down in one's log everything that happens. I could have written a good deal on something that occurred today. How one on board ship finds out the good and bad points of one another's character – if it be selfishness, it shows itself first, being in a place where there are so many inconveniences and discomforts, that every action, whether selfish or not so, it is immediately discovered. Everything is so circumscribed, that nothing escapes the notice of one's fellow passengers, very little escapes their ears, and you may be sure, where there is so little to do, scandals are rife. This ship is no exception to the general rule in this respect, but what's the odds, so long as you are happy. Fleas walked off with about two pounds of my flesh last night, which was not considerate of them, seeing how little I have on my bones.

Feb. 12. A fine day, off the Cape of Good Hope, A large number of Albatross swimming about all around us, we soon had hooks baited with pork out, and in about one hour we caught nine of them, one of which measured thirteen feet from tip to tip of wing - they all measured over ten feet they looked quite small in the water, but when we got them on deck they were bigger than swans in the body. A couple of hours after they had been flying about, several of the small bones in their wings had been converted into pipe stems, and already under way. Some of the superstitious sailors said we should have a gale for killing them, and so we had, for about 8 p.m. a breeze sprang up, which soon freshened into a stiff gale, but as we could keep our course, I did not mind it. Had the doctor and first mate in my cabin at night, gave them some grog. It is a lovely night, with a good moon.

Feb. 26. A dull day, fine breeze and still going as we could wish. It was found out today that somebody had broken into the stores, so there was a grand search, and in one of the single emigrants (men) mattresses was found about 60 Ibs. of flour. He will get about six months when he lands; he is a London fellow, a bad lot. A lot of eau-de-cologne had also been taken from a case. They had broken through a cupboard, and if a track of flour had not been left, probably nothing would have been found out about it. This caused a great deal of excitement. In the afternoon, Mrs Paine and myself cut out a coat for myself, and I washed the lining of it. I stayed up on deck very late, did some steering from 10 to 12 and had some grog with the first mate at midnight, it was very cold on deck.

Mar. 10. A dull day. but a fine afternoon. Service on poop only a short one had a row with the doctor at breakfast, the poor old black cook died this morning, about 6 a.m. and this was the occasion of my row with the doctor for the brute, when he was called this morning, and told the poor old man was dying, he did not go directly, but has water brought, and washed, and sent for a plateful of bread and butter and ate it before he went, and then the poor old fellow was dead. I can tell you this riled me and I could not contain myself; he deserved all I said to him and I did not spare him, I was so wild with him. The skipper told me, after breakfast, that he would like to see him have a jolly good cow-hiding, when he got ashore.

Mar. 11. Death on board ship makes one think. I am very glad it was Sunday. Like many men before him he was more honoured in his death than in his life. All day he lay on the foredeck with the Union Jack draped over his stiff, cold form. I felt almost glad for the poor old man, when at four bells in the afternoon, we consigned his mortal remains to the deep, deep blue sea, for he was terribly teased on board and I don't suppose his life had ever been happy.

The *Lady Elizabeth* docked in Freemantle at the mouth of the Swan River on March 12, 1878 after a voyage of 112 days. The following day Bush travelled the nine miles into Perth and within five days had met most of the significant local inhabitants including Mrs Lochée and her children with whom he had tea before going to the cathedral. He described the family as all being "very nice indeed" and would later marry the widowed Constance Lochée.

McDonald states that soon after arriving at Freemantle, Bush went jackerooing and his "ambitions were roused to become one of the gentry",[45] however Bush's own Log shows there was no time for him to do so. In fact the period from March 12 to April 2, 1878 was entirely taken up with establishing local contacts including Sir George and Lady Leake, E.W Landor, J Forrest, Mrs Shenton and "Bowra and Buck two old 96th men".

Expedition 1

On April 2nd 1878 Bush and Lodge then sailed on north a further 200 miles to Geraldton arriving there on 13th.[46] On May 9, 1878, accompanied by Thomas Soutter Lodge,[47] Hepburn Gales, John Giles and A. du Boulay, Bush set out into the interior to look for gold.[48] Bush kept a hand written journal, which seems to have been typed up some years later, perhaps by his second wife.

This first trip into the interior was a steep learning curve for Bush for it was

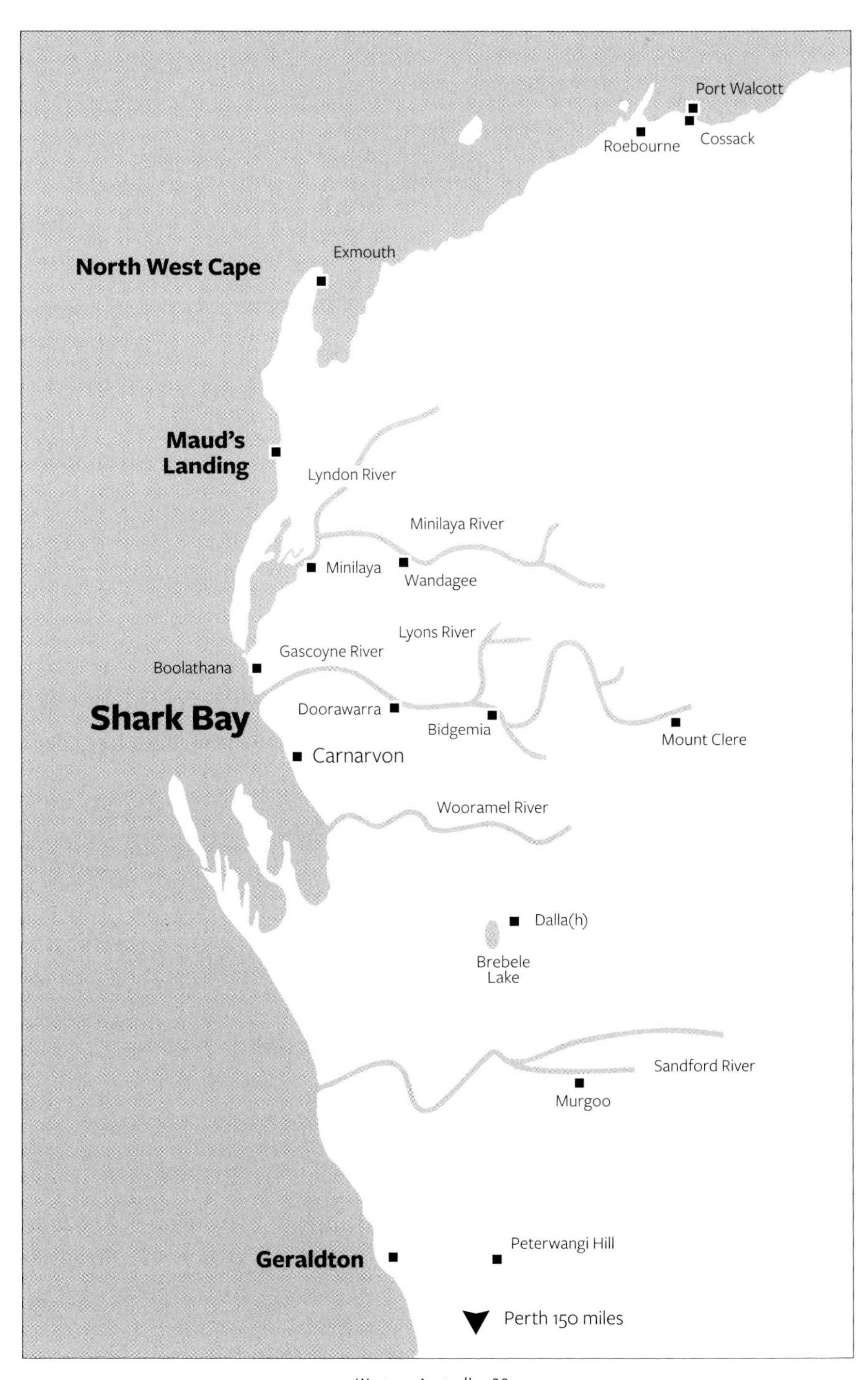

Western Australia 1880.

a very rough, waterless country but his journal shows his keenness to learn. The party arrived at Minnenooka the first evening. Owing to the rough terrain they soon found the trap they had taken unsatisfactory. On several days they wasted much time and effort tracking their horses which had wandered off during the night. Cooking was taken in turn and Bush seems to have been surprised by his success in making his first damper and jam tarts using salt pork fat. However their attempts at living off the land were hopeless; several attempts to shoot kangaroo and emu were unsuccessful. At Oolagong, which was Bell's cattle station they acquired a "black fellow and his woman" to help them but this did not seem to improve matters. Catherine Cameron, who also had access to Tom Lodge's journal reported that later, with food shortage becoming serious, they found a flock of the Lacy brothers' sheep and du Boulay persuaded the shepherd to let them have one which enabled them to eat well on their return journey to Geraldton.[49] Bush's log does not record this but later mentions dining off "very maggoty mutton"!

Their prospecting at Peterwangi resulted only in a little gold dust and they decided to go on to Mullewa. There they worked on a quartz reef using explosive charges but again met with no success. They finally arrived back at Geraldton on May 26, with their horses "quite done up", very thankful to return to comfortable beds and good food.

Expedition 2

Bush's next recorded trip was north to Cossack and Roebourne to investigate the commercial prospects of pearl fishing. He and Tom Lodge set sail on August 16, 1878 on the 65 ton Schooner *Rosette*, finally boarding after a "row with the skipper"! On board the following day he met Dr Bompas from Bristol who had been a house surgeon at the Bristol Infirmary where Bush's younger brother James Paul Bush was now working. Cossack was at the head of a tidal creek with a 16 foot tide and the *Rosette* arrived on August 27 after a long pull against the tide. Bush describes the town as a rum hole consisting of about 20 wooden houses "two of which have the impudence to call themselves hotels"! On the 28th Bush reports

Summary of Bush's Expeditions: March 1878 - March 1880

Dates	Route	Accompanied by
March 12, 1878	Arrived Freemantle then on to Geraldton arriving 13th April	Thomas Lodge
May 9-26, 1878	Expedition to Peterwangi in search of gold then Peterwangi to Mullewa	Thomas Lodge, Hepburn Gale, A du Boulay, John Giles
June?-26, 1878	To the mouth of the Murchison River	Unknown
August 16 - Sept 26, 1878	By boat 1500 km north to Roebourne and Cossack, then back to Freemantle	Thomas Lodge
September 26 - October 5, 1878	Back to Geraldton	Thomas Lodge
November 1878- May 1879	Set out in the SS *Rob Roy* "for the NW". Probably worked as jackeroo at Warra Warra, owned by the Lacy brothers or Yuin owner Frank Wittenoon or Murgo.[50]	
May 1879 – Sept 1979	Port Walcott to Mauritius on Schooner *Janet*	On his own except for crew
October 14, 1879 – March 7, 1880	Exploring N of the Gascoyne River. Arrived back 2 months overdue.	The Lacys, Frank Wittenoon, Walter Howard, Edward Sewell, Aborigines Pat and Cranky Billy
April 1880	Applies for leases in the Upper Gascoyne	

"After dinner (think this means lunch), as we were sitting in one of the rooms, there was a row between some of these pearlers, and one of them was shot in the shoulder with a revolver (some said it was an accident but that is bosh), it did not seem very unusual, for in a few minutes the event seems to have been forgotten. They are a lawless set up here, most of them drunk and always fighting, the scum of the Colonies, and that is saying a good deal."

Perhaps because of this event at 4 p.m. the same day the two companions set out in a trap for Roebourne 25 miles away which they found to be very much the same sort of place but it was also the home of Dr Bompas who they had met on the boat. They visited him the following day and found the house very comfortable. They were invited to stay there and met the Resident Magistrate Mr Sholl who in due course would prove to be a relative of Bush's second wife Marjery Scott.[51]

Over the next few days they experienced more fights, a "dead Corroborie",[52] a native riot, and a war dance. Bush was invited to see the Pyramid sheep station by one of its co-owners Mr Grant. This was about 30 miles from Roebourne and Bush spent a day looking round it and found it to be the best he had seen in the colony to date.

On September 6 Bush called on the Resident to pay his respects and the following day reboarded the *Rossette*. Three weeks later after a passage of fearful weather the two men finally arrived thankfully in Perth.

Expedition 3

In May 1879 Bush made the voyage from Port Walcott to Mauritius in the Indian Ocean, then under British rule, in the belief that there was an opportunity to export horses there as the climate in Mauritius was unsuitable for breeding them. He was responsible for looking after the horses under a charter arrangement for some of the north west settlers. Only five of the horses belonged to Bush. The 211 ton *Janet*, was fitted out to take 65 horses but Bush's log says they did not take the full number. As the other horses belonged to the Pyramid sheep station the idea may have arisen during Bush's visit to Cossack the previous year. Port Walcott was immediately adjacent to Cossack and was the main export port for the sheep stations of that region.[53]

Bush who had again been staying with Dr Bompas rose before daylight on May 6 and with two others drove the horses down to the shipping stockyard. They loaded them on the following day when Bush observed:

> "Let it be understood they are not like the horses that are shipped at home, well broken in and handled, but many of them have only seen human beings

> once or twice, they having always roamed at will, over some of the immense runs up here, so you can imagine it is no play shipping the brutes, and whilst they are being slung etc. you might see as fair kicking and bucking, combined with snorting and squealing, as one could wish".

Bush alone was responsible for looking after them during the 25 day voyage which was tougher than he expected. After a week of bad weather his log records

> "After breakfast, I had a regular cleaning up, the horses having been on board a week now. It was fearful hard work, and the heat and stench down in the hold, nearly knocked me up, some of the horses were very wild and I had the greatest difficulty in digging the manure from their hind feet. This has to be done as all the manure accumulates under their hind feet, thus raising the horse up to a foot or eighteen inches . I was at work with them from 6.00 a.m. to 1.00 p.m. and when I came up, was glad enough to have a pretty stiff glass of rum, which the Captain advised me to take".

As in his first log written on his voyage from England, Bush gives the latitude and longitude at the end of each entry. They also had 21 sheep aboard and when the captain decided to kill a sheep, neither the cook nor the crew of six Malays knew how to kill it so Bush had to offer to do the job. There was a general shortage of water on board and because of this some horses grew weak and began to collapse in their stalls and this meant Bush had to go round them twice in the evening to attend to them. After some very rough weather and extreme shortage of food, the schooner delivered its passengers and cargo safely to Port Louis on June 4, 1879.

On arrival in Mauritius Bush found himself welcome in what was a mainly French society. He took the opportunity to see two operas performed by a French Company; 'La Juine' (knowing of Bush's poor handwriting this was probably "La Juive" by Fromental Halévy).

> "The singing was pretty good, but I must say that I scarcely saw a good looking woman, either on the stage or as a spectator. Being French however they had got themselves up very well, which goes a long way."

Four days later he saw Il Trovatore which he described as being "not bad"

There was a small British garrison on the island and Bush enjoyed seeing a cricket match played between the Mauritus Club and the "88th". However the sales of horses did not go well and Bush only made $730 for his five horses which barely covered his costs. After a return journey marred by severe storms and illness he arrived back in Freemantle on July 15 and went ashore in the Police Boat. He immediately dined at Caesars, his favourite haunt, and called on Miss Kate Scott. He then drove to Perth and during the next few days his journal records visiting the Lochées, Mrs Mason, the James, Lady Leake, Mrs Howe, Mrs Jubb, Father Gilroy, F. Smyth and the Forrests. Other contacts were Ned Shenton and Bob Palmer and Tom Lodge, who he telegraphed as he was probably still in the Roebourne area. The journal ends on July 21, 1879.

Expedition 4

It is not clear what Bush did during August and September but on October 14, 1879 he and his new companions Walter Howard and Edward Sewell set out to explore north of the Gasgoyne River. This was not the first expedition there had been into the Gascoyne area but very little was known about it apart from the coastal area. In the Spring of 1858 Francis Thomas Gregory, the Government Surveyor, had set out from Perth with a group funded by Walter Padbury and others, returning three months later.[54,55] The Government Surveyor's report questioned the reliability of the seasons and this would prove to be a problem for Bush in later years, but it seems likely that the report was unknown to him at this time, having remained in the surveyor's office.

As the companions intended to spend no more than three months they took no change of horses which would prove to be a problem. They started out from Mungarra station (this appears as Numgrra in the typed version of his log) and after 32 miles reached Warra Warra station owned by the Lacy brothers. Ted Lacy had just returned from England and they toasted his return in rum and listened to his news. After three more days, and having travelled just under 120 miles, they had reached Murgoo. This was Frank and Edward Wittenoon's new sheep station where they waited for charts to arrive from Champion Bay about 230 miles to the west. While they did so they drew up an agreement as to how they would divide up the land they found which clearly shows that Bush had now decided his future lay in sheep farming.

On October 23 the party set out to explore. It now consisted of Walter Howard, Edward Sewell, Bush and two natives Pat and Sankey, with eight horses and three packs of ration of 170 lb each plus two revolvers and two other guns. They crossed the Sanford River and headed NNW for the Murchison River. This time they were more skilled at living off the land, shooting Duck, Teal, Turkey, Pigeon, Cockatoo and small rock kangaroo but shortage of water was a persistent problem. Though their route is not clear Cameron believes they travelled via Breberle Lake. They reached the Woomerel River on October 24, and followed it downstream. Eight days later they met a group of more than 100 natives "all painted up and heavily armed" but found them friendly and good natured. They followed the river almost to the coast and then turned WNW and aimed for the Gascoyne River. Finally after a day and a half without water they reached the mouth of the Gascoyne and Finnerty's Sheep Station on November 6. Here they were regaled with accounts of the hostility of natives and Bush commented:

> "I am afraid they overestimate the danger, but there is no doubt there has been a good deal of shooting about here".

They now travelled a further 15 miles north and reached Brockman's Boolathana Station. Charles Brockman had explored the area in 1872 and established the Boolathana Station fifty miles from the mouth of the Gascoyne the following year.

Bush says

> "Stayed with Brockman found him a very nice fellow but living very rough indeed, he made us quite at home. His accounts of the natives are rather reassuring, although some have had to be shot here. He knows how to manage them."

He and Brockman would remain lifelong friends.

Three days later on November 9 the explorers pressed on up the coast skirting the south end of Lake Macleod. For several days they had to manage without fresh water but oysters were on the menu and allowed them to survive, Edward Sewell nearly swallowing a large pearl! On November 18, the 36th day of their trip, they finally found a break in the coastal reef which they had been following for more than 100 miles. They thought this might be made into a suitable harbour and named it Maud's Landing. Turning south they made their way slowly back to Brockman's, managing about 25 miles a day but suffering even worse shortages of water. On November 29, Bush unwisely drank water which the horses would not touch and was soon suffering from dysentery.

When they finally arrived back at Boolathana Bush was much worse. The following day he was visited by a deputation of natives who brought their doctor to see him, believing he had been "buleed" (poisoned) by other natives. Bush describes how the doctor

> "...set to work to make me well, by pressing with great solemnity on my stomach, for about quarter of an hour, with both his hands, and then told me that I should be all right by night, I have no doubt that he did me as much good as many a soft footed practitioner at home would have done. It was a funny sight, to these black fellows round me, all painted up, and with all their arms and feathers. They all went in mourning for me, that is, they had blackened with charcoal all round their eyes. They used to come every day, and ask how I was, whether I was 'little bit mendic' or 'gwoba' or 'big fellow mendic' that is 'little bit ill' or 'all right' or 'big fellow ill."

Bush remained at Boolathana still suffering from dysentery and vomiting while the other two headed north to explore some of the country they had missed. By Christmas Day Bush was beginning to recover but the others had not returned and he was getting worried. With still no news, on January 6 he decided to go out with "a young fellow called Walter Ridley" a pack horse and a native and try and find them though they realised this was in the height of summer and might mean travelling 60 or 70 miles without water. On January 9th they found Howard and Sewell's tracks and learnt from a native that their friends were now returning along their outward route. While Bush was writing a letter for the man to take to them they saw their dust cloud approaching. Bush says

> "When they came up to us, they did look bad. Howard was ill and they had been starving for more or less three weeks . They had lost one horse and all the other horses looked terribly bad.

Giving their companions the last of their water Bush and Ridley set out to try and recover the kit that had been dumped 60 miles back and find the missing horse. They found the horse dead but recovered the saddle and other discarded items and then followed the other party southward arriving back at Brockman's on January 16.

They agreed that returning by the coast road was impossible so accepted the extra 200-300 miles going up the Gascoyne River and then across to the Murchison which they reached on February 16. On their way they noted that they had passed through some very good country. They finally arrived back at Murgoo on February 21, 1880 after a journey of 146 days and 1885 miles. They had experienced temperatures of up to 110° F during the hottest summer then on record and had suffered extreme shortages of water. This, their failure to bring spare horses, and the unwise excursion of Howard and Sewell, meant that their trip took much longer than they intended and they found a Government organised search party was about to set out to try and find them.

A month later in April 1880 Bush bought the first of his pastoral leases on the banks of the Gascoyne 100 miles east of Carnarvon at a place called Pindandoora. Bush renamed this "Lower Clifton Downs". One account describes his initial homestead as "a little paper bark hut on the banks of the Gascoyne".[56] According to several sources the local aborigines referred to the area as Bidjiia Mia meaning place of the Bidjie grub, and it is now known as Bidgemia.[57] His earlier companion Walter Howard acquired the adjacent lease further east along the river. A few weeks later Bush sent his first sheep up there in the care of Howard and Sewell while he set out to attempt to try to pioneer a coastal route which he might use in the future to export his stock; this he found but didn't subsequently use.

Ten years later Bush, now a rich man, was able to buy the 800,000 acre Mount Clere sheep station further up river to the east when it was put up for sale. The previous owner John Sydney Davis and his brother had been early settlers in the area and it was now supporting 20,000 sheep. Bush renamed

Believed to be the Bidgemia station after it was rebuilt by Robert Bush.

it "Upper Clifton Downs". Finally he acquired the Erraville Station from the Shaw brothers bringing his total holding to more than 2,000,000 acres in the east Gascoyne.

Until 1890 the colony only had an appointed Legislative Council under the control of a Governor. Early settlers in the territory had to provide amenities such as roads from their own resources, this despite paying rent to the Government; they felt they deserved something in return by way of police protection, a mail service and better local representation. In 1887 a local Upper Gascoyne Road Board had been set up by pastoralists to manage the 126 mile road joining Carnarvon on the coast to the junction of the Gascoyne and Lyons Rivers. The road connected seven sheep stations including those of Bush and his friend Walter Howard 26 miles further to the east. The group was vocal in expressing the views of the local Gascoyne pastoralists on the problems they were having with sheep and cattle stealing by the aborigines.[58] Bush became the Board's first chairman and as a result of its pressure on the Legislative Council a Post Office was set up at Bush's Bigemia Station in 1883. A local police station soon followed.

In the next few years there were increasing calls for a greater measure of self Government in the Territory. This culminated in the passing of the Western Australian Constitution Act of 1889, which established the State of Western Australia and gave the former territory an elected Legislative

Some of the local aborigines.

Assembly in addition to its Legislative Council. In 1890 Bush was appointed to the first Legislative Council of Western Australia and Robert Frederick Scholl became the first Gascoyne Representative of the Legislative Assembly.[59] By the mid 1890s Bush was a magistrate and President of the Northerners Association which he had founded. He resigned from the Legislative Council in 1894 when this too became an elected body but remained as an influential voice in Northwestern affairs.

An earlier rare and controversial critic of the pastoralists' treatment of aboriginals in the Northwest had been the Reverend J.B.Gribble, an Anglican missionary in the Gascoyne area. Cameron in her paper describes Gribble's arrival "to save heathen souls" as tearing the colony apart.[60] Bush was condemned by the missionary for his treatment of aboriginals and aired these complaints in Perth. These were refuted by Winthrop Hackett, (who like Bush he had been made a Vice President of Western Australia Cricket Association at its inaugural meeting in November 1885) who described Gribble as "a lying canting humbug."[61] In Bush's own writings there is nothing to suggest that he viewed the native Australians any differently from the majority of colonists at the time. His own accounts seem to suggest he viewed them with kindly amusement though he abhorred their treatment of women and their cannibalism.[62] In 1897 the new edition of G.W Rusden's *History of Australia* would describe Bush as "an authority on all native matters" who "employed a

Some of Bush's stock - date unknown.

Camel transport.

system of justice combined with firmness and kindness".

Bush, like others in the Upper Gascoyne, had been badly affected by the drought from 1889-1892 . He lost 54,000 sheep and this resulted in a debt of £50,000 owed to Dalgety and Company. Frederick Dalgety had founded his company in Melbourne in 1846. This originally supplied prospectors and sheep ranchers and advanced loans to ranchers in anticipation of their yearly wool sales. One report says that during the drought Bush was on the point of returning to England when Dalgety, by reducing the rate of interest on the loan from 8% to 7%, persuaded him to stay. His fortunes slowly recovered allowing the debt to be repaid. To improve his stock Bush now imported a valuable Vermont ram from America and several good ewes and rams from eastern Australia. The drought over, his combined estates soon supported 75,000 sheep. In 1890 he brought in a steam engine and hired an engineer to run it. This assisted in the shearing of his sheep and gave him powered wool presses. Soon his shearing shed was acknowledged as being the most modern in the colony.

During a second period of drought from 1895-1900, which is thought to have been the worst until recent times, sheep numbers in Australia overall were reduced by half and cattle by 40% (Australian Bureau of Statistics). But Bush was able to survive by bringing in Chinese workers from Singapore to dig wells and install wind pumps in his paddocks. He later claimed to have dug 100 wells and put in 1500 miles of fencing. When the rains finally returned Bush was once again able to restock and by 1905 was a very rich man with his 2,000,000 acres supporting 100,000 sheep, 10,000 cattle, 500 horses and 100 other animals (camels, mules etc.)

Bush married for the first time on January 28, 1883 in St. George's Cathedral Perth. His wife, the widow Constance Harper (née Lochée), was the third daughter of Mr Francis Lochée, for forty years the manager of the Western Australia Bank. Constance bore him two children but sadly she died in 1896. (See Appendix 1)

From what has been said already it will be obvious that Bush was a keen and able horseman. In this he took after his father who had been a founder member of the Western Australian Turf Association. In due course Robert Edwin would race many good horses and become a Vice President of the Gascoyne and Victoria Turf Clubs. There he would have met Dr Edward Scott, another JP, keen sportsman and later MP for Perth who would become Bush's father-in-law when he remarried in 1907. Bush remained an enthusiastic cricketer throughout his life and strongly supported the formation of the Western Australia Cricketing Association (WACA). This was finally established on November 12, 1885 by the merging of four major cricket clubs in Perth. Mr J.C.H. James was elected as President, with Bush as one of the 10 Vice-Presidents and the State Governor Frederick Broome as Patron. Initially they played on the Perth recreation ground but in 1889 a deputation approached Governor Broome just before he demitted office for a grant of land to establish a dedicated cricket ground. In 1938, during Bush's 13th and last visit to Perth, Sir George Kirwan, the President of the Legislative Association claimed at a reception in Bush's honour, that it was while Bush was staying with Broome in 1889 that he had persuaded the Governor to make the grant. Much work on the new site was necessary and it was not until 1893 that the ground was officially opened and the WACA ground is still in use today.

Several reports claim that Bush took part in the first inter colonial

This photograph appeared in Australia in 1933 as part of the special centenary edition of the Western Mail January 5, 1933 p.33. The caption reads *"Western Australian players and officials in the inter-colonial cricket match which was played against Victoria on April 1 and 3 1893."* Despite similar claims appearing elsewhere this was not the first inter-colonial match in Australia and Bush (back row extreme left) did not play in this game but was an umpire. (See text).

The same 1893 picture, far right, could be seen hanging on the wall of Bishop's Knoll's Billiard Room.

match between Western Australia and Victoria in 1893. However, according to Harte,[63] this had occurred more than 40 years earlier in a match between Victoria and Tasmania at Launceston on February 11, 1851, while the first encounter between mainland colonies was that of Victoria versus New South Wales at the Melbourne Cricket Club on March 26, 1865. However as far as the Western Australian press was concerned, the first such match was between Western Australia and Victoria and took place at the new ground in Perth on April 1 and April 3, 1893 with Bush in the Western Australian team, though it appears only as one of the two umpires! [64]

Robert Edwin Bush as Sheriff 1912.

Return to England

In 1905 Bush left Australia and returned to England, this may have been because the children of his first marriage were now of school age. He left William Scott to manage his Bidgemia (Lower Clifton Downs) sheep station[65]. Scott had been employed there soon after the turn of the century but would leave in 1912 to run his own station at Mooloo Downs. Bill Cream was then appointed in his place and in 1913 was reporting to Bush that 40,000 sheep were likely to be ready for shearing that year.[66]

Robert Edwin sailed from Hong Kong on board the SS *Empress of India* with his two children on the June 21, 1905 and arrived in Vancouver on the July 11, 1905 on route to England. Later that year he bought Bishop's Knoll. In March 1907 his friend, the surgeon and former Mayor of Perth Dr Edward Scott JP, sailed from Brisbane for England on the RMS *Orient* with this wife and second daughter Marjery. The family arrived in Plymouth on March 26, 1907. Dr Scott's son, James Edward, had preceded them three years before, entering Clifton College in September 1904. It seems that Dr Scott had come to England in 1901 both to visit his relatives in Devon and arrange for James to board there during Clifton College holidays. One assumes this choice of school for his son must have been influenced by Robert Edwin Bush.

On the May 27, 1907 Bush married Marjery Scott in the 50 year old St. Mary Magdalene Church, Stoke Bishop; she was then aged 21 and he 51. Almost certainly her brother John Edward would have attended the wedding as he was now a pupil at Clifton College and would become Head of School (Head Boy) in 1909 before going on to get a First Class Tripos at Cambridge. By this time it seems that their parents had decided to live permanently in England.[67]

Kensington Court Mansions.

By 1911 the two children of Bush's first marriage were at boarding school in Bristol. Charlotte who was 17 years old was a boarder at Mortimer House, a Private Boarding School in Clifton, and Robert Francis aged 15 was boarding at his father's old school of Clifton College. The rest of the Bush family were recorded in the National Census as living at Flat 25, Kensington Court Mansions, Kensington with this new wife, three year old daughter Marjory Elizabeth, two year old son John Edward and their three servants (a housemaid, parlour maid and nurse). The same Census has no entry for "The Knoll" as it was unoccupied but the Lodges were staffed. [68] (See Appendix 2) This suggests that Bush was already advising Dalgety Company Board which he would join as a Director the following year.[69] Frederick Dalgety had died in 1894 but Bush, who still owned his two sheep stations, would have provided the Company with up to date knowledge. His directorship, as well as a need to keep an eye on his two sheep stations, accounts for his several trips back to Australia after his return to England.

Having spent nearly 30 years in Australia, Bush was not as well known in his native Bristol as many of his peers. However in 1911, he was elected to the post of High Sheriff and his years in office did much to bring his public and commercial activities to the fore. He threw himself into civic life with gusto. Already a member of the influential Bristol Publicity Committee, Bush took on extra civic duties during the absence of Lord Mayor, Sir Frank Wills, when a party of businessmen and civic leaders visited Halifax in Nova Scotia to present a bronze relief from the citizens of Bristol to the citizens of Halifax as part of a ceremony to open a National Memorial Tower in the city on August 15, 1912.

Bush or his wife kept a scrapbook covering his year in office,[70] filled with photographs, press clippings and ephemera on a multitude of civic functions ranging from presenting awards at swimming galas to hosting the Canadian Premier and attending the opening of the King Edward VII Memorial Infirmary in Bristol on June 28, 1912.

An occasion he clearly relished was when he hosted a group of Australian boys that visited his Bishop's Knoll house as part of the Young Australia League's world tour. The League was formed in Perth, Western Australia in 1905 and the visit would have had particular poignancy for Bush. He was only too happy to help. [71]

The end of his year as Sheriff saw him take on another role – this time the Presidency of the Society of Bristolians in London. If Robert Edwin Bush was not as well-known at the start of his year of office – by the end of 1912, he was well and truly cemented as a key player in the Bristol establishment.

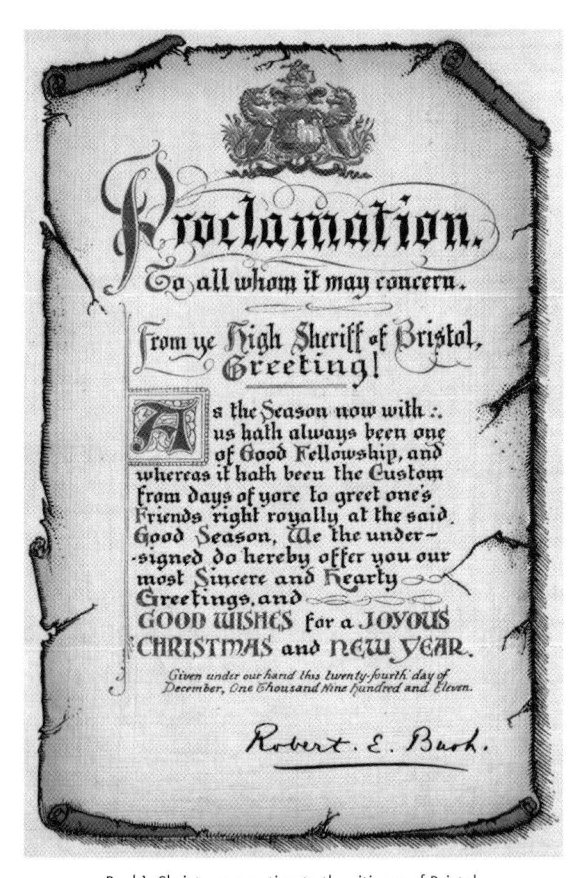

Proclamation.

To all whom it may concern.

From ye High Sheriff of Bristol,
Greeting!

As the Season now with us hath always been one of Good Fellowship, and whereas it hath been the Custom from days of yore to greet one's Friends right royally at the said Good Season, We the under-signed do hereby offer you our most Sincere and Hearty Greetings, and GOOD WISHES for a JOYOUS CHRISTMAS and NEW YEAR.

Given under our hand this twenty-fourth day of December, One Thousand Nine Hundred and Eleven.

Robert. E. Bush.

Bush's Christmas greeting to the citizens of Bristol.

CHAPTER 3

HOSPITAL SERVICES IN THE FIRST WORLD WAR

Military Hospital and Nursing Services 1908-1913

At the end of the Boer War, the British War Office was concerned that in the event of another war the medical and nursing services as they were then configured would be insufficient to cope with the probable demand. The peacetime needs of a standing army, in relation to medical care, were very small and specific, and to find thousands of trained and experienced personnel at very short notice without the expense of maintaining them in peacetime was a difficult problem to solve.

Although the Royal Army Medical Corps (RAMC) had been formed by Royal Warrant in 1898, once repatriated British wounded were the responsibility of home based charities and voluntary services, mainly provided by the Red Cross. This led Sir Richard Haldane, the then Secretary of State for War, to introduce a series of far reaching reforms between 1908 and 1912. Among these was the Territorial and Reserve Forces Act of 1907 which set up plans for co-operation between voluntary agencies and the Army. Two years later in August 1909 the War Office issued its 'Scheme for the Organisation of Voluntary Aid in England and Wales,' which established both male and female Voluntary Aid Detachments (VADs) to fill gaps in the Territorial medical services. By early 1914, 1757 female detachments and 519 male detachments had been registered with the War Office. The female detachments contained trained members of nursing staff, i.e. Queen Alexandra's Imperial Military Nursing Service and the Territorial Force Nursing Service and were reviewed and inspected annually.

Arrangements for dealing with the wounded in the First World War

A First World War soldier who was injured in the field would first be examined at a Regimental Aid Post close to the front line by the Medical Officer and his orderlies.[72] He would then be moved by stretcher-bearers either to an Advance Dressing Station, usually two miles behind the front line, or the Main Dressing Stations another two miles back. If further treatment was needed he would be moved to a Casualty Clearing Station by motor ambulance. This was a tented camp out of range of the enemy's guns (a minimum of 10,000 yards behind the front line). If required the casualty would then be moved to one of the base hospitals usually by train and the seriously wounded taken back to Britain by Hospital Ship.

For the first six months of the war, wounds were superficially disinfected and sutured in the clearing hospitals but death rates were very high (as much as 80%) due to subsequent severe pyogenic infection and gas gangrene caused by the untreated wound contamination. In 1915 Aberdeen Surgeon Henry Gray and the Australian Captain E.T.C. Milligan then attached to the RAMC published results of immediate wound excision and suturing which they had been using since November 1914. This was carried out at the Casualty Clearing Station to remove all foreign material and morbid tissue.[73] Under this regime the survival rates immediately improved. As a result a much higher number of casualties than expected survived to reach hospitals in England.

Bristol's war effort

The Great War began on July 28, 1914 with Austria-Hungary's declaration of war with Serbia. Britain declared war on Germany on August 4.

The war effort put in by the city of Bristol was considerable and out of proportion to its size. The Gloucestershire Regiment, with its headquarters and regimental depot at Horfield Barracks, was the main infantry unit for Bristol. At the beginning of August 1914, it comprised two regular battalions and a reserve battalion. When war was declared the 1st Gloucesters were stationed at Borden in Hampshire and were training at Rushmore Camp. The Battalion was mobilised on the night of August 12, 1914 and joined the British Expeditionary Force, arriving at Le Havre, 24 hours later. The 2nd Battalion was in Tientsin in China and set out to return to England on November 8, 1914 landing at Le Havre on December 18, 1914.

The two Bristol Territorial Infantry Battalions – the 4th and the 6th Gloucesters – were ordered back from their training camp at Minehead, Somerset and mobilised between August 4 and 9 1914. Based at Queens Road and St Michael's Hill respectively, the 4th and 6th Gloucesters left Bristol on August 10, 1914 for training in Essex before crossing to France and Belgium in April 1915.

Other Bristol-based Territorial Units, such as the 1st South Midland Brigade, Royal Field Artillery; the South Midland Royal Engineers and the 3rd South Midland Field Ambulance (RAMC) were also mobilised in the early part of August 1914.

The Bristol division of the Royal Naval Reserve mustered between 400 and 500 men before the war and was mobilised on August 2-3. A further 2829 men were recruited during the war by the Bristol Recruiting District.

With the regular army, reservists and territorial forces mobilised and either training or on their way to the front, attention turned to the recruitment of an additional 'New Army' of volunteers demanded by Lord Kitchener, the newly appointed Secretary of State for War. The Bristol Citizens Recruiting Committee was established to co-ordinate this recruitment across the Bristol area and soon formed two further battalions of the Gloucestershire Regiment – the 12th (Bristol's Own) and 14th (Bantams) Battalions as well as two artillery units of the Royal Garrison Artillery – the 127th and 129th Heavy Batteries. Several other service battalions of the Gloucestershire Regiment were formed in Bristol and other units recruiting men within the city included the North Somerset Yeomanry, the Royal Gloucestershire Hussars and the Somerset Light Infantry. By the end of the war, 26 military and naval units were closely associated with the City of Bristol, with 55,000 men enlisted from the Bristol area; around 6,000 men serving in these units lost their lives.

Bristol also made a major contribution to war effort in the air through the Filton based British and Colonial Aeroplane Company established by Sir George White and his brother in 1910.

Sir George White (1854-1916) was another remarkable self made local man who would have got on very well with Robert Edwin Bush who was his contemporary. Quite apart from establishing the British and Colonial

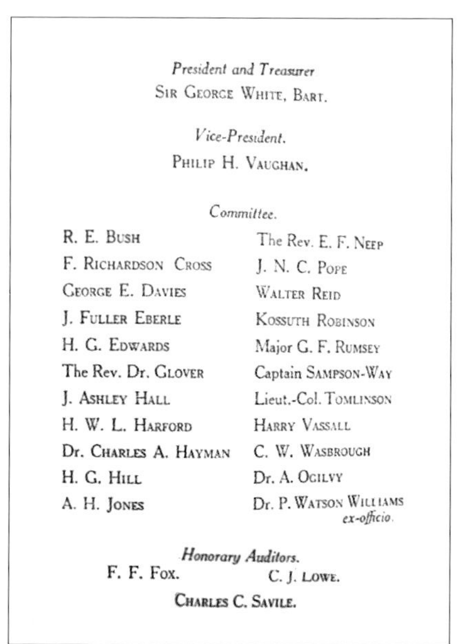

President and Treasurer
SIR GEORGE WHITE, BART.

Vice-President.
PHILIP H. VAUGHAN.

Committee.

R. E. BUSH	The Rev. E. F. NEEP
F. RICHARDSON CROSS	J. N. C. POPE
GEORGE E. DAVIES	WALTER REID
J. FULLER EBERLE	KOSSUTH ROBINSON
H. G. EDWARDS	Major G. F. RUMSEY
The Rev. Dr. GLOVER	Captain SAMPSON-WAY
J. ASHLEY HALL	Lieut.-Col. TOMLINSON
H. W. L. HARFORD	HARRY VASSALL
Dr. CHARLES A. HAYMAN	C. W. WASBROUGH
H. G. HILL	Dr. A. OGILVY
A. H. JONES	Dr. P. WATSON WILLIAMS *ex-officio.*

Honorary Auditors.
F. F. FOX. C. J. LOWE.
CHARLES C. SAVILE.

The members of the fund raising committee acknowledged in the programme for the opening of the Edward VII extension to the Bristol Royal Infirmary.

Aeroplane Company, White had by this time considerable interests in railways, docks and shipping companies. He had earlier been responsible, as secretary of the Bristol Tramways and Carriage Company, for introducing electric trams in Bristol, one of the first cities to do so.

In the years leading up to the War Sir George had saved the Bristol Royal Infirmary from debts of more than £15,000 and was knighted for his public service. In 1906 he was appointed President of the Bristol Royal Infirmary and had by this time established a fund to build a new hospital building. Robert Edwin Bush served on this committee and their efforts resulted in the building of the 1912 Edward VII Memorial Wing. While war was not contemplated at this time, during the opening ceremony performed by King George V and Queen Mary on June 28, 1912, it was announced that in the event of War this would be used as a war hospital. [74]

Bristol's War Hospitals

At the outbreak of the First World War, the British Red Cross and the Order of St John of Jerusalem combined to form a Joint War Committee. They

Lieut-Colonel J. Paul Bush, C.M.G, CBE, RAMC.

pooled their resources under the protection of the Red Cross emblem. In Bristol Sir George White was the first treasurer as well as a benefactor of the Red Cross in Bristol and so played a crucial role in establishing the First World War Red Cross Auxiliary hospitals.

As the Red Cross had secured buildings, equipment and staff, the organisation was able to set up temporary hospitals as soon as wounded men began to arrive from abroad. The buildings varied widely, ranging from town halls and schools to large and small private houses. The most suitable ones were established as auxiliary hospitals, which looked after patients who remained under military control. There were eventually more than 3,000 auxiliary hospitals administered by Red Cross county directors.

The 2nd Southern General Hospital

The 2nd Southern General Hospital, based in Bristol was one of five Southern Regional Territorial Force Hospitals formed when the Territorial and Reserve Forces Act came into effect on 1st April 1908.[75] From 1908 to August 1914, these contingency hospitals only existed on paper but the staff were all appointed, and once a year the Officers, NCO's and men undertook a month's training in camp. In the event of war they would be mobilised by the War Office.

Robert Edwin's younger brother J Paul Bush was born on June 30, 1857 and, like his brothers attended Clifton College (1869-1876). He went on to study medicine at the Bristol Medical School shortly before the Bristol University College was founded.[76] After junior posts and a period as assistant surgeon Bush was finally appointed full surgeon at the Bristol Royal Infirmary in February 1889. By this time he had shown himself to be a very able organiser having been hospital treasurer for more than one successful fund raising

The Queen Mary Ward of the 2nd Southern Hospital in the Edward VII wing of the Bristol Royal Infirmary made over to military use in 1914. There was an identical King George Ward.

effort.[77] Almost immediately he was sent out in charge of a field hospital in the South African War.[78] When he and his staff returned safe and sound in September 1890 he received the CMG (Companion of the Order of St Michael and St George) for his services.[79]

Bush reached the retirement age for an Infirmary surgeon in January 1913 after 31 years service,[80] but was soon in charge of the 2nd Southern General Hospital with the rank of Lt Colonel in the RAMC (T). Thus on the day general mobilisation took place J. Paul Bush assumed command of the 2nd Southern General Territorial Forces Hospital,[81] and the Matron of the Royal Infirmary, Miss A. B. Baillie, took up her duties as Principal Matron with control of all the Territorial Forces Nursing Staff in the region.

The original plan was that on the outbreak of war the RAMC controlled 2nd Southern General Hospital based in Bristol would take over 520 beds of the Bristol Royal Infirmary for treatment of military wounded. However by the time war was declared the Infirmary had found that the claims of the civil population were so great that it could not supply the agreed quota.[82] Instead they placed the newly completed Edward VII wing of the Infirmary at the disposal of the authorities, with its 260 beds fully equipped.[83] In order to make up the promised number the Bristol Board of Guardians of Southmead

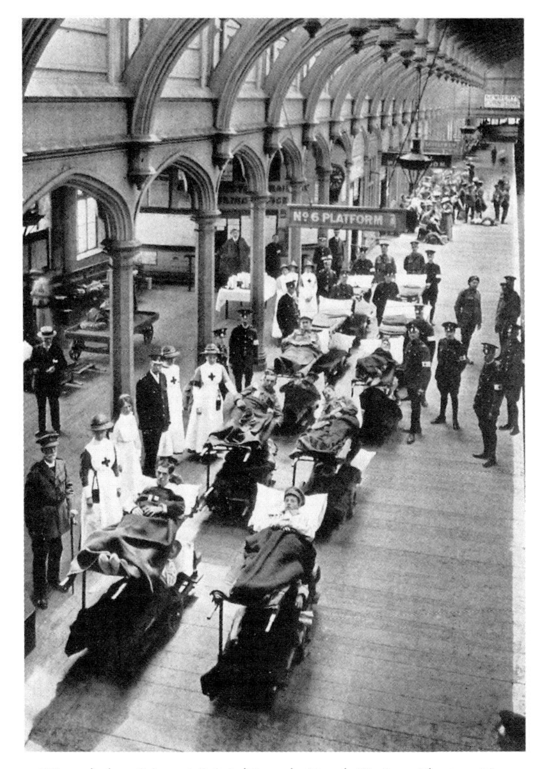

Wounded arriving at Bristol Temple Meads Station. The two tier stretcher trolleys fit the ambulances.

Hospital agreed to put 260 beds at the disposal of the War Office.[84] This was a "Poor Hospital" or "Workhouse Hospital" which was nearing completion at the time but had not yet been brought into service.

Three weeks later, on September 2, the first hospital train arrived at Bristol Temple Meads station bringing 120 wounded men from Mons. From the very beginning the reception of these hospital trains was highly organised. Three men's Voluntary Aid Detachments (VADs) and four women's VADs assisted at Bristol Temple Meads station, carrying out all the work in detraining and in feeding men during all hours of the day and night. Well trained Red Cross and St John's Ambulance men were always on hand and the convoys of wounded were rapidly dispersed. By the end of the war 417 trains had brought 31,640 stretcher cases and 37,771 "sitting cases" to Bristol and almost the same number had arrived in hospital ships at Avonmouth.

It immediately became clear that the planned provision of 520 beds at

Bristol was hopelessly inadequate and additional beds were urgently needed. In fact by the end of the War ten times this number of beds were in use.

Australian Forces involvement in WW1

By the end of September 1914 the war on the Western Front had ground to a halt and Churchill, as First Lord of the Admiralty, raised the idea of opening a second front with an attack on the Gallipoli Peninsula at a meeting of the British War Council. Churchill believed that knocking the Ottomans out of the war would undermine Germany. The Council however, led by Prime Minister Herbert Asquith and the Secretary of State for War Lord Kitchener, deemed the plan too risky but the continuing stalemate on the Western Front led to the War Council approving the plan on January 28, 1915.

On February 19, 1915 British and French ships began a naval assault on the Dardanelles but after a month the bombardment had failed and three Allied battleships had been lost to Turkish mines. Rather than concede defeat a ground force was hastily assembled in Egypt under Lieutenant-General Sir Ian Hamilton. This comprised a single British division sent out from England, a French colonial division from North Africa, and a small Indian expeditionary force.

The First Australian Imperial Force (AIF) under General Bridges had set out from Albany on November 1, 1914 with the intention of going direct to England where they would join Canadian forces encamped on Salisbury Plain for training in preparation for deployment on the Western Front. On November 27 while in transit on the Red Sea the AIF received new orders to disembark in Egypt and to train there and to form an Australian and New Zealand Army Corps (ANZAC) under the command of General Birdwood ready to join the Combined Mediterranean Expeditionary Force. Birdwood who was another Old Cliftonian, was given the temporary title of General Officer Commanding, Australian and New Zealand Forces.[85] (see also Appendix 3). The choice of a Bristol commanding officer might seem curious but during the latter part of the nineteenth century and in the first decade of the twentieth, large numbers of Bristolians left the UK to find work and new lives in Australia, Canada, South Africa and New Zealand but very much still saw Britain as their Mother Country and almost 700 members of the Australian Forces had been born in Bristol with more from the surrounding area.[86]

General Birdwood GCB, GCSI, GCMG, GCVO, CIE, DSO (See Appendix 3).

The Gallipoli invasion by the combined Mediterranean Expeditionary Force was launched on April 25, 1915 but soon ground to a halt. In August 1915 Sir Ian Hamilton now with eleven divisions under his command endeavoured to break the deadlock but by October it was soon clear that this too had failed and the decision was taken to evacuate all forces. This was completed by January 9, 1916 and by this time the casualties on both sides exceeded half a million men.

Six weeks later on February 21 the Germans attacked Verdun, and six British Divisions, including the evacuated ANZACs under the direction of General Birdwood,[87] were ordered to the Western Front where they served throughout the rest of the War.

Provision of Medical Services for the Australian Imperial Forces

At the outbreak of war the British War Office, in return for a very generous financial arrangement, had accepted that Australian sick and wounded would be treated in British Hospitals. But while these would provide the initial treatment the need to track the progress of casualties and provide convalescent care was accepted as an Australian responsibility. At the same time the War Office requested that 200 Australian medical officers and 200 qualified nurses be recruited into the RAMC. It was further agreed that two Australian Hospital ships, the Goorkha and the Letitia would make their way to England and be moored off Southampton to provide the major contribution to Australian medical services. In the event these ships were diverted to receive and

HMHS *Dongola* ferried wounded during the Gallipoli campaign.

transport casualties from the Gallipoli campaign and never arrived. HMHS *Goorkha* was mined in October 1917 and decommissioned while the HMHS *Letitia* was wrecked in thick fog off Nova Scotia the same year.

On December 15, 1914 the Australian Surgeon, General Williams, arrived in Britain believing that his hospital ships and 200 Australia doctors and nurses would soon arrive as the first tranche of his staff. He therefore set up his Headquarters in the High Commissioner's Office in London, where George Reid (later Sir George) the first High Commissioner and former Prime Minister of Australia and his Tasmanian wife were in residence and had already formed the Australian War Contingent Association in readiness for the coming conflict.[88] (See Appendix 4)

By early 1915, because of the diversion of Australian troops to the Gallipoli campaign the small number of Australian troops in Britain placed few demands on the High Commission in London. This changed rapidly following the landing of Australian & New Zealand troops at Gallipoli on 25th April 1915. These casualties were initially transported to their base in Egypt, which was soon unable to cope with their numbers, and wounded began to be sent to England. By November 1915 it was reported that 213 Australian Officers and 4677 men were in hospital in Britain,[89] and by the following month it was very obvious that the available medical services in Britain were inadequate to cope with the number of Australian casualties. The Australian High Commission with very limited resources needed a service to deal with the flood of Australian casualities and provide hospital and convalescent facilities. Much of this was undertaken by voluntary effort coordinated through the Australian War Contingent Association which had been set up under the presidency of Sir George Reid, the High Commissioner of Australia (See Appendix 4).

From mid summer 1916 there were never less than 50,000 Australians in Britain either in hospital, training, or in transit.[90] Once a wounded solider was deemed fit enough to leave hospital, he would be discharged to a Command Depot for the rehabilitative training after which they would be allocated to a battalion. However, initially the ANZAC troops found that there was no Australian base to which they could report. So on May 31,1915 a command depot was set up at Monte Video House in Chickerell, two miles from Weymouth. This then became the Australian Imperial Forces (AIF) Command Depot No.2.

Those not fit enough to resume front line service might be found alternative duties as headquarters staff or in the military police but most of those seriously disabled and those not expected to be fit for duty within six months as a result of wounds or sickness were repatriated through Weymouth.

The First World War greatly affected Australia and especially Western Australia as nearly 40% of West Australian men aged 18 to 44 years served in this conflict.[91] By the end of the War of the 416,809 Australian men who had enlisted, 60,000 had been killed and 156,000 wounded, gassed, or taken prisoner.

CHAPTER 4

THE BISHOP'S KNOLL WAR HOSPITAL

Robert Edwin Bush who maintained a great affection for Australia clearly realised very early in the War that it would not be "over by Christmas". He regarded himself an adopted son of Australia, although he never took up Australian nationality, but having made his fortune in Australia, Bush and his wife wanted to repay the country that made them so wealthy.

The declaration of War became generally known in Bristol by August 5. Three days later Bush and his wife determined to convert their house into a hospital for Australian service men. This they accomplished with astonishing speed. The decision to convert the house must have been taken in consultation with his brother Lt Colonel J Paul Bush under whose command the hospital would have to operate and on August 24, 1914 the Bishop's Knoll hospital was ready to receive patients. Robert Edwin's offer was acknowledged in a rather stiff formal letter from his brother dated August 31.

Just how radical the conversion of Bishop's Knoll was is described by "Leigh Woods" who was Archibald Powell the editor, writing in the first issue of the hospital's "Coo-ee!" magazine.[92]

> "It was in the happy pre-war days that I first had the pleasure of visiting Bishop's Knoll. The occasion was a dinner party and the guests were sportsmen, some with a well-established county cricket reputation and some whose names are as familiar in Australia and South Africa as here in England.[93] This was in the winter time and the charms of the exterior aspect of the Knoll were obscured by darkness. The next occasion was a garden party. It was a glorious day in

2nd Southern General Hospital.
Bristol.
31/8/14.

TO.
R.E.Bush.Esq.
Bishops Knoll.

Dear Sir.

I have been requested by the Deputy Director of Medical Services, Southern Command, Salisbury to tender you his grateful thanks for your generous and patriotic offer which has been classified and filed, and will be taken advantage of when the need arises. I further beg to state that I have the approval to use these 100 beds as supplementary to this Hospital as soon as this Hospital is fully accommodated. The D.D.ofM.S. has pleasure in sanctioning the appointment of Dr Nixon as Medical Officer in charge of these 100 beds.

I have the honour to be, Sir,
Your obedient servant,

J.P.Bush.

Lt.Col. R.A.M.C.T.
o/c 2nd Southern General Hosp.

Letter from J. Paul Bush to Robert Edwin Bush.

mid- summer and the scene even now is fresh in my memory the gay throng scattered about lawns and terrace, the superb view of the winding Avon with the woods of Leigh across the river, and the Bristol Channel and Welsh hills in the far distance, making a picture of peculiar charm.

How changed was the scene when next I crossed the Downs and visited the Knoll. The declaration of war had been made : the Germans were hacking their way through Belgium and France and everywhere up and down this land of ours preparations were being made for the home-coming of our wounded fighting men. Among the first of private citizens to offer aid to the Government, the owner of this beautiful mansion by the banks of the Avon lost no time in making his preparations for receiving wounded soldiers. He was ready to receive them on August 24th 1914, and the first arrivals from France actually came on September 13th. Since then many hundreds of wounded soldiers have found rest and the very best of medical attention at Bishop's Knoll.

The suite of rooms were dismantled, costly furniture, treasures of art and choice bric-a-brac removed and a complete equipment for dealing with one hundred patients installed. (A later account by Powell says that in addition to removing the furniture and wallpaper the fine parquet floors were protected with cork linoleum).

The handsome ballroom with the rich decorative features and the fine organ, which has proved such a great boon to the patients, was the main ward. It contains twenty-five cots, and these are ranged on either side and down the centre. The adjacent dining-room and the drawing-room across the hall are other wards, whilst the range of bedrooms, light and cheerful with the exquisite outlook, are also provided with cots, a spacious apartment – the billiard-room of happier times - being reserved for those well on the high road to recovery.

In the conservatory handsome foliage plants and rare exotics have given place to prosaic but exceedingly comfortable lounge chairs and a small billiard table is only forsaken after lights out. In the recreation room there is a full-sized billiard table upon which the weekly handicaps are played. Out-door recreations include clock golf on the tennis lawn, bowls on the well-ordered green and cricket or football in their due seasons.

Fortunate indeed are the lads who come battle-scarred to Bishop's Knoll. Not only are they set in the midst of natural beauty that will be hard to beat anywhere in our British Isles, but the whole atmosphere of the place is comforting. The red tape of officialism is practically unknown here. The Commandant, with thirty-five years of bush life in Western Australia to look

The operating theatre from the outside.

back upon, is never better pleased than when, in odd moments, he can sit with a group of the boys and yarn about the land away yonder under the Southern Cross. The Commandant's wife and daughter are closely identified with the care of the big family who have the run of the mansion, and the sisters and nurses take a personal interest in every "case." How true this is the letters which come from men returned to duty clearly show (see Chapter 12).

There is much one would like to say about Bishop's Knoll, but the Commandant will have nothing in the way of eulogy for his "bit" in the war. Indeed, it was only after a deal of persuasion that he consented to have these bare details set down. Of the many friends of the hospitals, and how they have helped to make the stay of the Australian patients in Bristol agreeable, I shall have something to say later on."

On September 2, 1914, after the first battle of Mons, the first batch of wounded soldiers arrived from Temple Meads at the Marlborough Street Section of the 2nd Southern General Hospital, in other words the Edward VII wing of the Bristol Infirmary. It was from here that the Bishop's Knoll Auxilliary Hospital received its first patients 11 days later. Auxiliary Hospitals did not receive

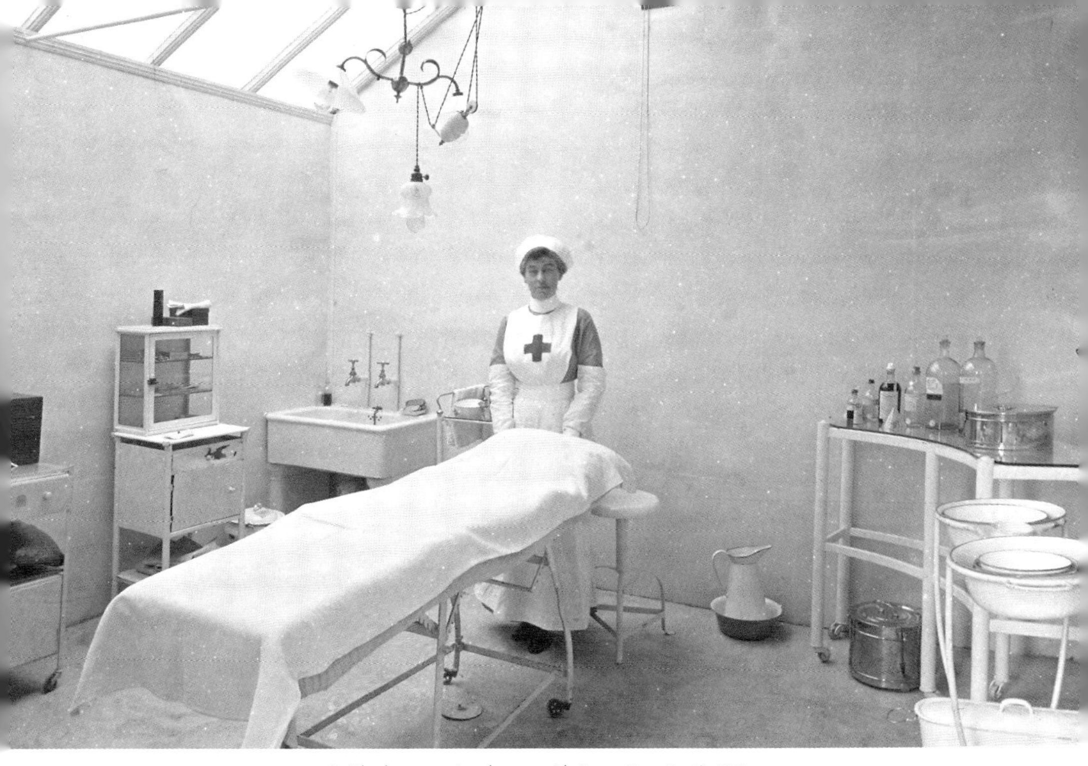

Inside the operating theatre with Nurse Nora Austin VAD.

patients direct from the Front, but acted as relief to the 2nd Southern General hospital which now comprised wards in the Bristol General Hospital as well as the Bristol Royal Infirmary, and Southmead.

The acceptance of the well equipped Bishop's Knoll as a full British military hospital was soon confirmed by the Army Council in a letter from the War Office dated December 30, 1914. This meant Bishop's Knoll became part of the 2nd Southern General Hospital rather than a separate auxiliary hospital.[94] Wounded could now be sent to it direct from the front and its inclusion brought the total number of 2nd Southern General Hospital beds to 1040.[95]

A dedicated operating theatre had been added in a specially built temporary extension outside the main entrance of Bishop's Knoll as no other suitable room could be found.[96] (Trooper Lennox reports that before this some operations were carried out in the ward.[97]) The photograph opposite confirms that this free standing room was of light construction, with a corrugated iron roof and walls.

It was now a fully functioning 100 bedded hospital equipped and staffed at Bush's own expense. Powell says that over the 4 ½ years of the War it cost him £100,000, equivalent to £10 million today.

The 1040 beds now available to the 2nd Southern General Hospital in December 1914 were still not nearly enough so Lt Col Paul Bush approached George White the Chairman of the local Red Cross for assistance. This led to the establishment of several further Red Cross Auxiliary Hospitals staffed and equipped by the detachments of the British Red Cross Society. Twelve of these were located in Bristol and others scattered over the counties of Gloucestershire, Somerset and Wiltshire.[98] By late 1914 Bristol Red Cross Hospitals had been opened at Cleve Hill, Cossham and Almondsbury. In neighbouring Gloucestershire hospitals were opened at Cheltenham, Gloucester, Lydney, Stroud, and Tewkesbury. In Somerset hospitals were opened at Weston super Mare, Clevedon, West Harptree, Shepton Mallet, Newton St. Loe and Bath. Ultimately there were 21 auxiliary hospitals under the control of J Paul Bush as the Commanding Officer at the 2nd Southern General Hospital and what had been 520 beds available to the group at the outbreak of war had risen to 5789 by 1917 of which 4000 were in Bristol.[99] (For a full account of all these hospitals see Stone G.F., Wells C. *Bristol and the Great War*. J.W. Arrowsmith, Bristol, 1930 pp 135-178.)

Robert Edwin Bush had always wanted to treat only Australians at Bishop's Knoll and so had initially offered his 100 bed hospital through the Australian War Contingent Association. His offer was accepted but subject to the condition that the administration for the hospital should be carried out by Australian officers and the soldiers treated by Australian doctors and nurses. Bush could not agree to these conditions and so from September 1914 all British and Commonwealth wounded were accepted. This decision would however have financial consequences for Bush. According to John Sandes, writing in the Sydney Morning Herald in 1918,[100] the Australian Government had made Australian earnings expended for patriotic purposes during the War free of tax but the Prime Minister of the day, Mr W.M.Hughes, ruled that because Bush had not placed his hospital at the disposal of the Australian Government this did not apply to him!

The first Australians treated at Bishop's Knoll arrived as part of a mixed Allied Expeditionary Force in February 1915,[101] (According to his mother these were Cpl Lawton Greig of the 3rd Company Australian Motor Transport Service and his colleague "Mr Knight" who could have been either Claude Roland of

Receiving casualties from Temple Meads before the operating theatre was added in front of the main entrance.

the 5th Company or James William of the 4th Company).[102] This led to friendly rivalry between the British and Australians being treated there. Powell related how he was working late just before Christmas (the year was not specified) at the editorial offices of what was to become the Bristol United Press, when he received a telephone call from an Australian soldier at Bishop's Knoll. The problem was that the soldiers wished to present Mr and Mrs Bush with a Christmas gift but could not agree who should present it; the British soldiers insisting that the honour should go to their Sergeant Major. Powell resolved the matter to the satisfaction of all parties and the presentation was duly made on Christmas day by the Australian Sergeant Major! [103]

Not one to give up, Bush made continuing efforts during 1915 to achieve his original wish of treating only Australians. In March 1915 the Surgeon General of the Southern Command had written to the Australian Divisional Command at Romsey Hants, advising them of Mr Bush's wish and asking them to "transfer any cases from your unit which you decide to send...........to the section of Bishop's Knoll." Whether this informal request was acted upon is unknown.

On June 27, 1915 Bush again wrote to the Secretary of the Australian High Commissioner's Office to further explain the position and enlist his help.

Above: Ward 1 before the War. Below: Ward 1 1914-18.

I think if I take your letter paragraph by paragraph I may be able to place before you more plainly my views.

1. My offer made some months ago through the Australian War Contingent Association was to place my 100 bedded hospital (which I have been running under the War Office since the 2nd week in September) at the disposal of the

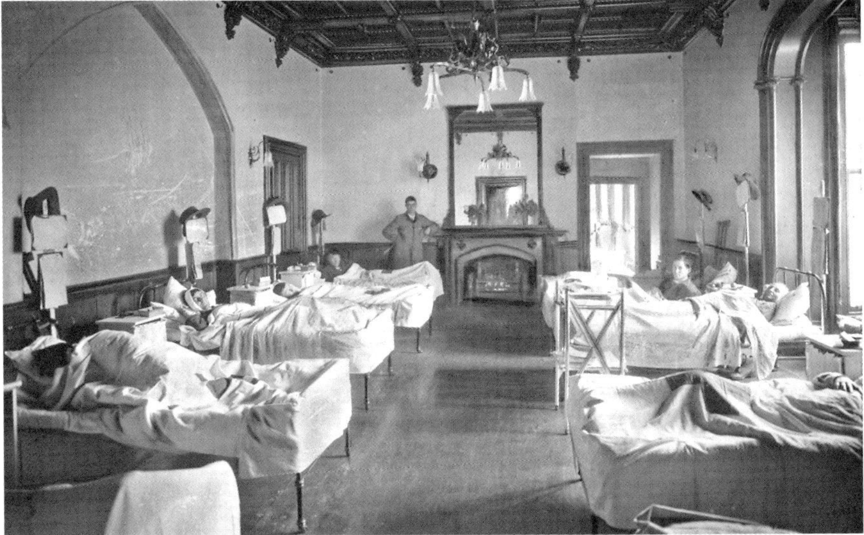

Above: Ward 2 before the War. Below: Ward 2 1914-1918.

Commonwealth Authorities for the reception of sick and wounded Australian sailors and soldiers. I offered this as an on going concern with an equipment of medical and nursing staff, orderlies, servants etc etc, free of all cost to the Commonwealth, and engaged to run same until the end of the war bearing the entire expense.

Above: Ward 3 before the War. Below: Ward 3 1914-1918.

2. Personally I can see no reason why because this hospital is nominally part of a military hospital it should not be devoted to the sole use of the Australian sick and wounded under the District Command.

I am very keen indeed to admit only Australians to this hospital and if I can do so and save an expense to the Commonwealth of anything from £700 to

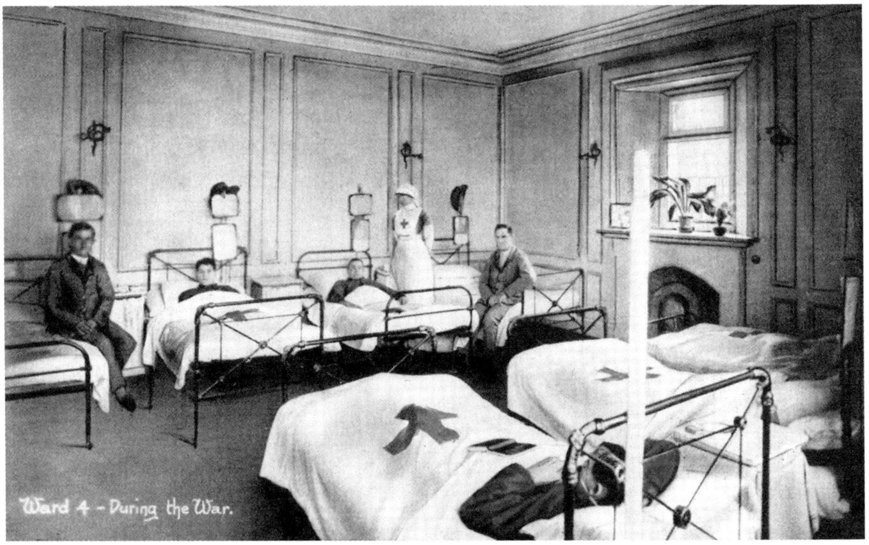

Above: Ward 4 before the War. Below: Ward 4 1914-1918.

> £1000 a month which the running of a 100 bedded hospital would cost, I should be only too delighted to do so.

Having been duly inspected by Major Dunhill of the Australian Army Medical Corps in June 1915, success was finally achieved following a letter to the War Office from the Australian High Commissioner, Sir George Reid, dated

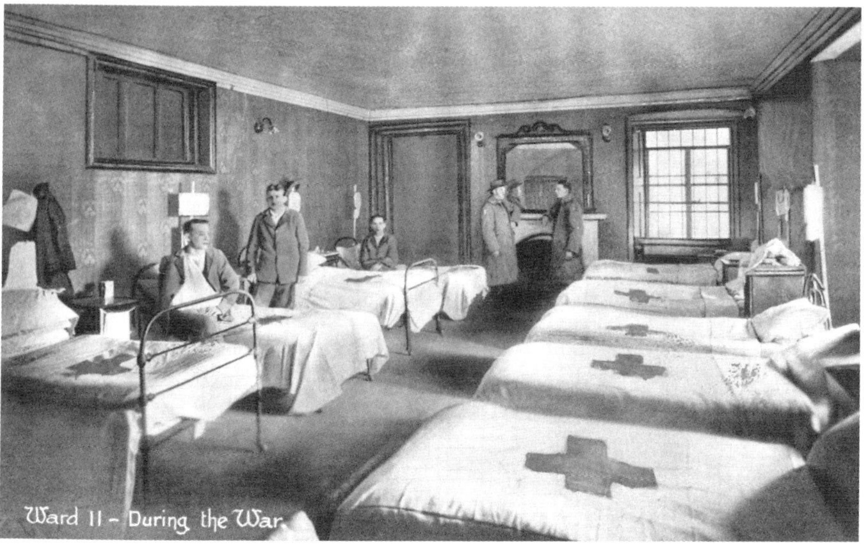

Above: Ward 11, the Billiard Room before the War. Below: Ward 11 1914-1918.

September 30, 1915 after which the War Council agreed and only Australians were to be treated at Bishop's Knoll. Maybe the letter was preceded by a telephone call as Trooper Lennox reported that the first batch of Australians from the Dardanelles arrived at Bishop's Knoll on September 15, 1915.[104] Perhaps as a quid pro quo Bush had accepted the Chairmanship of Sir George Reid's Australian War Contingent Association's Matinees Committee and organised a successful fund raising event held at His Majesty's Theatre London on November 19, 1915 in the presence of the King and Queen and the Princess Royal. Many famous artists gave their services free of charge but Clara Butt and Nellie Melba were unable to attend but donated £100 each.

Like those soldiers being treated or convalescing elsewhere in England, patients at Bishop's Knoll wore a blue uniform with a red tie, known as "Hospital Blues", to indicate they were wounded serving soldiers. There were constant complaints about the poorly made and ill fitting uniforms. On October 20, 1916 *The Times* recorded that a Mr Randell, "is to ask the Secretary of State for War on Tuesday whether he is aware that the blue uniform supplied to the wounded soldiers seems to be defective". Bush made every effort to ameliorate matters and it is clear that nurses were also employed as seamstresses. As a result the Bishop's Knoll inmates were regarded as the smartest dressed of those wounded seen in Bristol.

Soldiers recovering at Bishop's Knoll were still subject to army regulations and Powell records that Military Hospital rules were displayed in every ward but that Bush considered that these were not very suitable for the Australian volunteer soldier. When each new draft of wounded came in he always addressed them pointing out the rules but adding "I have in my own mind a few rules I regard as absolutely necessary." These were not given by Powell but clearly had the desired effect for he records that only one man was ever carpeted for speaking rudely to a sister and he never heard bad language on a Ward except from a soldier coming round after an operation! [105]

The wounded were accommodated in 13 wards, five in converted living rooms, including the billiard room, and the remainder in bedrooms on the first floor. Bush records that the average stay in the hospital was 42 days and the longest 21 months.

By the end of the War more than 2000 Australian non-commissioned soldiers had passed through the hospital which was reckoned to have been the best in the south of England. It is noteworthy that while a number of wealthy British families offered to turn their mansions into convalescent hospitals later in the War they were usually only prepared to accept officers; for example Ashton Court's hospital for officers opened in 1917.

Mrs Marjery Bush and Robert Edwin Bush.

The staffing and running of the hospital

While Robert Bush was the 'Commandant' in charge of organisation, he also worked tirelessly as an orderly and made regular trips to Temple Meads station to collect the Australian wounded. Mrs Bush was the Quartermaster and personally oversaw the work carried out in the kitchens, assisted by her step daughter Charlotte when she was not required as a nursing auxiliary and by Robert Edwin's niece, though which one is not made clear. Powell says that Mrs Bush undertook the cooking for the patients and staff for the whole period of the War.[106] It should also be pointed out that in April 1914 she had given birth to her daughter Diana Mary and in March 1916 when the hospital was full of British and Commonwealth soldiers, Paul Tobin was born. After the war Mrs Bush was awarded the OBE for her services.

The Lady Quartermaster

By Gunner W. Matthew [116]

Our Q.M.S. she is a dear,
Of men and maids she has no fear;

Her job is hard, for stocks are short,
Don't grouse at her, but be a sport.
Your tunic may not be the best,
Your cardigan may be scanty,
Your breeches, putties and the rest
Have come from near Levantie.
These are the things she cannot help,
Hers not to reason why;
The "Heads" will send these "togs" along,
And to fit you she must try.
So boys, when out in France again,
And your hearts are beating faster,
Just spare a thought for Bishop's Knoll,
And the Lady Quartermaster.

Sister in Charge Miss G. Prout with her Red Cross Medal. She was also a regular contributor to "Coo-ee!" as GYP.

The nursing staff consisted of seven trained nurses and around 25 Red Cross auxiliaries, under the Sister-in-Charge, Miss G. Prout. These were supported by the Bristol 12th detachment of VADs, under their Commandant Mrs M. E. Herapath, the 41 year old wife of a Brush Manufacturer who lived near to Bishop's Knoll in Downleaze, Sneyd Park. A complete list of all staff who ever worked in the Hospital between 1914 and 1918 is given in Appendix 6.

Our sister in charge

by Number 12.[107]

This appreciation of Miss Prout appeared in "Coo-ee!" in August 1917. As there were only ever seven trained nurses working at Bishop's Knoll Hospital one must assume that several left during the first two years of the war and that "Number 12" was the twelfth qualified nurse to be appointed.

From the time she comes on duty, after breakfast, to make her morning round, looking as if she had just, stepped out of a bandbox, to the time she goes off

Bishop's Knoll Nursing staff.

duty at night, she is here, there and everywhere like a flash of lightning, but missing absolutely nothing on her way. Do not flatter yourself if you are a newcomer or feeling lazy, that something you may have left, thinking that 'it won't matter this once' will escape her eagle eye: beds out of line, castors turned out or quilts of unequal length, dusting or sweeping skimped, will at once be noticed, and smaller things which you may fondly hope have been overlooked have all been seen by Sister.

On the other hand, no one could be quicker to praise where praise is due, or more appreciative of work well done or extra trouble taken with one's daily round, and knowing that only the best is good enough, praise from her is much prized and cheers us on our way. Her unfailing tact in dealing with all sorts and conditions of men, combined with a keen sense of justice, make her one of those rare beings, a woman well fitted to rule and to be in authority, and those who work for her cannot fail to realise it. Coming as she did from a large base hospital, where the dividing-line between a pro.(bationer) and staff nurse is very distinct and a Sister a being altogether apart, she yet manages a crowd of partly-trained VAD's with such patience and success, that she is a real friend to them all, and at the same time maintains the necessary discipline of a hospital. Many a newcomer, rather wobbly about the knees, has started work

Left: The Principal Medical Officer, given in various accounts as Dr Miles and Dr T G Myles, Right: Captain Kyle.

Left to right: Dr Ormerod, Dr Lees, Dr Parsons.

in the wards in fear and trembling, but has soon revived and been spurred to do her best by the knowledge that work well done will always be rewarded by a few words of encouragement and praise. The writer will never forget, when starting as a raw and stupid pro. with only a month or so of hospital training behind her, how her first dressing was done under Sister's wing, with Sister herself doing the pro's work in order that she might best learn how to do it, and her patient instruction and her kindly encouragement and praise when it

The morning ward round.

> was done.
>
> Though a very clever surgeon has been lost to the profession, that loss is our gain, and we are more than thankful that Fate has sent her to us. Long may she stay where she has gained the admiration and affection of all.

There were four doctors attending the hospital and these all lived locally. Dr Henry Lawrence Ormerod, at Westbury on Trym; Dr Henry Francis Parsons, a near neighbour of The Heath, Sneyd Park; and Dr Edwin Lionel Lees of Chesterfield House, Clifton. The Principal Medical Officer given in various accounts as Dr Miles and Dr T G Myles appears to have been George Thomas Myles of 147 Whiteladies Road, Clifton. A Captain Kyle was in overall military charge, this is likely to have been Henry Greville Kyle RAMC whose address in the Medical Register of 1915 is given as Westbury Road, Bristol. Captain Kyle would later become an Officer of the Order of St. John of Jerusalem.[108]

While most accounts mention these medical staff only as "Doctors" they had quite distinct roles. George Thomas Myles was Principal Medical Officer; Henry Lawrence Ormerod was the surgeon, Henry Frank Parsons was the physician, and Edwin Leonard Lees was the anaesthetist. Captain John Alexander Nixon was initially in overall charge of the "medical management"

Bishop's Knoll Hospital
(100 beds)
(2nd SOUTHERN GENERAL HOSPITAL)
Stoke Bishop, Bristol.

SURGEON IN RESIDENCE required immediately. Salary £250 per annum, with board, lodging and laundry. Must have had recent experience in major operative surgery.

Applications, stating age and qualifications with copies of testimonials, should be forwarded to The Commandant, from whom further particulars may be obtained.

Advertisement for a surgeon.

but was soon replaced by Captain Henry Greville Kyle who was also called upon to operate on severe abdominal cases. Their qualifications are given in Appendix 5. It is not clear how these doctors were recruited but certainly Dr T.G. Myles volunteered his services as soon as he learned of Bush establishing his hospital in August 1914.[109] It would appear that these services were paid for by Bush as the above appeared in a local paper in 1914.

As has been mentioned, Bishop's Knoll soon had a fully equipped operating theatre and it is clear that a great deal of operating was undertaken with regular lists. Today one would expect surgeons to have a Fellowship of one of the Royal Colleges (FRCS) awarded by examination but none of the Bishop's Knoll doctors had the qualification. This was not unusual at the time for although the FRCS had been awarded since the late 18th century this was to eminent surgeons by election rather than examination. Lt Col J Paul Bush under whom these men were nominally responsible similarly only had an MRCS and only one of his two former colleagues who were surgeons at the Bristol Royal Infirmary had an FRCS.

In this poem, by Miss Prout the Sister-in-Charge, it is not clear who the SMO was since this title is not used elsewhere. However the fact that the "Blue Boys" are described as standing to attention for the SMO strongly suggest that this is Captain Kyle though it could have been Dr Myles who is described as the Principal Medical Officer. Either name, with that of Dr Lees, would enable the last line of the fifth verse to rhyme!

Our SMO he is a man
  Of navy blue clad neatness.
He likes his staff all on the plan
  Of smart and quiet fleetness.

Ward 1 he enters for to see,
  He bids us all "Good morning."
If things are not as they should be
  Then we must all take warning.

His quick eye glances round about,
  The Ward looks as it oughter;
Nurses are ready, and no doubt
  Soap, towel, and hot water.

He passes up and down the rows
  Of Blue Boys at attention;
Inspects their wounds, chest and trench toes,
  Too numerous to mention.

On operation days he's seen,
  Gloves cap and gown's the style,
And oft accompanied he's been by
  By Doctors-------- and ______

If things get missed, alas! Then he
  Will really look most pensive;
Those instruments are dear, you see,
  Exceedingly expensive.

The chaplain, Bishop Alfred Clifford.

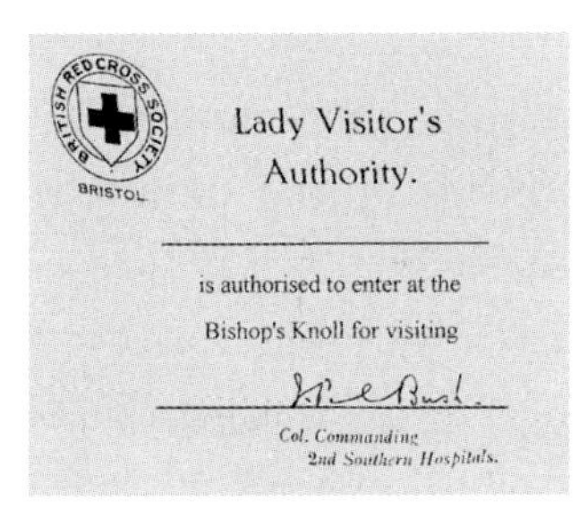

British Red Cross Society
Bristol

Lady Visitor's Authority.

____

is authorised to enter at the Bishop's Knoll for visiting

Col. Commanding
2nd Southern Hospitals.

Visitors Pass.

He works so hard, and if we do
Our best and slacken never,
We may be sure that he will too
Praise us, for our endeavour.[110]

The Bush's youngest child Marjorie Elizabeth (Betty) with Charles Lapham the coachman in 1912 (See Appendix 2).

It was inevitable that Bush given his firm Anglican faith would appoint a hospital chaplain and who better than Dr Alfred Clifford, the inaugural Bishop of Lucknow for 17 years who in his retirement was now the local vicar of Stoke Bishop. He was assisted by the Rev W. Whitehead as Sub Chaplain. Church parades on Sunday were a major feature of hospital life in which music played a significant part. The needs of Roman Catholics were met by Cannon Lee the Roman Catholic Chaplain and visits of the Padre Father Iles. There were also other regular visitors organised through the Red Cross, these were carefully chosen and issued with passes authorising their access to see patients.

While the hospital was being converted Robert Edwin Bush and his family moved out. Several accounts say they moved into the Lodge but this cannot be so as it was already occupied by his coachman, groom and chauffeur and in any case was far too small for the Bush family of four and at least four additional servants. Sandes says they moved into a cottage "close by".[111] In fact they moved to the "Oak" next door, a large but much less grand house, which Bush either rented or purchased for the duration of the war. The Oak does not appear in the 1911 National Census indicating that the house was fortuitously unoccupied at that time.[112] However the Lodge on the Oak estate was still occupied by Henry Sweeting and his family. Henry and his two sons were market gardeners. Given the large areas under glass at the rear of the Oak this was clearly a commercial undertaking. Reports say that the Bishop's

Showing the extensive gardens of the Oak and the smaller garden of Bishop's Knoll.
This is a photograph from the Tozer collection - part of the archives of the Sneyd Park Local History Group.

Knoll itself, which only had a typical Victorian domestic garden, was largely self sufficient in fruit and vegetables. Bush also kept a Jersey cow and pigs with the milk being stored in pans kept in the cellar.

However as a hospital Bishop's Knoll would have needed the Oak's entire output as well as its own to feed the staff and inmates. Chapman says that, according to local residents, at one time there was a gardening staff of 18 men and boys many of whom lived nearby,[113] but only three are listed in the Census of 1911. The fact that some of the male staff would have volunteered or been called up explains why the VADs were put to work in the kitchen garden when "off duty". (See page 147).

Perhaps more should be said about the role of VADs at this point for their input was considerable. Not only were they essential to the running of the hospital but they were also crucial in raising the morale of the recovering soldiers. Nothing more clearly shows this than this poem written by a Bishop's Knoll soldier (perhaps Pte AG Davis).

The VAD Brigade

Angel Davis.[114]

I thought I knew each regiment, battalion and brigade,
Until I got to Bristol, by Red Cross train conveyed,
And saw upon the platform a company in blue,
Of goodly wives and daughters, and little flappers too.
I whispered to a comrade, "Pray tell me, who are these
With smiles upon their faces?" He answered, "VAD's,

They're called the 'Pillow Smoothers,' they have another name,
The 'Very Artful Darlings,' and well they play the game."
I'm but a shy young Anzac, not used to women much,
I've always dreaded nurses, and hospitals, and such;
How was I going to stick it, until my wounds were well?
A crowd of them, all fussing—far worse than shot and shell.

I lay upon a stretcher, a little girl tripped up,
My cigarette she lighted, and held my coffee cup.
And "Could she write a post card to send to any friend?"
Or "Would I like a pillow?" she bucked me up no end.
I had no friends in Blighty, and when the pain got worse,
I never could have stood it, without that little nurse;

A father, mother, sister, and sweetheart all in one,
If I had not adored her, I must have been a Hun.
But what if I should lose her? I know, I'll put a ring,
Upon her wedding finger, to claim the little thing;
And when the war is over, if I should lucky be,
That "Very Artful Darling" perhaps may cross the sea.

Such views were widely shared.[115] They were also feared by many a VAD parent who could see losing their daughter to an Anzac. It was not only Angel Davis who had in mind marrying a VAD after the War.

English Girls God bless 'em

Gunner F Jackson [116]

What do I think of English girls? What do I think of them? Well, I shouldn't just like to tell you all I think, me being a bashful sort of chap and scared to death when skirts is around. Female society ain't my line exactly. We ain't used to women folk round about the parts I come from, and those we do see, well—you don't get duchesses straying around in the bush.

The first English girl I saw in the old country was taking tickets from rough great galoots like me on a railway station. Gee! how we stared at that gal! Pretty as the pictures on the almanac in my old shack way back home, and she said, "Thank you!"—said it so sweet that it seemed to make a fellow want to take his hat off and tip-toe off the station. Since then we have seen something of how English girls are doing their bit. Ever been in a munition shop? I have, and when I read columns of slush about "gallant Anzacs," I wonder if all your editors are clean crazed—or is it the Censors—not to keep all those adjectives for your girls at the lathes, at the arsenals, on the buses, and in thousands of other jobs.

Trenches are 'ell, but what of all these dear little kids—God bless 'em—spoiling their lovely complexions on ten-hour shifts, soiling their pretty little hands, and slavin' like big buck navvies for the likes of you and me? Makes a chap feel cheap, all this talk about heroes and nothing about heroines.

I ain't read nothin' about handing out VCs to those kids who carried on at the big high explosive shops with the Zepp engines a-buzzing up above 'em. Let these same girls give the glad eye to lonely fellows like me though, and there's columns in the papers by the Jeremiah Johnnies who don't seem to be doing much to win this war themselves. Look at all the stuff we read about the Flapper. Pretty rotten time some of us fellows would have had, I'm thinking without her. Leave us to the tender mercies of the "Oh-my-poor-man" sort of female woman, and not many of us would be troubling about week-end passes I guess. The Plain* ain't so bad as that. (* Salisbury Plain Camps)

The English girl? She's great. She's winning this war just as sure as any Anzac, and I'm for telling her. The Plain ain't just a Garden of Eden, but it's not so very far from Bristol, where there are girls—real English girls—who don't

Clifton, Bristol May 3rd
To the next of Kin,
4441 Pte. T.A. Jackson
26th Batt. : A.I.F.
Mr Bush thinks that you may like to know that on Anzac Day, April 25th, we took flowers to all the Australian Graves in Arnos Vale Cemetary.

The Graves looked quite lovely heaped with flowers.

You will see by the enclosed photos, that the Gallant Dead sleeping so far from home, are never forgotten by us, who owe so much to them.

Yrs, with grateful Sympathy,

K Swinton
V.A.D.

A note from VAD K. Swinton to the family of Pte T.H. Jackson. This accompanied the Remembrance Card for the 1925 Anzac Day pilgrimage to Arnos Vale.

> wait round to be interdooced to a chap, even when he 's big and ugly like me. And don't you go thinking they are any the worse for that. Here's one that ain't going back to the old shack by himself when the Mad Dogs 'muzzled.

It also is clear that at Bishop's Knoll the VADs shared the burden, if such it was, of maintaining contact with Anzacs and their families after they left the hospital.

Even 13 years later VADs and nurses were still attending the annual Anzac Day service at Arnos Vale Cemetery with Bush and his wife. In the report of this event in the Western Daily Press this poem from a VAD was included, as much a tribute to Bush as to the occasion.

Soldiers Corner Anzac Day

The graves are green this April day.
No April tears can wash away
The memory of what has been.
We travel back the after years
From divers lives, delights and fears,
Till every thought has reached one goal:
Again we are one corporate whole.
This April day the graves are green.

The graves are green this April day.
No April smiles can smooth away
The sorrow of what might have been.
Beside their flowering graves he stands,
Who gave them once with generous hands
Succour and home: and all that will
And heart of man could give: And still
He keeps the tryst. He has no need
Of words. He gave them deeds.
This April day the graves are green.[117]

Staff and patients, Robert Edwin Bush is on the left in the white jacket. Less well patients were in the Wards.

Recuperating patients convalesced in the extensive grounds of Bishop's Knoll and numerous pleasure trips were organised for the more mobile soldiers by Archibald Powell. In addition there was an extensive programme of entertainments organised for all Bristol Blue boys by the Inquiry Bureau (see Chapter 8). Regular excursions were made to Bristol Zoo, Bristol Art Gallery, Cheddar Gorge, Burrington Coombe, Langford House, Yatton, Bath, Weston-super-Mare, Berkeley Castle, and Salisbury. There were also trips on the river and regular evening entertainments provided by visiting local artistes. Music included that provided by Robert Edwin himself who played on the organ in the Ballroom now Ward 1.[118]

Leaving Bishop's Knoll on one of the many outings organised by Archibald Powell.

Weston-super-Mare picnic outing. Robert Edwin Bush is standing in front of the middle char-a-banc.

During a boat trip on the River Avon.

Bishop's Knoll visit to the Zoo with Lord Mayor Barclay J. Baron and veterans of the Crimea.

A visit to the Bristol Art Gallery organised by the Bristol Inquiry Bureau.

Many Commonwealth Emergency hospitals produced their own postcards to enable the men to write home showing where they were being nursed. This one says *"This is the back entrance of the Hospital. It is some place isn't it. That glass affair is the Conservatory where we had billiard tables phonographs, games books and goodness knows what. I wish I had some thousands. I would buy a place like this to live in for all of us after the war.* Charles".

CHAPTER 5

BISHOP'S KNOLL'S "COO-*EE!*" MAGAZINE

The Bishop's Knoll Hospital magazine was published every month from November 1916 until October 1917. This was not the only such magazine in Bristol; a short lived Magazine of the Second Southern General Hospital had appeared in April 1916 costing 4d. It was well supported by advertisements but was later renamed the "Kit Bag" of which a further five copies appeared.[119] There was also the "Dinkum Australian", about which nothing is known except that it is mentioned in a letter of February 1920 from J.W Arrowsmith of Bristol in response to an enquiry from Australia.[120]

THE MAGAZINE OF THE 2nd SOUTHERN GENERAL HOSPITAL

FIRST NUMBER
APRIL —— 1916

PRICE FOURPENCE

The short lived Magazine of the 2nd Southern General Hospital.

"Coo-ee!" was by far the most successful of WW1 hospital magazines through the efforts of its editor Archibald Powell, a reporter on the Western Daily Press, supported by Robert Edwin Bush's energy and finance. It would seem from a letter which Powell wrote to Bush on the eve of the latter's departure for Australia in March 1919 that *"Coo-ee!"* was Powell's idea. He also said that he greatly regretted that he was not able to have given as much time as he should have done to the task when his increasing workload as a reporter forced him to

give up the editorship in 1917.[121] This was clearly not what Bush himself thought, expressed in a postscript to the book which Powell was later asked to write by the Director of the Australian War Memorial, then located in Melbourne, for inclusion in their library.

A POSTSCRIPT [122]

"No account of the work of Bishop's Knoll Hospital is complete without reference to Mr A. G. Powell *not only* on account of his highly successful work as Editor of the Hospital Magazine "Coo-ee," which speaks for itself, but also for what was of even more importance, in that he constituted himself a kind of god-father to all Australians who came to Bristol, but more especially to those admitted to Bishop's Knoll. For Mr Powell to see a lonely Aussie in the streets of Bristol meant to that lonely one immediate friendship and hospitality. As a city, Bristol laid itself out to try and make the Australians feel at home, but I am sure no Bristolian did anything like as much as did Archibald Powell for the lads from "down under." I could go further and say no Englishman made more friendships than he did amongst the Australian soldiers. Many of them bless him for helping them out of sundry scrapes that they occasionally got into. He very kindly relieved me of all the work connected with the "outings" of the boys from this hospital, and undertook in the most enthusiastic manner the obtaining from three to six prizes regularly every week— for our games tournaments — which meant that from his friends he extracted some five hundred prizes for these events, which gave so much occupation and interest to the patients, week by week, and which made them forget their wounds and the necessarily somewhat monotonous life in hospital. Bishop's Knoll Hospital is much indebted to him; as are many hundred Australian soldiers whom fortune sent to this Queen City of the West. Probably this is the last service that he will render to Bishop's Knoll in connection with its war work. I sincerely thank him for this last goodness."

ROBERT BUSH

The title *"Coo-ee!"* was suggested in a competition run for patients at the Bishop's Knoll hospital by its Commandant for which Bush offered the prize of "a case of pipes". It was won by Sergeant Douglas Woods (who one trusts

"Coo-ee!".

was a smoker!).[123] The name derived from the practice of Australians shouting "Coo-ee! Come and join us!" during a recruiting march from Gilgandra, New South Wales, to Sydney in October 1915.[124] However, long before this the call was used by aborigines and then more generally by colonists in the outback to attract attention as the call carried well over long distances.

"Coo-ee!" was subtitled "The Journal of the Bishop's Knoll Hospital Bristol" and carried a dedication in its first issue (see over).

In what amounts to the first *"Coo-ee!"* editorial Powell says:

> "We are greatly indebted to the Vandyke Printers for the cover (*the only part in full colour*) and to Messrs Partridge and Love Ltd,[125] for material concessions in the matter of printing. Without the generous help of these well known Bristol firms Coo-ee would indeed be, for us, a far cry. Every bit of the literary and artistic work is voluntary, and our thanks are specially due to journalistic friends on the Bristol Newspaper press for their substantial help" (*Vol. 1 No 1*)

This Volume is

DEDICATED

to the First Thousand sick and wounded Australian Soldiers who were patients at Bishop's Knoll Hospital.

It is not unfitting, I think, that the first volume of "COO-EE" should be dedicated to those brave men from Australia, to whom it has been my privilege to minister: it has been not only a privilege, but it has also been a great joy to my wife and myself, to do all that was possible to alleviate their sufferings and to create a home-like atmosphere around these fine fellows so many thousands of miles from their homes and loved ones.

Amongst other distractions from the inevitable monotony of hospital life, our Magazine—"COO-EE"—has been one of the most successful; for I know that all the patients look forward to its monthly issue, and many are enabled to forget their aches and pains while contributing to its pages.

I should not like to close this brief foreword without testifying to the patient courage and fine discipline of these Australian soldiers during the time they were in my care. Ninety-eight per cent. of them quitted themselves like men—using the word "men" in its highest and best sense—and at the same time were almost womanly in the tenderness they showed to their more helpless companions in adversity.

I hope that this volume of "COO-EE" will recall many happy memories of Bishop's Knoll, when in happier times old patients look through its pages.

ROBERT BUSH.

Dedication to Issue 1 of "Coo-ee!".

"Coo-ee!" was soon circulating widely outside the hospital both to other UK camps and hospitals, as well as to parents and families back in Australia. Each issue cost 6d and was available from six booksellers in Bristol.[126] It could also be delivered to any address in the UK or abroad at a special rate for soldiers

of 7/6d post-paid for 12 issues. For others in the UK the annual subscription was 10/-, both subscriptions to be paid to the printers: Messrs Partridge and Love of Broadmead, Bristol. It was reported that over 100 copies were printed of later issues.

Vol. 1 No. 1: November 10,1916 (48 pages)
Vol. 1 No. 2: December 20, 1916 (40 pages)
Vol. 1 No. 3: January 20, 1917 (40 pages)
Vol. 1 No. 4: February 20, 1917 (40 pages)
Vol. 1 No. 5: March 10, 1917 (36 pages)
Vol. 1 No. 6: April 19, 1917 (38 pages)
Vol. 1 No. 7: May 21, 1917 (36 pages)
Vol. 1 No. 8: June 16, 1917 (38 pages)
Vol. 1 No. 9: July 10, 1917 (38 pages)
Vol. 1 No. 10: August 24, 1917 (38 pages)
Vol. 1 No. 11: September 18, 1917 (36 pages)
Vol. 1 No. 12: October 20, 1917 (42 pages)

The publication dates of the 12 issues of "Coo-ee!".

While it might have been seen as a private journal it is clear from a paragraph in the third editorial it had to be submitted for approval by the Press Censor.

The Editor Archibald Powell, was not a near neighbour of Robert Edwin Bush. In 1915 he was 48 years old and a reporter on the Western Daily Press and was living at 46 Linden Road, Redland. Born 1868 in Bristol, his first job had been with E.S. & A. Robinson a Bristol paper, printing and packaging company. He then ran away to sea for three and a half years. When he returned at the age of 23 he joined the Institute of Journalists as a pupil in 1891 and in 1893 joined the staff of the Western Daily Press.[127] Quite when and how he and Bush met is unclear but it was almost certainly through Gloucestershire cricket. Powell was an amateur cricketer, and in an article in the Bristol Evening World in December 1933, said he wrote as one who was privileged to have the right to play at the Gloucestershire County Ground at Ashley Down in Bristol "right from the start". This must mean that he turned out to play for the Bristol Press Cricket Club who rented a pitch there in 1888 when development work at the ground was still going on.[128] There is a record of a single innings game played on the Gloucestershire County Ground on July 11, 1893 between F.R. Alderwick's XI and Coalpit Heath in which A.G. Powell scored a duck for Alderwick's![129] Powell would later write a book on W.G.Grace and his sons.[130] Powell also dealt with the requests made during the First World War through the Western Daily Press for cricketing kit by serving Bristol units.

Powell at 48 years of age was too old for military service but he had good

Leslie Powell MC.

reason for wanting to "do his bit". His eldest son Leslie Archibald Powell, a naval Petty Officer,[131] had by this time served six months with a naval unit at Gallipoli and was soon recommended for a commission. Later as Flight Sub-Lieut. RNAS,[132] Lieutenant Powell RFC was awarded the Military Cross for "gallant fighting in the air" on the Western Front.[133]

Quite how much effort Powell senior put into the production of "*Coo-ee!*" and the social programme for the soldiers at Bishop's Knoll which will be described later is indicated by this letter sent just prior to the printing of the first issue of "*Coo-ee!*"

Oct 31st 1916 **16 Linden Rd Redland Bristol**

Dear Mr Bush,

I have fixed up a round the town trip for Friday next for a party of 26, we shall go to Redcliffe church, the Council House and then to tea at the Constitutional Club. Afterwards to the Picture House. On the following Friday a similar trip while on the 24th we shall I think be the guests of the Cornish society, the programme being a drive to Portishead and Clevedon and back to Stuckey's to tea with members of the Society. This has not however been definitely arranged. On Saturday Paymaster W.H. Cole R N V R, will with your concurrence take the chair at the concert. He is giving the prizes and his wife will distribute them. Mr Charles Inman is arranging the programme and it will be a very good one.

All the copy for COO EE except list of patients is in hand and Mr Love and I are making up the pages. It will I am sure turn out well but the next number will profit by our experience. I have been rather troubled over Sir Newton More and Sir........ letters. There is not a line that is otherwise than a tribute to B.K. and it seems rather discourteous to dismiss such prominent personages with a small par (sic) when we are making a big display of the Hon F Young's letter. It would be quite the best thing if you could send them each a copy of Coo-ee and ask them to give our enterprise their benediction. You could perhaps explain that their previous letters were not quite what you had expected. I am starting on the next number and I am hoping you will be able to get Lewin to do something for us. Holland has given some first rate drawings as well as the recruiting sketches but I don't want to dampen his enthusiasm by asking him do to much. Mr Cowlin of Yatton would like to have Robinson and three others to tea at the Picture House on Thursday next. Could you give them leave to remain out till six o'clock. I have asked Robinson who knows Mrs Cowlin to make up the party. They are to meet her at the Picture House at 2.30 p.m.

Yours very truly,
A.G. Powell

Archibald Powell frequently wrote in "*Coo-ee!*" under the nom de plume of "Leigh Woods" and this seems to have been his earlier practice for other papers including the Scotsman. This short insert comes from the first issue of "*Coo-ee!*"

Lieut. Leslie Powell, (i.e. Archibald Powell's eldest son) whilst serving in Gallipoli captured a native puppy. It was christened Archi Baba. One day this pup gave rise to a discussion on dogs in general. A Scotsman said, "If you want to know anything about dogs you should read the Scotsman. A fellow writes an article every week about 'em, and he seems to know all about every hair on their body."

"What is his name?" asked Lieut. Powell. "Leigh something," was the reply.

"Is it Leigh Woods? "asked Lieut. Powell.

"That's it," was the reply.

"Funny," said the Lieutenant.

"Why funny? "asked the Scotsman.

"Because 'Leigh Woods' is my father," was the unexpected rejoinder.[134]

Archibald Powell and his dogs in 1918.

It was clearly the intention of Bush and his committee to continue publication of "*Coo-ee!*" until the end of the War but they were faced with increasing difficulties. This announcement appeared in "*Coo-ee!*" in April 1917

> We would draw our readers attention to the new Government Order which will next month abolish the custom whereby magazines were "on sale or return" at all newsagents. The Order is due to the stringent necessity of conserving the paper supply, and our readers are requested by the Management Committee to place a definite order for the delivery of "Coo-ee!" every month. Unless this is done, many readers will be unable to secure a copy. The general public are little aware of the many adversities under which newspapers and magazines are today handicapped, due to restricted imports of raw material for paper-making but we feel that readers of "Coo-ee!" will assist us in every way by at once placing an order with their newsagent for delivery each month. Copies can, of course, be ordered direct of the Publishers.[135]

By October 1917 the editor could claim that "the journal originally promoted in the interests of Australian wounded nursed at Bishop's Knoll Hospital... has since been adopted by Australian soldiers generally as 'their particular organ' in this country".[136] However the magazine was subject to the same restrictions which had caused all newspapers to be reduced in size and many magazines to cease production altogether,[137] and the October 1917 issue would prove to be the last though this was clearly not intended at the time as the Editorial in that issue advised:

> "When "Coo- ee!" is next issued it will be found to have slightly altered its aspect. Our friends the printers have, despite a heavy handicap in the matter of paper shortage and depleted working staff, managed to publish our magazine for twelve months in the proportions originally decided upon, but the time has come when economy in production is absolutely necessary. The little magazine, we are assured, has been such a source of pleasure to patients, old patients, the staff and friends of Bishop's Knoll Hospital, that we were loath to let it disappear altogether. Thus it comes about that Coo-ee! will have to conform to the exigencies of the time, and appear with fewer pages although this is compensated for by the use of smaller type. We would appeal respectfully to our many friends and subscribers to give us their continued support, so that "Coo- ee!" might continue its useful service in giving pleasure to wounded soldiers."

Each of the 12 issues of *"Coo-ee!"* was produced and printed to a high standard and contained vivid, cheerful and moving accounts of the experiences of soldiers and staff as well as reports of the hospital's daily life and social activities. Several issues contained articles in different font size or line spacing suggesting that these may have been collected from other sources – perhaps those rejected from Bristol daily papers which Powell would have written or had access to. The *"Coo-ee!"* articles were enlivened by cartoons drawn by Private George C Holland of the Gloucestershire Regiment who intended to publish these after the War, but as far as is known this did not happen.[138] This was perhaps because by then many hundreds of similar cartoons had appeared in print elsewhere in widely distributed magazines such as in Punch.

"Coo-ee!" was an immediate success. In a little more than a week the first issue was sold out and the editor had received many letters of commendation

Private George C Holland.

and many favourable press comments.[139] As the editor could later claim:

> "Coo-ee is a journal originally promoted in the interests of the Australian Wounded nursed at Bishop's Knoll Hospital Bristol, but has since been adopted by Australian soldiers generally as 'their particular organ in this country'. It is not a commercial speculation. No fees are paid for any contribution and printing and distribution are done at actual cost., Any profits which may accrue will be devoted to the comfort of the Australian wounded."

The editor also surmised at the time that :

> "Years hence copies of Coo-ee will be much prized as souvenirs of the World War"[140]

Given that 100 years later bound volumes of *"Coo-ee!"* are to be found in reference libraries in England and Australia and all issues are also available on the internet,[141] such a prediction can be seen to have been fully justified.

The distribution of copies beyond Bristol was made by the YMCA and the editors reported on the rush for copies at the YMCA hut after a concert at the Salisbury Plain camp. Almost immediately articles for publication began to be received from soldiers based at Bishop's Knoll and further afield. So while the first issue had articles by Archibald Powell and Robert Edwin Bush alone (writing under the pseudonyms of "Leigh Woods" and "Dinkum" respectively) there were later regular contributions by soldiers, staff and other authors.

In each issue there was a list of the names and numbers of those still resident at the Hospital with those who had been there longest heading the list. The first issue in November 1916 also gave the details of the onward postings of soldiers who had recovered and their units but this was not included in

Honorary Executive Committee	
Chairman	R. E. Bush Esq. J.P. Commandant of Bishop's Knoll Hospital.
Vice Chairman	F. A. Wilshire Barrister-at-Law.
Hon Treasurer	Paymaster W.H. Cole RNVR.
Hon Sec.	L.V. Manning, Western Daily Press.
Editor	A.G. Powell.
Assistant Editors	L.V. Manning and T.Jay.
Art Editor	Pte George C Holland.
Commericial	F.T. Love; W.T. Pearce.

The cartoon which appeared at the front of each issue of "Coo-ee!".

subsequent issues (see Appendix 8).

Initially no indication was given in *"Coo-ee!"* as to its organisation and this is very likely to have been an ad hoc arrangement, but by the 12th issue, perhaps because of the publication's considerable success, a clear management structure had emerged (see above).

Private Holland's cartoons had appeared in the first issue and as he was now artistic Editor he must have been employed locally after his discharge from the Hospital. Judging by the subject of his first cartoon this is likely to have been in the Bristol Recruiting Office. He was intending to produce postcards of these and sell them for the benefit of wounded soldiers but so far no examples have been found.

It is enlightening to read how those of influence in Bristol viewed the city and its place in the world at this time. The Royal Edward Dock had been

The "Coo-ee!" Journal cover was designed by Robert Edwin Bush, it shows the house with the Australian Commonwealth forces badge above and the Coats of Arms of Australia, King George V and Bristol below.

opened at Avonmouth in 1908 in the hope of recovering Commonwealth trade from Liverpool. The article below was written by G.F Stone and appeared in "*Coo-ee!*" in December 1916. Admittedly it was aimed at influencing the Australians who were passing through Bishop's Knoll Hospital, some of whom would eventually make it home.

Imperial Bristol

G.F.Stone

When the Powers of the Grand Alliance assume the commercial offensive at the conclusion of the war, the importance of Bristol as an imperial link will be accentuated. Already the European struggle has imparted a tremendous impetus to the prestige of Bristol and it may not be generally understood in the city that through the length and breadth of the United Kingdom there are on the main highways thousands of sign-posts bearing the words, "To Avonmouth". This, however, is a theme which cannot at present, and for obvious reasons, be descanted upon, but all roads seem now to lead to Avonmouth, which is an integral part of the municipality of Bristol. That, in itself, is a premonition of the enhanced status of the city and the port; for it is a fair assumption that if Bristol and Avonmouth have played important parts during the war, they are likely to enter more definitely into the Imperial system when peace has been re-established. Some critics may, perhaps, take exception to the designation of the city as "Imperial Bristol"; but it is surely possible to so describe it, if it becomes, or is now, one of the trading centres of the British Empire. The picturesque and material aspects of Bristol, ancient and modern are being dealt with by a more able pen than mine; but it is the business aspect of the situation that demands attention, and we must be prepared to put forth an immediate effort to organise all our resources, so that the enemy may gain no advantage when the time for action arrives. Citizens of Bristol are well aware that the geographical position of the port is such as to confer upon it almost unique opportunities for development.

The present Sovereign, when he cut the first sod of the Royal Edward Dock (1902), declared Bristol to be "the Gateway of the West." And so it is. As such it is a heritage of immense value, and it is the bounden duty of those who have come into this heritage, not only to zealously guard it, but to enhance its worth for the benefit of posterity. In Australia, in Canada, in New Zealand, in Tasmania, and in South Africa, the knowledge of Bristol's potentialities has been spreading for years past, and this has been in no small measure due to the assiduous and tactful "missionary crusades" embarked upon by Mr Henry L Riseley, who is probably about as familiar a personality at the Antipodes as he is in his native city. On this foundation there ought to be raised a stable and permanent superstructure of commercial relationship; and when the troops that are now in our midst as our welcome guests return to their overseas homes, they may be moved to say a few kind things about Bristol and its scarcely veiled fortunes.

Bristol, including Avonmouth, is the natural port for the discharge of cargoes consigned from Canada. It lies nearer than any other first-class port in this country to the Ocean Gateways of the Dominion and to the Atlantic seaboard of the United States. Steamers to and from Bristol and New York effect a saving of 126 miles if the rival terminal port were Southampton, and 34 miles if the starting-point were Liverpool. In these days of exorbitant freights and costly coal this is a consideration, and it is one that has evidently influenced the decision of the Cunard Company to use Bristol as a terminal home port. By sea and rail Bristol is appreciably nearer to London than either Southampton or Liverpool, for the railway between the Metropolis and the western port has recently been shortened and the service otherwise accelerated. Those who have not had an opportunity of inspecting the installations of machinery and other dock equipments at Avonmouth will scarcely realise that these are the most complete and modem in this country. When the carrying power of British shipping is being subjected to the most exacting tests, the rapid discharge and distribution of goods are desiderata, for it must be remembered that Bristol is the focus of a vast radiating system, and embraces within easy range a densely populated industrial area in the Midlands. In fact, Bristol ought to be, and will probably become, the natural port for the supply of overseas commodities to Birmingham and the congeries of industrial communities of which it is the centre. That is a point which ought to carry great weight when the assumption of a general commercial offensive is under consideration. As a writer in a London magazine rightly observed, "As a distributive and concentrative centre the case for Bristol is unassailable, always providing that the dock accommodation and equipments are adequate." This sentence was penned fourteen years ago, before the Royal Edward Dock was constructed. During the interval, progress that may be justifiably described as marvellous has been made in the equipment of Avonmouth for every conceivable class of overseas traffic, and what Bristol cannot provide in the matter of modern facilities is not to be had elsewhere in the United Kingdom. The docks at Avonmouth can accommodate the largest steamers afloat, and if there is a tendency to increase the tonnage of ocean-going steamers, then Bristol will be quite prepared for the change. Bristol, which was once only second to London as a British port, is steadily moving towards the recapture of that position, and in the years that lie ahead it will be more and more clearly realized that amongst the other "Imperial" seaports Bristol will take high rank.

As the gateway for Canadian produce and mails Bristol has no serious rival, but the port is also advantageously placed for the transaction of business with the Antipodes. East of the Suez Canal all steamers are, of course, on an equality as regards the distances to be traversed to New Zealand or Australia. But west of the Suez Canal vessels chartered to Bristol have an advantage, since from Port Said to London the mileage is 3,232, and to Bristol 3,070, and thus 102 miles of sea journey are saved on the run to Bristol. The congestion on the Thames is also a factor in the situation, and the frequent and dense fogs which descend on that great highway create additional risks and delays. The Bristol Channel and the Estuary of the Severn are comparatively free from fogs, and there is, moreover, the additional advantage that a steamer bound for Bristol can steam full speed ahead until almost abreast of the entrance to the Avonmouth Docks. The contiguity of the coal-fields to Bristol renders fuel cheap, whereas coal has to be either sea borne or rail borne from long distances to both London and Southampton. Taking it all round, traffic between the Antipodes and Bristol can be more economically and promptly conducted than by way of London or Southampton: and the striking computation has been made that a vessel starting from Port Said (which is the point at which the equality of competing and westward-bound steamers comes to an end) could discharge her cargo at Bristol and deliver it by rail in

London a full day before a London-bound vessel could get rid of her goods. If, therefore, Bristol is incomparably the port for the Dominion of Canada, it is also the best home terminal port for the reception and distribution of all kinds of goods, perishable and non-perishable, from Australia, New Zealand and Tasmania. If the Overseas Dominions at the Antipodes meditate the increase of the exportation of meat to the Homeland it may be interesting to all those engaged in the traffic to learn that meat can be delivered, ex-ship at Avonmouth, in the great London mart in less than four hours, in the Birmingham district under two hours, and in the teeming and absorbent markets of South Wales in much less time. These may be, perhaps, prosaic details; but when a great problem like that which will soon confront the Empire has to be grappled with, it is carefully analysed and marshalled detail that counts. A seaport capable of successfully performing these most essential economic functions - a seaport that is a vital link not only between the Motherland and her Overseas Dominions far to the east and far to the west, but a link, in certain respects, between all the remotest outposts of the empire is well entitled to be classed as "Imperial". And so Bristol will remain "Imperial Bristol" and further lustre will assuredly be added to that distinction, for the future holds for Bristol all that her devoted sons most ardently desire for her.[142]

The Contents

"Coo-ee!" contained regular features apart from the editorial. These included "Ward Gossip" by Dinkum, that is R.E. Bush himself; "Should Auld Acquaintance" - news of former patients by Sister Miss Prout (GYP) ; "Entre nous" by Thomas Jay, one of the two assistant editors, containing amusing war related paragraphs from the British Press and "Stranger than fiction", odd war-time coincidences by "L.A.P" who remains unidentified.

There were other occasional articles on a variety of subjects intended to amuse or enlighten the Australian visitors but which had nothing to do with the life of the hospital. Many of these were written by Powell and the assistant editors Manning and Jay, and included "Ratting", "English Pastimes", and "Pantomimes". A surprising inclusion each month was a week by week retrospective rainfall report for all the regions of Australia. Quite why this should be can only be guessed at. Bush probably got such reports from Dalgety and Company as these were of great significance to the survival of farming stock and thus the fortunes of the company. Maybe, since many of the inmates of the hospital would have come from farming backgrounds, Bush included these out of interest or had been asked to do so by one of the soldiers.

The present author did consider reproducing the entire content of all issues of "*Coo-ee!*" here but apart from the question of size this would detract from the main purpose of this book which is to give a clear picture of the life of Robert Edwin Bush and of the hospital he created and ran. This means that many excellent articles have been omitted including the series by G.F. Stone on the History of Bristol. Selected articles from the twelve issues of "*Coo-ee!*" Magazine have been grouped in the following chapters (6-12) to give an overview of the organisation and workings of the hospital and its inmates.

Every Anzac should buy a copy of "COO-EE" the Journal of Bishop's Knoll (Australian) Hospital Bristol.

A voluntary literary & artistic effort in appreciation of the noble part played by Commonwealth soldiers in the cause of Empire, forming an interesting Souvenir of . . this stirring war time . .

You will be helping your wounded Comrades by supporting this Magazine as profits (if any) will be expended on their behalf.

PRICE SIXPENCE

PER COPY.

CHAPTER 6

PATIENTS' ACCOUNTS OF THEIR WAR

The Natural History of a dugout

Gunner Frank E Westbrook [143]

Frank E. Westbrook.

Gunner Frank Westbrook was a cut above the average. The account below appeared in the first issue of "*Coo-ee!*" as did the announcement that his collection of poems "Anzac and after", had been published.[144] This was one of the first books of poems to appear and the only one to contain poems actually written at Gallipoli. While these are unknown in England they are well appreciated in Australia and the book is still in print.

Frank was born in 1889 in South Yarra, Victoria and was an early recruit to the Australian forces. He enlisted as soon as War broke out and described his former occupation as a cook but in fact he had held many jobs including sheep shearer. He joined the Field Artillery Brigade of the Australian Imperial Force as Trumpeter but soon held the rank of Gunner of the 4th Battery of the 2nd Brigade which had the distinction of taking ashore the first gun on Anzac beach. Frank had left Australia for Egypt on His Majesty's Australian Transport *Shropshire* on October 20, 1914 bound for Egypt. While in Egypt he wrote his first poem and had his first brush with authority.

The Australian troops had been stationed at Mena Camp in Egypt and before embarking for Gallipoli their behaviour while on leave in Cairo had been a cause for concern by the military authorities. Under instruction from Major General Sir William Bridges, commander of the 1st Australian Division, Charles Bean raised the matter in a dispatch, which was published in various Australian newspapers in January and February 1915. Bean who was another Old Cliftonian, had won a scholarship to Oxford where he read law. Returning to Australia he later resigned a legal post to become a reporter on the Sydney Morning Herald and in 1914 was successful in securing for himself the appointment of the official war correspondent to the Australian Imperial Force with the rank of Captain.[145]

Over the following weeks, Bean's dispatch came in for a good deal of attention in the Australian press, and a number of letters were published there. Westbrook penned his scathing satirical poem, *'To Our Critic"* which lambasted Bean for having defamed the Australian troops in Egypt, describing him as a "whining wowser". Initially published in the *Egyptian Mail*, the poem was subsequently circulated widely in Australian newspapers during April 1915 and eventually elicited an apology. It would seem that this was Frank Westbook's first effort at poetry.

After several months of action at Gallipoli, Westbrook was evacuated to the island of Lemnos in October 1915 suffering from what was known as the *Gallipoli Gallop* (severe diarrhoea). Here he wrote further poems. He was then sent to England to convalesce. One of his poems is written from Epson in December 1916 and others from London. By the summer of 1916 he was at Bishop's Knoll as one of the first Australians to arrive there, but by November 1916 was sufficiently recovered to be posted to Salisbury by which time his poems had been published. Remarkably by June 1918 he was still in England where, on the 21st of that month, he married Winifred Eggleton who came from Gloucestershire. He returned to Australia after the war and wrote no further poetry as far as is known. This is one of his articles for *"Coo- ee!"* based on his experiences in Egypt and Gallipoli.

I am glad I was not Pharaoh when his plague of flies came. I'll just bet the old fellow called on his trusty henchmen to swing the punkahs more energetically than ever, and begged his many women to curse with him when the flies flopped into his royal kuss-kuss and coffee. Flies have not altered much I dare say since those times, for they still have a most ingenious knack of alighting on your food when it is on the brink of one's mouth, and it sets one guessing as to whether one has bitten fly a la Anzac on bully and biscuit or biscuit and Tickner's marmalade. They also have a fierce antagonism to a piece of netting that is designed to shield a sleepy Bill-Jim's face from their persistent attentions. Old Pharaoh was lucky in a way; he could kick his slaves if they failed to keep the versatile fly from his regal dusky visage. I have heard it said that for every fly one killed a thousand came to see fair play. Well, I "dunno," I think someone here in Anzac has been killing them for a long time, and this season the blighters are out to recover some of their debit account. I wonder how Jacko the Turk endures it? Perhaps, like the "Gippos," he has them well trained.

I have a vivid memory of the gamins of the gutters and bazaars in Cairo sharing with a mangy dog and a regiment of flies a dilapidated hunk of sugar-cane. They never bother. Doubtless they are fatalists, and say, "What is to be will be" consequently Mr Fly is quite at home at any old place with these people, wherever opportunity offers. I am flapping the door of my dug-out and waterproof sheet, combined with some empty sandbags, to drive them out, but they merely go out and beckon others. But tonight I will have an awful revenge. When the night stars lower and the temperature drops a good many points, and my enemy develops cold and sticky feet (a soldier's complaint), he is at my mercy. For I make a cone-shaped flare out of a newspaper (that has come to me from home, and sealed with a kiss from dear, sweet lips—what base use is it reduced to), and set it aflame, and soon hundreds of wingless and legless little fiends of torture are either consumed in the flaming fire of vengeance or scatter themselves in pitiful array across my couch, composed of blankets, bags and some stray pieces of dug-out. Even in death's throes they hide with a stern resolve to do their duty in my blankets. Some crawl down my back now that I have retired to rest, and hold a parade in wingless glory across my anatomy. I crush them with an iron hand, and then ruminate on their remains, and a picture rises of the flies at work on a dead Turk just over the edge of the wall of my dug-out. So much for them.

Then I have a dim recollection of a Biblical statement that Pharaoh was afflicted with a plague of lice. Worse and worse! Poor devil, what a fate! I can picture him in an astute and yet undignified position, while his slaves searched his nether garments for the royal enemies. Gee, I know and understand and a Bill-Jim would sooner go without his army cracknels and bully for supper than miss this undress parade, for his night's rest depends on his success in the hunt and slaughter. System is everything, and one learns to start methodically and go from head to heel with great care, and turn over every seam and lapping-end, puttee, socks and all. They survive boiling water and any precautions one may take to prevent their activities. Where their intelligence emanates from is marvellous, considering their size. They will wait till your puttees or leggings are put on and secure, and then will attack you in the calf of the leg. When one girds on the equipment of a swaddy (sic), they make a fine de-bouching movement between your shoulder-blades,[146] where you cannot scratch. They have learnt the soldier's art of digging in to cover, in the earth, for kill them as you may, they arrive in battalions each day for the slaughter, and they stand not on the order of their coming (or their going).

I am glad I am not Pharaoh; he could have all his wives, concubines and slaves thrown in. The flies are quiet now, and the roof of my covering shows tiny glimpses of a star-gemmed sky. I pause to scratch ere I settle down with the old black pipe, and picture another blue night sky, slashed with the brilliant gems of the Southern Cross. Out of the drowsy mists of approaching sleep I hear the cracking of stock-whips (it is only the Mauser bullets looping the loop on their way over), the rush of the galloping hoofs and the crash of horns. The tall, gaunt trees—gum trees in blossom—the wattle, the waratah, the dry creeks, the old homestead and the green corn. Can I forget them all?

So sleepy—a pair of brown eyes are beckoning me into dreamland. So long.

An incident on patrol

Private R.C. Hooper[147]

You have asked us Mr Editor, to jot down some of the happenings of our soldiering. Well, here is a little yarn which may or may not be worthy of a place in Coo-ee. Anyway, it is an incident showing what goes on when there is fighting to be done, and which isn't likely to get noticed from the war correspondents.

A patrol went out from our lines at Anzac- a NCO and four men. It was just after dark and our business was to see if Jacko was making any alterations or embellishments to his trenches. After crawling on our hands and knees through thick scrub for two hundred yards or so we came near enough to make out the Turks' trenches. We were resting for a while, when Jack and Bill started an argument and nearly came to blows. This is the burthen of their difference.

JACK: "I don't reckon there are any Turks at all in those trenches! They always keep very quiet of a day excepting for a few rifle shots that come from up and down the line from one shooter."

BILL: "Oh, rot! They do that of a day just to draw yer on. You'll find plenty in the second line. Why just hark at 'em barking now, that's more than one rifle; they carry on like that every night as though they were mighty scared at something or trying to scare us."

JACK: "Rats! You think you know everything just because your number's nine and you're an old hand. I say there are very few Turks in those trenches, and with a few men I could take the whole of the trenches."

BILL: (whose blood is up) "I've been across here since the bally show started. You came because they made it too hot for you at home. Why you've only been here a month, and you try to persuade me there's no Turks over there. You must be off your rocker, and if you have much more to say I'll straighten that blanky nose of yours."

Jack could not stand this and decided to have it out with Bill right on the spot. Both were proceeding to unfurl their tunics, when up came the sergeant.

"What the devil!" says he. "Silence! Down men, down! Retire as sharp as you can: a big patrol of Turks is trying to cut us off!"

Every man was very quiet as we retired to our own lines, and Jack had the chance to see a few Turks fall. A few shots were exchanged, and Jack got a slight wound in the leg, but not severe enough to leave the firing line. We managed to get to our lines safely and no sooner were we in than the Turks' lines were all ablaze with machine-gun and rifle fire, thinking we were going to attack. So Jack came to the conclusion that there were more Turks in the trenches than the eye could see.

Nursing Sisters

Lieut. Ripon ASC[148]

Many well-deserved tributes have been paid to the fighting men of the British Empire, and their deeds have always received the publicity of the Press throughout the English-speaking world. But what of the Nursing Sisters of the Empire? This question can easily be answered. They have made equal sacrifices to the soldiers, and in some cases even greater. I have seen them at work in various theatres of war, and know that their great pluck and attention to duty, and this often in the face of trying physical conditions, is not fully realised, although their praise is constantly on the lips of brave men in the fighting zones.

The curt Admiralty announcement of the sinking of the hospital ship Asturias will, however, make the indifferent think of what grave risks our brave women face in helping our helpless against the barbaric Hun. Some of my best friends were on the staff of the lost ship when I was aboard, and they brought brightness and gaiety into the lives of many a tortured man. I can well remember my introduction to members of the nursing profession whilst on active service.

When stationed on a desolate island in the Aegean Sea rumours had got abroad that nurses were coming to commence their noble work in our midst. It was bitterly cold there at the time, and when a cold north-east wind sprang up tents were blown down, whilst the sand and dust made it almost impossible to breathe without getting a lot down one's throat, as well as almost blinding one. There was also a great deal of sickness, the chief cases being those of dysentery, jaundice, and typhoid. How anxiously the arrival of the nurses was awaited may be gathered from the fact that there were no women on the island. This once led to a very humorous remark. As is perhaps known to many, some of the men in the East wear a long flowing robe, which might easily be mistaken for a woman's skirt. A fresh arrival from England noticing one of these costumes from the back, said to his companion: "Bill, what a treat to see a woman after ten days at sea!" It would be impossible to describe that man's face and his disappointment when he realised his error.

At length the day arrived when the nurses were to be disembarked from the hospital ship in which they had made their journey across the oceans. Somehow work seemed to be finished particularly early that morning. At any rate, by the time the nurses had reached the pier there was a long double queue of soldiers waiting to welcome them, and through which the nurses had to pass to the field hospital. Their light baggage was soon carried by stalwart soldiers to its destination.

Meanwhile the nurses had the ordeal of being cheered to the echo, and hearing light bantering remarks. How pretty and charming they all appeared to us men, and how our hearts went out to them in sympathy and admiration for having come to such a desolate spot. And they seemed to understand why we had forgotten our manners. In fact, our cockney soldier friend, who was so disappointed at not finding women on the island, summed up our feelings towards our new comrades very cogently in these ungrammatical words: "There are no wimmin here, but nurses, and they are heroes!"

Quietly, without complaining and without any fuss, the nurses set about their work of mercy in wards which were merely marquee tents. They felt the discomfort keenly, but many a man's misery was made lighter from the fact that the hardships were shared by them in so light-hearted a manner. Perhaps he contrasted the sacrifices they had made with those of himself and comrades, and determined to be brave for their sakes. Who knows? It was known, as a matter of fact, that the sight of their bright, cheerful faces alone accounted for the saving of the lives of many, whilst their careful and experienced nursing saved many more.

Their living quarters were huts, more or less sheltered from the elements, and they did their own cooking. However, much of the heavier work was done by orderlies. In the course of time I became a patient myself, and had, therefore, a much better opportunity of appraising their splendid work for the ailing officers and men who came under their charge. Occasionally, too, they would have to minister to one of their own sex who had broken down through overwork in trying climates. All the nurses took their work most seriously and conscientiously, as a matter of fact they appeared happiest when busiest. As with the soldiers so with them. They frequently had arguments between themselves as to whether Canadian, Australian, New Zealand or English made the best nurses, and which was the best country.

Certainly some Australian sisters on the hospital ship which brought me home thought of asking to return to Australia when they knew that they were going to serve in an English hospital under an English matron. Subsequently I met the same charming ladies whilst visiting London for the first time, and they admitted quite frankly that they had been agreeably surprised at all they had seen in the motherland. They also expressed pleasure at the warm and cordial welcome they had been given by their English colleagues. It was also very pleasing to find that sisters of the Regular and Territorial Force appreciated the help and assistance rendered by members of the VAD However, in England I found that the ladies who waited on wounded soldiers at meals received no official recognition whatever in the shape of a badge or uniform, and they looked upon this as a justifiable grievance. Certainly the work is very arduous, and nearly all give up the morning or afternoon in which to help the convalescent soldier.

The nurses at the home hospitals made a great fuss over the invalided warriors, and they seemed to know of an infallible cure for the moderate cases. It simply consisted of "feeding well," and assuring them that they would soon be able to go to their own homes. In conclusion, it is only right to remember that many nurses have laboured where virulent diseases are rife, and that some contracted illnesses which proved fatal, and their bodies were buried in the same little cemeteries where some of their soldier patients had preceded them. With the exception of the inscription, the crosses on their graves were the same as those of our soldiers.

Simpson and his Donkey

Leigh Woods[149]

Simpson's Donkey.

The story of John Simpson Kirkpatrick (known as John Simpson) caught the public imagination. This is just one of the many accounts given by grateful comrades. Twenty-two years old, British born John Simpson Kirkpatrick was an unlikely figure to become a national hero. He deserted from the merchant navy in Australia in 1910, and worked there in a variety of jobs. He only enlisted in the AIF, because he expected it would give him the chance to get back to England; but he found himself at ANZAC Cove on April 25, 1915, and was killed less than four weeks later.

> There is a halo of romance and mystery about Simpson. Who or what he was before kitting it out in khaki, nobody seems to know or care. 'Tis quite enough for Australians that for a month or more he was the hero of the Anzac drama, a man who said very little but who did big things, searching out the wounded giving them first aid, and then with the help of his donkey taking them back to a place of safety. It is said by some that Simpson was not so crazy about rushing to join up when the fiery cross first flamed through the cities and townships and out to the back blocks as most of the boys, and that his girl chided him for his slowness. However that may be, Simpson was away with the first contingent, and was among the first crowd ashore at Anzac. On the second day of the landing Simpson and his friend the donkey met. There was no formal introduction, and there was no special reason why Simpson should take to the donkey or the donkey to Simpson. The fact remains, however, that from the first the attachment was mutual. Perhaps the poor beast was nervy as a result of the pandemonium going on around, and looked for comfort from human society. Perhaps Simpson was fed up with things in general, and

found in the dumb beast that silent sympathy for which he yearned, but which was lacking in his boisterous comrades. Anyway, they cottoned on to each other, and for a whole month were inseparable pals. Exactly how many lives they saved will never be told ; some say scores, some hundreds. Every day Simpson went away up Shrapnel Gully with the donkey by his side, or following behind like a big, well-trained dog, to search for some mother's boy who might be lying in the scrub bleeding to death. Ever and anon they returned after a successful foray. Did the beast know when he was bringing a broken soldier down the gully that he must tread warily and avoid jerks? Of course not, but there are plenty of Anzacs whom it would be better not to contradict when they say he did.

It was a queer sort of beast that donkey, a regular bantam in size, save for his ears, which were unusually long and generally carried at the half lop. When his ears went to the full cock the boys knew it was time to look for cover for it was a sure sign that Beachy Bill had spoken, and that a big shell was on its way. And the donkey knew the value of cover as well as any one, otherwise he would have been cold meat in small joints long before Simpson made his last trip up the gully. It was in the palmy days of the snipers that Simpson and the donkey did their business. Often a poor chap took a bullet through the lung, or had his legs smashed without anybody knowing it, until the donkey smelled him out or Simpson found him.

And so this life-saving work went on. One day the donkey got in the way of a stray bullet and had to be left, but not for long. His master came back with a couple of comrades, and they half dragged and half carried the animal back behind the lines. A few days later he was up and about again, a bit lame, but just as keen on the job as ever. Late one afternoon he came down the gully with a wounded man on his back, but Simpson was not there. As soon as he had delivered his charge he turned round and trotted up the gully again. Somebody followed, and saw the creature stop and sniff at a form lying quite still on the ground. It was Simpson, with a hole through his great big heart.

(The picture of the donkey is from a photograph in my possession, taken by Trooper W. F. McIver of the 4th Light Horse – Leigh Woods.)

Two issues later the editor published the paragraph below which was abstracted from a letter he had received from Brigadier (later General Sir) William Birdwood who was now stationed with his 1st Anzac Corps in France.

> "I am very interested to see that Simpson's donkey, whom we knew on the Peninsula as "Murphy", is referred to. He was one of a batch I bought on the island of Lemnos the day before we effected our landing on the Peninsula in April, when I fully realized the water difficulties with which we would be faced. I therefore obtained about 100 small donkeys to carry tins of water which I am glad to say they did with great success."[150]

About a mule - a Remount camp episode[151]

The account below appeared anonymously but in the next issue in January 1916 the editor confided that it been written by Mr Lionel V. Manning who would later appear in the *"Coo-ee!"* management as one of the two Assistant editors.

> Herbert Augustus Simmons arrived at the Remount Depot wearing red hair and the happy expression of an alligator after it had a weekly meal. He had nothing to laugh about as far as we could see but you could tell he really was pleased with himself, because the smile did not come off even when the ambulance passed him, bearing the bruised and battered body of poor old 'Darky' Peters who had been having a one-sided argument with the pet of "J" lines — better known as "The Terror" — over a little matter of a dandy brush. Not an encouraging sight, you would have thought, to greet the eyes of a fledgling recruit, who probably had been making up his mind he was coming to a sort of Home for Tired Tommies and convalescent Column-dodgers.
>
> Not that Nobby was dead - not by any means. The only part of him not swathed in bandages was his face, and that from a strictly moral sense was a pity, for his language was making the stretcher bearers blush, and both had been at the Depot some weeks. Well Herbert Augustus smiled, and he smiled some more when we showed him the Depot's casualty returns for the week. So just to keep him cheerful we coaxed him onto the canteen (dry) and told

him the wondrous tales of The Terror most of them true, for where the Terror is concerned, truth is stranger than fiction.

Nobby led off with a striking (the word titled the subject) dissertation on mules in general, touching lightly upon their pathetic devotion to soldiers, and leading up in easy stages to The Terror's superiority over all other mules in heel and toe work.

"It's this wye wiv Terror," he explained soothingly, "'e ain't jest hartful, Ordinary mules is hartful, extraordinary mules is clever wiv it but Terror, 'e's a bloomin' Senior Wrangler. Ordinary mules jest kicks you when you ain't looking but Terror makes you think 'es yer best pal on earth, an when you're doing 'im a kindness 'ee kicks yer 'cos 'ee knows 'es going to 'urt yer feelins, as well as break yer leg; 'es a hartist, that's what 'ee is. 'Ee's never bin groomed yet, nor ain't ever likely to be."

We further pointed out to Herbert of the Sunny Smile that if this charming ornament of "J" lines had not been born a mule, he would certainly have been the world's very best feather - weight boxer. He enjoyed all the characteristics beloved by the fancy. He was nimble on his pins, had a terrible left with which he had never been known to miss, and could feint with his off hind fetlock like Freddy Welsh. As for ring craft, he could waltz you into any corner of the stable he chose before handing you your pass out check.

Herbert let us talk ourselves dry — it was the dry canteen, you will remember — and then he quietly announced : "I shall groom The Terror tomorrow." Just that. Uttered in plain, matter-of-fact tones, as if he was asking Nobby to pass the margarine at breakfast, only more polite. Lord! How we gasped. Under pressure he let us into his secret. He was, it seems, a young man with a system. He could tame fire-eating mules whose favourite meal was khaki, at one sitting. "Make 'em so tame, me lads," he said, "they will follow yer about jest like a little dawg." And the system was - KINDNESS!

When we recovered a little, we tried to explain that the last man who had experimented in the Come-into-the-garden-Maud business was still in hospital, and it was for saving him from the cruel fate of being eaten alive that Nobby had been recommended for his DCM which letters are short for "Don't Coax Mules". Furthermore, that The Terror had sworn an extra specially sanguinary vendetta against silly asses of Herbert's sort.

But Herbert Augustus still smiled confidently. He said he had a cousin on his wife's side who lodged with a man who had the tip straight from a retired lion tamer. So we let him go blindly to his fate.

Next morning at stables we stood by for trouble, and Nobby, who has tender heart on pay days had his first-aid outfit handy. The Terror, the minx behaved like a flipper with a curate, not too bashful, but just enough to draw him on. She led off with the gladdest of glad eyes, and, as Herbert turned on the baby talk, she nestled up lovingly.

Nobby says he saw her wink in our direction at that precise moment, but Nobby, being an untrustworthy person is not to be relied upon for detail. As he applied the dandy brush tenderly Herbert cooed a haunting lullaby. It only wanted spot-lights, slow music, and a beauty chorus to make it look like a chunk out of revue.

The Terror kept up the play-acting so long, however, that we began to think she really liked playing Juliet, and was going to let her Romeo off by merely biting his ear. The grooming was finished, and Herbert had actually said a fond farewell and promised to send round flowers in the morning, when he made the bloomer. He turned away.

We picked him up a full yard beyond the spot which had hitherto been regarded as the Terror's best effort in the drop-kick line. Herbert Augustus's system had been badly shaken. We laid him in the next cot to "Darky" Peters, and as we left the ward we saw his lips move. Bending low, I caught these words : "Me for the next draft, sonny". There are worse things than front-line trenches.

My friend Curly

Leslie A. Powell[152]

Another article by the editor's eldest son

He was an Australian, a fine, big, strapping fellow while I was quite small. When I say small, I was just half an inch over Bantam size, and no doubt it was because of these differences that we chummed up. Anyway, we just met—

I well remember the occasion —in Lemnos Harbour. Curly's ship (I always called him Curly because of a little fair wisp of hair which peeped from under his slouch hat, and always seemed to be trying to get into his eye) had run short of tobacco and cigarettes, and our ship was lying quite close, one of a hundred or so huge transports waiting to convey their cargoes of men who had answered their country's call at the very beginning, to that place where such glorious deeds were later performed called Gallipoli.

Sitting on the forecastle head one afternoon, I noticed on his ship a handkerchief being waved, and as I thought it was intended for me, gave an answering wave. Whereupon my Australian friend commenced semaphoring, and this message came to me :- "We have all run short of baccy and fags, and have not had a smoke for three days. Have you any to spare?"

I replied to the effect that if they sent a boat's crew over in a couple of hours' time they would not be disappointed. In due course the boat's crew arrived. In the meantime I had organised a collection of baccy and fags, and had gathered together something like four pounds of various brands of tobacco, a few cigars, and close upon 2,000 cigarettes. The dozen or so Australians who comprised the boat's crew spent the evening with us in a smoking concert on the lower deck and went away after dark followed by cheers from us and good wishes on both sides.

We met again, Curly and I, somewhere about April 29th. It was at Walker's Ridge, Gaba Tepe. We had just taken part in an advance, and had had to retire again. I spotted a man some distance away being pursued by about fifteen to twenty Turks. I was one of a machine-gun crew, and I immediately pointed this out to my comrades, and we opened fire on the pursuers, who were either knocked out or retreated. An instant later Curly stumbled into the trench. I need not go into details of this meeting: suffice to say it bound us closer together.

Some months later, when we were both in Alexandria, we had many good times together. Our next meeting was in the Lybian Desert, where we were giving a military lesson to the Senussi.* One day, having gone out to give battle to these disturbers of Egyptian peace, a column of cavalry were passing on their way to an advantageous position from whence to charge. Suddenly, with a "Cheer oh, Smiler!" (as Curly called me) I saw my Australian pal.

Poor Curly! The next I saw of him was on a Red Cross wagon with his thigh ripped open by a Senussi bullet. He was still as cheery as ever, and as I lit his "gasper" and shook his hand he said : "See you again in Blighty soon: we are sure to meet."

Sure enough we did meet. I was visiting a cousin who is a nurse in a London hospital, and while there talking to her someone came up and tapped me on the shoulder. It was Curly again!

*The Senussi Campaign took place in north Africa, from November 1915 to February 1917. The Senussi were a religious sect resident in Libya and Egypt, who were persuaded by the Ottoman Empire to attack the British in order to divert British forces.

How I came to Bishop's Knoll

Bombardier W.G.Haynes.[153]

When a company of people is together it very often happens that everyone seems to stop talking simultaneously, and a very marked silence follows. This same thing frequently occurs in France, for sometimes all the guns stop firing, and a peaceful silence settles round that portion of the line where you may then be stationed. It was during one such temporary lull in the firing that I first got into conversation with our then new officer. The officer was Lieutenant Robert Bush, well known in local circles, and this conversation took place in an artillery observation station at the beginning of the spring of 1915.

When an officer and a Tommy are alone in an observing "crow's nest" where death may come at any moment should the enemy artillery decide to shell them, it is only natural that the difference in rank is often forgotten, and they enjoy a somewhat affable chat. How the conversation started I do not know, but I remember that the Lieutenant suddenly remarked, "Oh! then you are a Bristolian!" Receiving my reply in the affirmative he took a photograph from his pocket, and handing it to me, he asked whether I knew the place on it. "Yes," I replied, "It is Cook's Folly," "No" he said, "It is not Cook's Folly, but stands just below there." He went on to tell me that it was Bishop's Knoll, his home, and that his father, Robert E. Bush, had converted it into a Red Cross Hospital, and many wounded had already received treatment there. "So," he said with a smile, "if you get, wounded do not fail to go there."

Just then the lull in the firing was broken by the enemy artillery, which commenced to shell our battery, and we, of course, replied by shelling theirs. Consequently our conversation ended abruptly.

It was about the middle of May 1915, that I was wounded, and after an operation in a field hospital was shipped to England. A week later I found myself in a hospital "somewhere in Kent." This was a good distance from Bristol, and thinking I would like to get nearer home, correspondence commenced with a view to enabling myself to take advantage of Lieutenant Bush's invitation: "If you get wounded, do not fail to go there."

Six weeks passed, during which time I was viewing some of the most beautiful scenery in Kent; then one night a telegram arrived stating that I was to proceed to Bristol next day. So I arrived at Bishop's Knoll the following afternoon, just after my arrival the Head Sister told me that someone wished to see me. I remarked, "What! So soon?" She seemed amused, and took me out into the grounds. Pointing to an invalid's chair she said, "He's in there," and before I could ask who, she was gone. I walked over as directed, and imagine my surprise when I saw lying in the chair my lost Lieutenant himself. For a few minutes I was rather confused, for he was the last person I had expected to see. Anyhow I was glad to see him there "safely" wounded, for things may have happened very differently. He told me where and how he had been wounded. It transpired that he had been riding along a road to seek out a new position for the battery, when a shell burst near him. His groom, who was an old friend of mine, had been hit very badly, and the Lieutenant had been wounded in the leg by a piece of the high explosive shell. His horse was, I believe, killed, and the Major with whom he was riding died of wounds the next day.

I remained at Bishop's Knoll for about six weeks, and spent a very enjoyable time. I found out that Commandant R.E. Bush works very hard during the day, assisting and superintending the preparation of meals, as well as running the whole of the work in connection with the hospital. Often during the evenings he would come into the splendid ballroom (or Ward 1), and play tunes to us on the superb organ that stands at the far end of the ward on a raised

Patients and nursing staff outside Bishop's Knoll war hospital.

platform. Whenever he played "Onward Christian soldiers!" he would remark: "Ah! Here's one with a chorus," and the men would join in the singing of this hymn very heartily.

It is a pleasure for me to be able to relate that I was present at Southmead Hospital on September 7th, 1915 when the King and Queen visited it. I saw Commandant and Mrs Bush presented to their Majesties, and am very proud to tell that King George himself spoke to me for some minutes. I do not mind admitting that my heart sank within me when I heard my name mentioned, and then saw His Majesty walking toward the place where I sat. I soon found that my "fears" were groundless, for the King soon puts you at your ease when he begins to speak.

Now, had it not been for Lieutenant Bush saying, "If you get wounded, do not fail to go there," it is quite certain that this article would never have been written.

Lieutenant Robert Francis Lochée Bush eventually retired with the rank of Brigadier (See Appendix 1).

CHAPTER 7

LIFE AT BISHOP'S KNOLL HOSPITAL

My stay at Bishop's Knoll

Trooper J. Lennox [154]

Well! I don't know how to begin, middle, or finish this task set me.

To begin with, I can only remember a leg on a splint, which was somehow hanging on to a body, that being myself, but wishing all the time to change places with some other leg. I can remember the Battle of Neuve Chapelle as if it were yesterday. The day of my knocking out was March 12th, 1915, From that day till the 16th it was all "leg". But after that, the day of arrival at Bishop's Knoll, there have been so many other interests to think about, that my leg itself has become a back number in my thoughts.

Trooper Lennox.

It was a pretty smash up, and I think Dr Ormrod must have been an artist as well as a magician to have brought the leg to the shape it is now. It was day-time when we arrived. Outside it looked very different, not having the operating theatre just opposite the front entrance to the hospital, where it is now. This was not built until after my first or second operation, which took place in the wards. After this the weeks passed without very much to mark them, except for the excitement of the new fellows coming in, amongst them being the good old ones – Stocks, Fergusson, McLeod, Bonnor and others. Those were Jolly days. Things began to go with a swing.

As the summer months came along and I was able to get about on crutches, I was one of those fortunate ones taken on those glorious Thursday outings arranged by the Bristol Inquiry Bureau, which we all looked forward to week after week, visiting Cheddar, Weston, Clevedon, and the old historic Castle of Berkeley, and many other places of interest. Apart from these we were taken out for weekly excursions, picnics, garden parties and long country rides by Mrs Seddon who accompanied us on every occasion. These were thoroughly enjoyed and appreciated greatly by all.

We did not have "passes" in those days. So to while away the time we got up a band and gave a concert and although there have been many concerts since (and some of them marvellous achievements) that first concert, given by that first band, was the best of the lot. It was composed of combs and tin cans, but the greatest feature of all was the conductor, "Hannah." He looked a treat in a great frock coat, top hat with flowers on the top, an eye-glass, and button-hole all complete. And that band played when it could blow, and when it couldn't it just quietly left off one by one. After the concert we were given a grand tea by the Sisters, and although the band gave a good performance, it was really at its best at the table.

The summer was soon gone, and then, about the 15th of September, the first batch of Australian sick came in from the Dardanelles, and with them "the old order changeth, giving place to new."

We had the much-longed-for "passes." The coach-house was turned into a billiard room, fitted with a lovely billiard table. Now there started more concerts and more outings, and all through the winter we had regularly two concerts a week. Some of the singing and playing at these has been great, and there is something in the programme for all to enjoy. About Christmas time, some of the men being very fond of music, they got up several concerts among themselves, and invited a lot of friends. All who were here for Christmas will have that day in their memory for a long time to come. For a long time before, the Sisters were busy getting ready to give us all a great time. We were all to be dressed in fancy costume – that was all we knew. "Bubbles" (alias Bromley) and I were Pierrots. Everyone had to be something to make the fun as great as possible.

The Christmas dinner was a great affair. Mr and Mrs Bush carved the huge turkey, and all the other Sisters were busy helping. Then came plum pudding and after that fruit, but our appetites seemed to have quite gone by that time, and we were "sorry we had had enough." After dinner there was the great excitement of dressing up, and all appearing in different costumes. The Sisters all dressed up too, mostly in Dutch Costumes, and we all joined round the laden Christmas Tree, which was covered with presents for all, and were given out by the Commandant. Afterwards we had games, then supper, and then to bed very late.

Christmas Pierrots.

It is a day long to be remembered, and having been here so long into this year, I am wondering whether it may be possible that I shall see another Christmas Day at Bishop's Knoll.

This year since Christmas has gone on wings. We have had two concerts a week right through the summer months, and outings galore sight-seeing around Bristol, special visits to places of interest in and around the city; competitions in games of billiards, bowls and cards, all of which add to our book of memory those things which we shall have to read over and over again long after the war is over, when we are back in our own quiet homes, in all parts of the Empire. I and many other chaps will think again, not of the misfortune of being knocked out of the running, but of the luck of being sent to Bishop's Knoll Hospital, one of the most beautiful homes of this England, for which anyone of us would gladly fight any enemy trying to disturb its right and honour.

Who's who at Bishop's Knoll

by Cobber[155]

As most people know, the average Australian soldier has a habit, more pronounced than other soldiers, of giving everybody a nickname, and it matters not whether they be statesmen, officers, nurses, or friends, they all come in for a pet name. This, of course, does not mean that they are less admired, neither is it an indication of any disrespect, but just part of the nature and disposition of the men from "down under", just anything that is not conventional. For a long time it has been suspected by the sisters in a certain hospital not a hundred miles from Bristol that the patients, mostly Australians, when speaking among themselves, were in the habit of referring to the sisters, doctors, and other beings necessary for the recovery of sick and wounded men, by names which do not appear on their birth certificates. To such an extent did they fear the worst, and one brave sister (oh, sister, why did you?) threw out the suggestion to one of the patients that he should make a list of these names 'Barkis was willin' but it is said that the following list was received with very shocked feelings : "Cuckoo" ; "Snowdrift" ; "Mother Goose" ; "'Arry Lauder" ; "Gentle Mary" ; "Irish Mist" ; "Mummy" ; "Annie Laurie" ; "Cluck-Cluck" ; "Mother 'Ubhard" ; "Sister Susie" ; "See-See" ; "Jinks"; "The Boss".

A day in the Ward

GYP[156]

This the first of several accounts by GYP, Sister-in-charge Miss G. Prout.

This particular morning the ward was roused rather earlier than usual, as a busy day was expected. There were to be four operations that morning, and

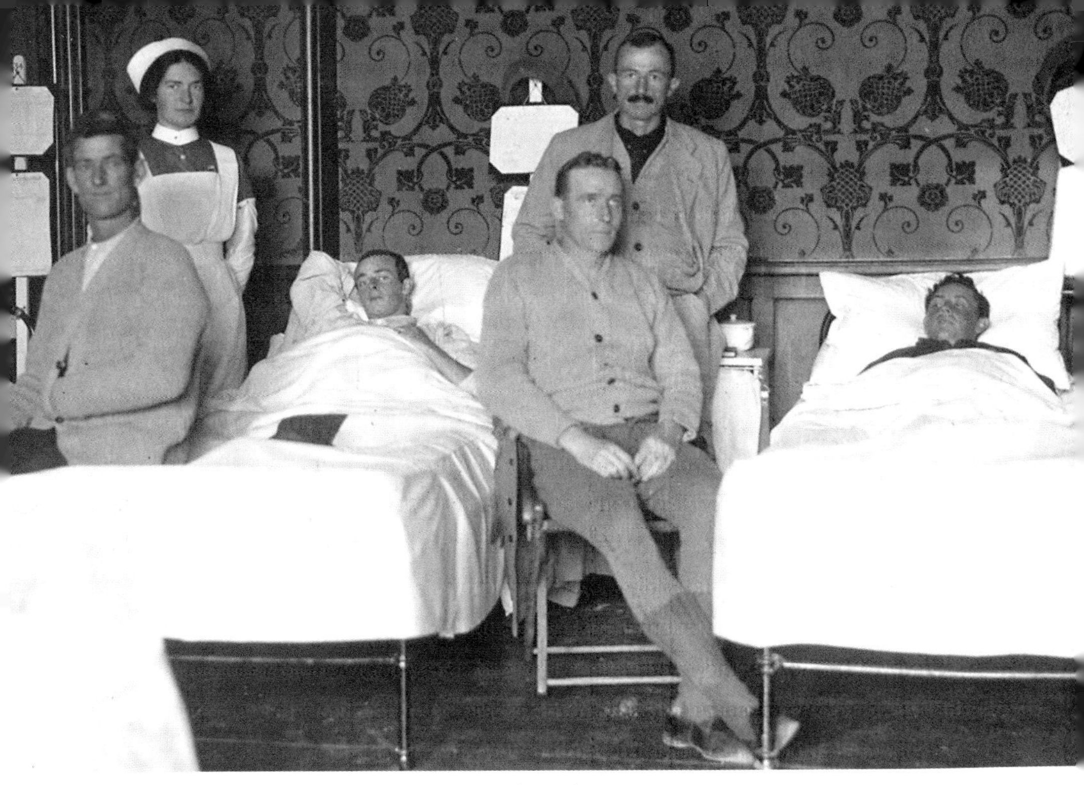

In the Ward.

all preparations for these cases must be well over by 7 a.m., and, of course, the usual routine of ward work had to be gone through as well. From 7 to 9 a.m. the sisters were busily engaged in bed-making, dusting, and a general cleaning up of the ward, not forgetting the very pleasant duty of arranging the beautiful flowers that had been sent in from the conservatories. It is not very hard to realise how precious these flowers are to patients who lie so patiently day after day in their beds. Sievwright (one of the longest residents) loves his violets, and Stuart and Jackson their narcissi, and all suggest that they should be placed on their lockers quite close to them. A large box of Australian whortle had arrived by the morning post, so every soldier was satisfied and happy, the bed-patients having theirs in special vases by their sides and the convalescent ones sporting theirs as a button-hole.

Guest was the first one to be sent in to "See the Pictures," as the boys call it, and is soon in his theatre garb. "Do you mind if I clear out until the scent process is over," says Love, who has had three operations, and has no great affection for the Ether Meth that is being rubbed on the patient's arm ready for the Scopolamin injection he must have an hour prior to his operation. Before long Guest is drowsy and comfortable, and hardly realizes that he is being carried away on a stretcher, to return later, perhaps a little sick and headachy, but very glad that all is over and satisfactory.

The bed is re-made specially, hot blankets and bottles placed ready, and the next case proceeded with. Thompson is quite prepared to go cheerfully through his ordeal, and laughs and jokes until the last minute. He also laughs and jokes after it too.

By 1 p.m. all cases are back in the ward. Morrison will not be troubled with his "Hammer Toes" again, and Jackson is cuddling his shrapnel. Poor Jackson, he has had a rough time of it, but he is satisfied now, and means to mend straight away, and can even smile when Dale jokingly promises him a visit to his "Prickly Pear Farm," where he shall have "Bardees" every day for dinner.

The early afternoon is spent in conveying fairly convalescent patients to the garden or cosy conservatory where they can watch an interesting and keen game of billiards, and the ward is left in peace and quietness, except for the now sleeping patients and the Sisters moving here and there giving afternoon medicines and feeds, etc.

Bishop Clifford has just entered the ward, and his visit is highly appreciated by all the soldiers. They are always pleased to see him and to have a few moments with him, and are glad to hear he is taking the evening service at the hospital.

Four o'clock comes, and it is tea-time. Sievwright, who has not yet been able to leave his bed, is quite sure he can enjoy a good cup of tea and a newly laid egg, with a piece of thin bread and butter. He does too, and we are all looking forward to the warmer weather, when he and Whitrow can be lifted out into the garden, where they will develop appetites like the traditional hunter.

Tea is over, and the patients who have undergone operations that morning are asked if they would object to the singing of the hymns at service. "We should like it," they all say, so the ward is quietly prepared and chairs are arranged for the staff and convalescents. It is very pleasant to hear the organ, the mingling of the mens' voices singing the well-known hymns, and to listen to the earnest address of the Bishop, and we all strive to be present at the service if possible. After service, if Fortune smiles and there is time, the Commandant may give us an organ recital, and this is thoroughly enjoyed by all the patients, who come from the various wards to listen.

The evening's work must now be commenced, and from six to eight-thirty is a very busy time indeed. Beds are re-made, flowers removed, lockers cleared, and the ward is left quiet and orderly, ready for the evening dressings. One VAD is preparing the suppers, and another is busily taking the temperatures of all the patients.

"I'll take your temperature, Paddy," says Sister to a patient whose temperature is reported normal. Paddy generally runs an evening one, but by some miraculous means he has been below 98.4 the last two nights, and Sister is suspicious.

"Oh, Sister, you have me altogether," says Paddy, "now I shall have to stay in bed in the morning." And he does, for his chart shows 100.2, and he is very sorry for himself at being caught. Never mind, Paddy, in a very little while you will be up with the first and to bed with the last if great care is taken of you, and you leave off playing your pranks.

Patients are washed and their wounds dressed and made comfortable for the night. There is a good deal of coughing going on somehow tonight, and more than one patient requires a dose of the beloved Syr. C.C. Michael is trying to look as if he rather enjoyed his H.M., as the Sister is telling him it is really "quite nice," but it is a bit of a failure, for he makes a grimace and shakes his head vigorously as he hands back the empty medicine glass.

Eight thirty, how time does fly. There goes the bell for closing down, and after a few busy, and it must be owned, noisy moments all patients are tucked up safely into bed. Prayers are read by the Sister of the Ward and lights lowered, and soon all are dreaming of the whortle country, (i.e Australia) where we trust they will take back bright and pleasant memories of our hospital.

Night on the Ward

Spero[157]

Perhaps it is at night-time especially that those working in a military hospital realise more fully the grim tragedy of war. During the day there is so much to do and so little time for thought, and besides the men seem to have a secret code which compels them to keep a tight hold upon themselves and refuse to admit pain—that plucky make-the-best-of-all-things mood which we have all got to know so well, for a few months of war turn out as stern a stoic as ever was trained by Zeno of old. (Zeno of Citium was the founder of the Stoic school of philosophy, which he taught in Athens from about 300 BC).

"Shut up growling, and think you are lucky to be alive," they would say to a grouser, and one-armed Jones will grin with delight if he can fling an orange across the ward and catch Smith unawares—an additional twinge of pain is no matter to either if it brings a laugh with it.

It is at night-time that the suffering wells uppermost. Perhaps a "take in" has arrived, another trainload of mangled men, with the same expression in the eyes of all, for none of them return without it. One feels a wave of sympathy go through all the wards, resulting in a special quietness—one could hear a pin drop long before the usual time for sleep, and as one passes down the ward one sees few smiles, and one knows that the thoughts of all are with the new-comers. Each man remembers his own journey back to Blighty, when each jolt was like a red-hot knife, and to be even gently moved needed a tight gritting of the teeth to suppress a cry, and as for the thoughts of bed, rest, and quietness, why it seemed such a heaven as to be too good to be true!

It is in the stillness afterwards, when wounds have been dressed, and ghastly enough some are, and the poor fellows sink into a sleep of utter exhaustion, that the watching Sister seems brought up close to the very spirit of suffering, the silence is full of it and the things of day seem very far away. She looks down Ward. No. 1 perhaps, with its beautiful white carved and panelled walls, its mirrors and organ, and instead of seeing dancing youth she sees long rows of beds. She looks at the sleeping faces, some so boyish in spite of drawn lines of pain, and she sees in her mental vision the mothers of these men praying in a distant land. Her thoughts are often broken by a sharp cry, a groan or an order hoarsely shouted by a man who in his dream undergoes an experience even more intense than the actual one passed through, for what has been bravely borne in actual life probably causes an appalling fear in his sleep. It is then the mind seems to shake off the waking control and wanders at its own free will, and no medical treatment can touch it, for the psychic portion of the brain is beyond the understanding of any doctor, however clever he may be, and only Time the great healer can restore the harmony and obliterate, to some extent, the terrible memories.

So the night wears on until daylight again floods the wards, and all get going again, determined to took upon the brightest side; for even the least imaginative know that behind all the blackness will dawn an era so full of blessedness that this great sacrifice will have been worth it and the tears of millions will wash away many of the old stains of the past.

Night at Bishop's Knoll - another phase

Hoctus[158]

As Spero so truly says, it is especially at night that those working in a military hospital realise the horror of war, and many and varied are the forms it takes.

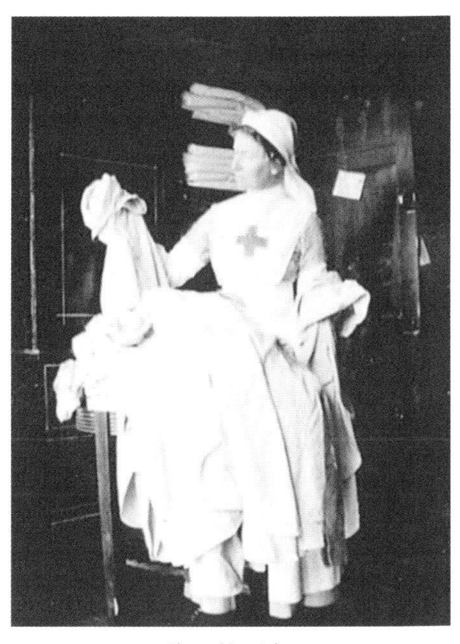

Clean shirt night.

Each night will have its own, and in addition there are special nights with their own fixed horrors, and of these the chief is known as "clean shirt night." Great is the rivalry between the various wards, and keen the competition for shirts of the most brilliant hues and the latest thing in pyjama suits, and on this particular night (it happens to be Friday, of course), the moment the preliminary cleaning and polishing has been scurried through, one creeps with as noiseless a step as possible — and it is remarkable that at night every board has an explosive creak which it never has by day, and even a slipper sounds like a marching boot! — to the stack of laundry baskets at the top of the hospital. Armed with a torch, one lifts the first lid, which goes up with a heart-rending creak audible of course to the would-be sleeping day staff, only to find that one has been forestalled. Miss Smith, whose usually dainty feet are at night enveloped in weird and particularly noiseless wrappings of her own invention, and which makes one think she is suffering from trench feet, has taken time by the forelock, and the worst has happened.

Alas! those very favourite pink and green shirts or the new pyjama suits are no more. One by one grasping VAD's steal up, each hoping to be the first on the scene, and get the pick of the basket for the "ward" her own of course! Then the fight begins, and for about an hour the following may be heard: "Will you give me that black and white one for Flynn, if I give you this one for Stuart?" "Well, I've got two left arms in my arms and you have only one, besides this fastens at the back, and I must have it for Sutton." "You've got the pyjama trousers belonging to this coat and Sister says I can have them for Phillips."

Or "You might let me have that blue one because all my Ward is going to be blue this week" and "Do you want ALL those because there isn't one left for anyone else," until the luckless people trying to sleep must long to throw the baskets at us.

At last everyone has staggered down with her collection, and peace reigns above. Not so below, for on examining Smith's favourite shirt, it is discovered that "those day people" have left it unmended, and Julian's pet coat has no buttons. Oh, "those day people" - nothing is too bad for them to do, and anything that goes wrong may be safely laid at their door, though when one is on day duty all crimes are committed by "those night people!" Eventually the garments for each patient are collected, and one enters the ward laden with clothes of every description, to be greeted with "Sister, my dressing has slipped," and Miller is found wearing the dressing that should be on his leg round the back of his neck. When this is done, Smith wants his heel rubbed, and Julian's bandage is too tight; White wants a drink, and Crowfoot's splint isn't comfortable.

At last, when the grey and chilly dawn is breaking, one realises that "shirt night" is over for another week, and perhaps after all life is worth living.

In March 1917 Bishop's Knoll Hospital had an outbreak of Mumps and was put in quarantine which meant that all outside visits were cancelled and the staff were very much left on their own resources until the following month. The mumps vaccine did not generally become available until the late 1960s and before that time every effort was made to ensure that children had experienced the disease at an early age before reaching adulthood when there were serious side effects. It would seem that confirmed cases were taken to the Ham Green isolation hospital outside Bristol. One soldier wrote from there to Robert Bush explaining that he was in a ward of 10 where the youngest was three years old and the oldest 15 years and that he was kept awake most nights by the younger ones "howling for their mamas"![159]

In quarantine

GYP[160]

In last month's Coo-ee you may have read a little about the leisure time of the staff, but in this issue I should like to show you that your Australian boys here do not waste much of their spare time either, and know fully well how to make the most of their hospital days.

I suppose it is hardly necessary to state that when the sick and wounded soldiers are first admitted to Bishop's Knoll Hospital, they cannot feel very fit for anything but the restfulness of bed, and are quite content to stay there, secure in the knowledge that all that possibly can be done, is and will be done for their comfort and welfare, so that before long they may be fit and strong once more.

It is always a matter of great wonderment to me how quickly patients sufficiently recover from their wounds and ills to take a keen interest in the lighter side of hospital life. Even those sad cases—and the Commandant and Staff are always more than ready to take their full share of these—which we all know must eventually be medically- boarded and sent back to Australia, are wonderfully bright and happy, and share in the amusements and pleasures that are constantly being arranged for the entertainment of the patients. The time I particularly wish to draw your attention to was—Quarantine.

Pierrots.

This is how it was. An annoying but quite natural thing happened. Private McPhee awoke one morning with a headache, sore throat, high temperature and colour, and a few other symptoms we did not like, and after a thorough sounding, and the round of the medical officers, he was diagnosed as, well I won't say what but anyhow infectious, so was promptly conveyed to the isolation hospital a little distance away, and we were in quarantine for three weeks.

All sorts of rules and regulations came into force then. Picture palaces must not be visited, the kind invitations of the Inquiry Bureau to concerts had to be refused and tea-parties were things of the past. In fact, passes and pleasures outside the hospital gates were strictly "taboo."

Having to recognise the inevitable, our convalescent patients of Bishop's Knoll were not slow to grasp the situation. Instead of grumbling and growling, a few of our most enterprising ones set to work and made the most of rather a bad business, and soon had arrangements fixed up for the entertainment of the entire hospital.

Private Francis, whom we all had regarded as rather a quiet sort of person, quickly proved himself "Master of Ceremonies" and in less than an hour an illuminated programme was hanging in the hall, inviting all to attend the marvellous "Pierrot Group" concert that afternoon at 4.30 p.m. It is really wonderful what a transformation can be executed with a few brilliantly striped

Private H Sievwright (4768) had one of the longest periods in residence at Bishop's Knoll recorded there from November 1916 until July 1917.

pajamas, some flowered cretonne treasure-bags as hats, and a pound of black darning wool, and with the aid of an obliging and interested staff the very startling and effective troupe you see here came into existence.

Private Francis is on the left, sitting down, and I wonder if the working party would have recognised in his fascinating head-dress a pale pink knitted theatre stocking that had been sent in a little time previously.

Private Wade, in spite of his quaint and laughable figure, made a most competent pianist, and one could scarcely imagine that the reckless Jehu, the son of Nimshi, was a patient who had been admitted with eleven wounds only a few weeks ago.

That day was a huge success, and fired with enthusiasm, Mahoney, a champion billiard player, and Private Jones, arranged tournaments for the Staff and patients with equally good results. Private Sievwright, who unfortunately cannot use his arm, is by no means out of the game, but takes his part as "Marker."

It is a great blessing for us that those early days of spring were warm and bright, so our bed-patients did not do badly either. Congenial little parties were conveyed to the grounds for a few sunny hours, and apparently much enjoyed. White had mended the gramophones, so that we got the strains of "Blighty" mingled with melodious voices wafted to us, as we go about our duties in the wards.

Photography is all the go too, and MacLeod and Murray have proved themselves experts in this line, and have given us some very interesting groups.

It is scarcely an exaggeration to say that we hardly felt the necessary confinement with such a bright lot of patients, and although we one and all indulged in a temporary fit of irresponsibility when we were pronounced "free," we felt we had not wasted the golden hours, and it was with real regret we said good-bye to the Blue Boys, who had so largely helped the hospital to enjoy what quite easily might have been a weary and tedious three weeks while we were "Prisoners of War."

Another outbreak

The account above, published in April, refers to an outbreak of mumps in March 1917. However the following account which appeared in the March issue of *"Coo-ee!"* shows that earlier in the year there was one of measles. One can surmise that because many of the Australian recruits had come from isolated communities they had not been exposed to this common childhood disease before. Such an outbreak in adults today is a serious matter, the more so among group of weakened recuperating soldiers where pneumonia or encephalitis can be fatal.

The Lighter Side of Hospital Life

unattributed[161]

Having for a while been shut off from the outside world owing to the measles, sport not being barred, our billiard and card tournaments have proved a great boon.

Most people will know that when a crowd of fellows find themselves with plenty of time on their hands there is always a chance of something happening that is not in accordance with the rules of decorum. The old adage about Satan finding a job for the unemployed is as true now as ever, so it is well, perhaps, that we should have these competitions of skill and luck to look forward to and occupy our time.

In addition to the chance of coming out on top oneself, there is always the hope that a pal or one who so far has been unlucky will win a prize, so that all through the week the interest is maintained. Then, of course, there is the staff billiard competition. The games in which our good friends the Sisters take part are real good sport, and last week's competition was tremendously exciting, for in the final Miss Gardner, who proved the winner, only beat her opponent by one point.

We have often wondered how our good friend the originator of these competitions managed to come out every Saturday afternoon with a bag full of prizes. He must have a heap of friends in the city. Some of the prizes, however, have been presented by old patients, and I should like to throw out a hint that this is a direction in which practical interest in Bishop's Knoll might well be shown.

Patients come and patients go, but the work continues and will continue until the war is over; therefore every bit of help we can give to help our friends keep our wounded comrades in good heart should be given without stint. We were very glad to hear on Saturday, the 24th February, that Sergt Douglas Woods and Private R. C. Hooper had provided prizes.

The competitions for the staff have been won by Sister Collen, Miss Graham, Miss Swinton and Miss Gardner. We have sadly missed the charming concerts given by Madame Marion Glass, Mrs Christopher George and the Inquiry Bureau since we have been in quarantine, but necessity being the mother of invention, we ran a couple of shows on our own. The press was not represented, which perhaps is as well. Miss Colthurst obliged at the piano, and the patients who contributed were Privates White, Williams, Campbell, Mitchell, Love, Sleeman, Flynn, and Lance-Corporal Lorenzten.

Others who have been generous in this way during the past few weeks include Messrs. Pleasance & Harper, jewellers of Wine Street, Bristol, Messrs. Stiff and Co., the well-known starch manufacturers, Bristol, Mr Coeford of the Bristol Liberal Club, and Mr Cummings of Maynards, sweet manufacturers. The prizes during the past month have been won by Sergt Murray, Corporal Alien, Privates McFee, Hewitt, Sleeman, Knevitt, Brooks, and Williams (Billiards), and Corporal Alien, Ptes White, Williams, Knevitt, Yates, Love, and Bone (Cards).

On the 16th the concert finished up with a very amusing sketch by the "Dug-out," entitled "The Rookem Telephone Company," in which the offenders were Privates Knevitt, Yates, Farndon, White, Corporal Alien, and Sergt Murray. With the aid of some old civvy clothes and a little grease paint the characters were well made.

On the 24th we had a grand Inquiry Bureau Concert, the company comprising Miss Gertrude Winchester, Miss Gwilliams, Miss Baker, Mr Baker, Mrs Hillier, and Mr Lionel Saunders.

A kitchen reverie

by Spero[162]

How hopeless it is for a "never-saw-itself-in-print-before-Coo-ee-days" individual to even attempt to describe the kitchen; it needs the pen of Jerome K. Jerome at least to do it justice, for the flow of wit which accompanies the work is as unquenchable as Kitchener's Army! The amount of cooking needed is just tremendous, but it all goes so easily that one gets the impression of sunshine and happiness with the work thrown in.

As this is a truthful article, and not written for an evening paper, we must own we do occasionally hear the voice of our Commandant, "Not quite so much talking" and though he is a person who carries much weight, yet up to the going to press of this month's Coo-ee we have never heard the talking abate one inch. Our Commandant adds to his wide range of worldly wisdom an almost uncanny acumen in the domestic and culinary line; in fact, it is a bit aggravating sometimes, for in pre-war days, though we women were not let do much, we certainly were supposed to come out top in domesticology; but our Commandant not only knows the best way of doing everything, but the worst of it is he is nearly always right. There is nothing he will not turn his hand to, from carving great joints to opening tins, which job for some occult reason no one seems particularly keen on.

We must say our head cook, who is the wife of our Commandant, can open them beautifully, but she generally has a badly lacerated hand after, and looks as if she had been holding a bayonet the wrong way up. By the by, our head cook does not wish to be mentioned in this dispatch, but that is grossly unfair, for if the centrepiece is left out the whole thing will collapse. She finds nothing too much trouble, and cooks for the whole hospital (at present ninety-eight, not counting the staff), joints, stews, soups, fish, those nice little pasties you all like so much, as well as "specials" for the worst cases, and a hundred other things besides. With it all she is never too busy for a smile and kind word for

The Kitchen – Bush carving.

everyone, and is beloved of all. Most of us get that said when we are safely off this planet, and those left are afraid it might be nasty to contradict it. She also ranks as first wit.

Then comes our second cook, who has steadily cooked since the German Emperor made her, almost from the beginning of the war. She can cook, too, pies, puddings and cakes. She is a bit of a martinet, too, in her way, and knows how to stick up for her rights. If she had only been a Suffragette, we should have had the vote years ago, and have got quite tired of it by now. Then we have another worker who, besides her work in the kitchen, has since 1914 handled the house linen, suits and millions of socks in a really masterly manner. For wit she runs a good tie with the second cook. As you know, wit is a commodity which nourishes in the soil of Bishop's Knoll, the wards are simply full of it, so whether it percolates from the wards downwards or wells up from the kitchen we leave to you; for ourselves we are always in favour of upward growth.

Also we have a Gravy-Maker in Ordinary; in fact, we may be said to possess two ADCs, they might even aspire to the title of Generals. Last but not least there is the upstairs Pantry-maid-door-opener-telephone-answerer-and-spoon-polisher. She comes under the title of General Service, and deserves it. She too loves the kitchen, and possesses a weird aptitude for suddenly appearing when the second cook in her nicest mood makes a presentation of one of her succulent little cakes all round. We shall never cease to wonder

The Commandant and his roses.

Sister and her dog Billie Collers.

if it is a case of telepathy through the channel of the lift, second sight, or an abnormal sense of smell, and we are all too polite to ask. However, they all get a warm welcome, for a chilly atmosphere is a thing unknown in Bishop's Knoll kitchen.

Off Duty – a wander round the grounds of Bishop's Knoll

GYP [163]

I was walking along the higher lawns one lovely day in May, and it seemed to me that the illustration on the cover of Coo-ee did not convey nearly a good enough impression of our Australian hospital and its lovely grounds. I thought, perhaps, a short description of how and where the staff and patients spend part of their free time would not be altogether unacceptable to our friends Down Under.

You will have read the account by Leigh Woods of the hospital itself in the November number, and if not, you will of course secure a copy as soon as possible and do so. I am not going to write about the sick and wounded this time, but just to please one of them, and also because I fancied you might

VADs Miss K. Swinton and Miss V. Saville.

Updating hospital record charts.

be interested to read a little about the hospital and home where your boys are brought back to health and strength. You see it happened like this. A very young blue boy who is badly wounded said to me one day.

"Sister, I often see you going to the grounds. What do you do there and what is the garden like? I wish my people could see this place and know you all."

As he must stay in his bed all day - he is not even well enough yet to be carried into the garden - I feel I should love to do as he wishes, and if he can forget his pain for a while and read this, and if it gives him any pleasure at all to send it to his far-off home, I shall be more than satisfied.

This very afternoon I happened to glance along the drive and saw our Commandant inspecting one of his prize rose trees. In the little leisure time he has he can generally find something to look after, and appears to take a pleasure and interest in it too. He seems fairly satisfied, and makes his way across the lawns, prodding now and then at the plantains and dandelions which somehow will appear and offend his critical eye.

Our Night Sister has been freshening herself up after her hard night's work by running round the grounds with "Billie Collers," her dog, and is just taking him back to his kennel, where he will be safe and sound until she sees him at 9 p.m., for to be quite candid he is a bit of a "runner away."

I have to stop for a few moments and "shoo" the ducklings back to their proper home. They are trespassers and are waddling across the lawn after their foster-mother, the buff orpington, as fast as ever they can, I know they will go the same way their brothers and sisters went a little while back if they persist in going along that broad drive that leads to destruction. They are all back in the farmery presently, and I go through the five-barred gate and cross the paddock to the kitchen garden beyond. Here two of our VADs, Miss K. Swinton and Miss V. Saville, are working on the land, and they look very pink and heated with their exertions.

I stop to watch them for a few seconds, and think. They work hard in the wards all the morning and evening, and are generally off-duty from two to five in the afternoon. I am sure you will agree with me that it is most patriotic of them to spend part of their play-time like this. I try to persuade one of our senior Sisters to come round with me, but she has had a strenuous morning, and prefers to rest quietly under the trees writing letters. She laughingly holds up her blotter to me, and I see she is using one of your blue boy's charts.

All sorts of things are happening in the garden. Everything is so young and fresh and green that it is simply a pleasure to stroll around enjoying the mere fact of having nothing to do for an hour or two. Just by the ramblers I come across a very jolly group, and although they did not see me I saw them. In a secluded spot of the garden Miss Bush and a few of her friends were improving the shining hour by sorting socks for soldiers. I am afraid it must have taken them some time to fill the basket Miss Bush was sitting on, as I know what sorting socks means only too well.

"I believe there are two Sisters sitting under the oak," says a blue boy I happen to meet. "May I snap them?" And he does. I feel sure the Sisters will not mind, as the boys love these little odd snap-shots, and like to send them home. After all, it is a very picturesque spot in the garden, and the Sisters do not look too bad.

Turning round the corner I find some of the patients having tea out of doors. This is quite an established feature now the warm weather has set in, and the soldiers enjoy it so much. Amongst the group you will find Privates Roberts, Marshall, Robinson and Bankier, all amputation cases. I stay to chat

Sister Lambert and Miss Philip back from their ride about to go on duty.

with them for a little while, and they are all very bright and happy. Roberts is as brown as a berry, and even Marshall's pale face is getting a copper tint.

I must hurry now, though, as it is almost time to go back on duty. The gong I know will sound for tea in a few moments, and I see Sister Lambert and Miss Philip coming down the hill. They are returning from an afternoon's ride, and, like myself, are freshened and ready for their evening duties. We exchange a few words ; they pat their horses "good-bye," and then go quickly through the hall and up to the tower. Soon we are all back at work, forgetting play-time in the interest and welfare of the patients at Bishop's Knoll.

Ward Gossip

by GYP [164]

This by the Sister – in - charge Miss G. Prout written in April or May 1917. It is full of comments many of which only the staff and patients would understand.

The hospital is again full-up, and the Medical and Nursing Staff can find more

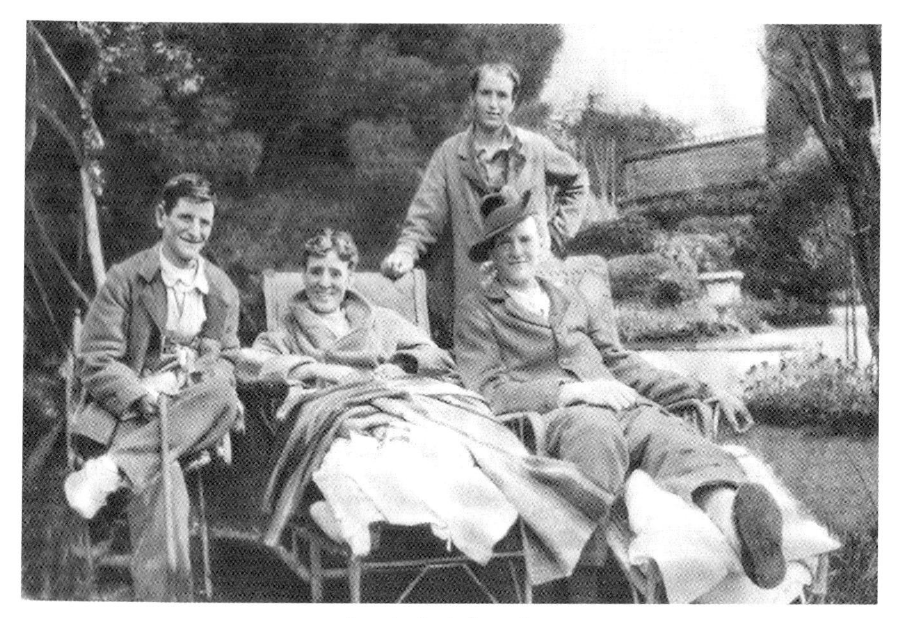

Convalescing in the garden.

than enough to do. We are sorry to say that many of the new patients are severely wounded, but trust they will make a speedy recovery.

Ward II. has made a good start. Already several of the patients there have been carried on stretchers into the garden to enjoy the fresh air and lovely weather we have been having lately.

Some of our older Australians have been quite sarcastic concerning our English climate, but are more than ready now to take our word that the sun does sometimes shine in England.

It is an open secret that a Dug-out King is to be elected very shortly. At the time of going to press the honoured one is not known, but we trust he will be worthy of the position. Davies of shrapnel fame admirably held that post for many weeks, but he has left us some time ago. Who votes for Love? By the way, Private Love enjoys the morning battery, and would not miss it for worlds!! It enables him to get through his vast amount of secretarial work cheerfully and willingly.

Ward VII. is quite a favourite spot now. The new paper is most engaging, and Scott and O'Reilly say they dream of the long, long trail every night. Several petitions have been handed in to make that ward their abode —when the beds are vacant.

A poet in Ward IV. has more time to write now, as several of the argumentative patients have left and he gets a little peace. He writes very nicely too, and we wish he were a little less bashful and would send some of his efforts in "Coo-ee!". It would be much appreciated. Perhaps Guest would have some influence there.

It was delightful to see Sergeant Stumbles back again, and walking round the wards just as though he had never left us over a year ago. He had been sent back to Australia, but gained so much strength in six weeks that he re-enlisted and was returned for duty to England. He looked awfully fit and well, and brings us good news of Calligan, another old patient of Bishop's Knoll.

Although Beyer is pretty bad, he does not object to being shut up in his steam tent bis die. He has always a smile and cheery word when we "do the round." Whyte in the same ward is equally interested in his water-court and yards of tubing, and thinks they are doing him such a lot of good. It would be rather nice to know Smith' s views— in Ward II.—on the same subject.

Ward III. wants to know if the oxygen apparatus introduced there is a German bomb, timed to go off at a certain hour. Yes, if any talking above a whisper is heard after 8.30 p.m. we are certain of it. But Ward III is almost a model ward as we have two excellent non-commissioned officers there in Reg. Sergt-Major Old and Sergeant Cooper, who keep good order and discipline. The rest of the Three-ites are so cheery and good-tempered though, that they do not find it at all difficult. White and Fox are very bright, and only hoot each other when an argument starts about going back to give Fritz another nasty blow, and to spend a few more happy months in the trenches. Cunningham, in Ward III., was a take-in all alone. He somehow got lost the day before, and we missed one amongst the patients admitted. However, he came to Bishop's Knoll the next day and was very glad to be with his own countrymen—who had already settled in—once more.

We are so sorry Brownfield has gone, he gave quite good hints on billiards. Jackson is taking his place very nicely though and the Sisters will still take the first prizes on Saturdays.

Now that so many patients are confined to bed all day, the Commandant is finding it quite a nice piece of work to get the round of the hospital with the three and sixpences. However he gets over it in his usual cheery way. I always heard that an Australian is permitted few expressions if he had a ticklish bit of work as well as lots of other things to do, but I find I am quite mistaken.

Our Gallipoli patients went off very happily to the fine outing on the 25th April (Gallipoli Day). The cars kindly lent by Mrs Strachan and Mrs Wynne-Jones were most tastefully decorated for the occasion, and there was quite a competition to ride down in these two. Reg.-Sergt-Major Old, Stuart, and others eventually won, and went off with much merriment and noise.

It is very nice indeed to welcome back some of the senior VADs; just lately they have been quite pink at 8.30 p.m. You see, they are very conscientious, and like to report themselves up to time. What we should do without them I really do not know, and I hope they won't read the Times too much.

Bowls, clock-golf, and other out-door sports ought to be all the go just now, and we are on the look-out for some champion players.

Quartermaster Jenkins is a new member of our Staff, and we hope she won't find the blue boys too trying when they get fussed if their tunics are not just the West-End cut.

Congratulations to the Lady of the Pantry who served up the many teas so very nicely on the 28th April.

We all wish Miss Diana Bush very many happy birthdays. The little lady was three years old on the 21st April, so comes into this number all by herself.

We greatly regret that Sister Meek was called away from the hospital suddenly, owing to her mother's serious illness. We miss her very much, and trust she will accept our deepest sympathy over her great loss.

Send off from Bishop's Knoll "Good luck be with you"

Sister GYP.[165].

"Hurrah! Hurrah!! Hurrah!!! Three cheers for Bishop's Knoll."

Again we hear this cheery shout as another batch of our Australian wounded and sick went off this morning some to duty, some to light duty, others to the Convalescent Camp at Southall. We are always sorry to see them go, these

Saying goodbye.

nice, frank sons from overseas. They have made themselves very dear to us by their interesting personalities and happy disposition, for with very few exceptions they one and all help each other and us, to lighten the daily routine of hospital life.

We like to think that our boys value the good opinion of the Commandant, the Medical and the Nursing Staff, and we believe they do. It would hurt us very much indeed if any patient who has passed through this hospital did not consider us his friends, and look upon Bishop's Knoll as his English home.

They are not off for a few minutes though. Private Thomas just realises that he has not said "Good-bye" to a bed-ridden comrade in Ward IV, and Cpl Walker must leave instructions for his mail to be kept for him until he returns for his furlough. We know he will, too ; they all do, and nothing gives us greater pleasure than to see their brown, sunny faces a few days later, and to hear them say: "Well, Sister, here we are again, may we look up Mr Bush and some of the boys?"

Their khaki-clad figures are bustling here and there in and out of the Red Cross van half-a-dozen times for one thing or another. Fortunately, the ambulance driver is remarkably good natured. He laughs and chats with them

Final photographs.

indulgently, and gives them a few minutes' grace.

You fathers and mothers in far-off Australia, we wish you could see your boys this bright winter morning — healthy and strong again — as they bundle helter-skelter into the conveyance, tumbling over each other, and laughing uproariously at the endless banter that is being kept up. Nevertheless, we catch a wistful glance back at the hospital now and then, and we know they are feeling as sorry to leave us as we are to lose them, for we feel confident that, although sick and wounded, their stay with us has been a happy one. It would gladden your hearts, and make you feel prouder than ever of your soldier boys, who have left home and dear ones to back up the Old Country, and to show what good men and true can come from "Down under."

Sandwiches are handed round to each soldier, snap-shots taken for our albums, good wishes exchanged, and the final hand-shakes given. At last they are off, and as they go round the curve and up the drive, the echoes of their hearty cheers and their good-bye song, "Good luck be with you," come back to us ; and because we are Englishwomen and nurses, we do not say much, but instinctively repeat for each one in our hearts, "God bless you". And the sound of that chorus the boys love so, and are always singing, lingers in our memories for many a long day.

CHAPTER 8

KEEPING THE TROOPS HAPPY - ACCOUNTS OF OUTINGS AND ENTERTAINMENTS

There were both internal and external events at Bishop's Knoll. Apart from the permanent staff at the hospital, a large group of outside people contributed to the welfare and entertainment of those recovering there. Many events were organised by Archibald Powell. There clearly was some twisting of arms needed though it is plain that a strong sense of "noblesse oblige" was felt by many wealthy Bristol citizens and landowners. As large was the programme of entertainments organised for all hospitals by the Bristol Inquiry Bureau. Two articles by the Editor, albeit under different names, are included here as they cover different aspects of this remarkable organisation

The work of the Bristol Inquiry Bureau

Leigh Woods[166]

"This report you gave me is a real, human document, and it gave me great pleasure to read it. I shall send the report to Lord Stamfordham,[167] and hope the King may have time to glance at it. You and your friends are doing as fine a work as I know, and it does you all great credit. If every hospital centre would follow your example, it would really help us and our work."

This letter was written some months ago by Sir Frederick Milner,[168] and it

Lord Stamfordham and the King.

had reference to one of the most remarkable of War Relief organisations in this or any other country - the Bristol Inquiry Bureau."

Where to begin or where to end in an attempt to set down the varied phases of the work, goodness only knows. Like many another great organisation, which the war has brought into being it began in quite a humble way. When the first contingent of wounded soldiers arrived in Bristol, the headquarters of the 2nd Southern General Hospital, Mr H. E. Townsend, called upon the Commanding Officer, Colonel Paul Bush, and asked if he, as a civilian, could do anything to help. His services were promptly accepted, and he was told off(sic), I believe, to deal with a mass of correspondence from anxious relatives making enquiries about their soldier friends.

Almost the first thing done was the institution of a complete card index (personal and regimental) of all admissions in the area, by which means information is immediately available to relatives of patients. For instance a Scotchman or an Irishman, whose home is far distant, comes to Bristol sick or wounded, and is admitted to one of the hospitals. The War Office makes his relatives acquainted with the fact, and naturally they want to know details of his condition. Naturally they write to the hospital, whereupon the Bureau, by means of their card-index system, can tell in a few moments at which hospital

Jock or Pat might be, and back goes a letter - a sympathetic missive- giving all particulars anxious relatives desire to know.

Another phase concerns men posted as missing. A list is sent periodically to the Bureau, by the War Office, of men who have disappeared. Then the searchers — members of the Bureau — set to work. Perhaps John Jones of the Welsh Fusiliers has been lost sight of after action at the front. The searcher's first duty is to find out if there is in his particular hospital, a man of the same regiment and battalion. If there is, he is at once interviewed, and asked if he remembers John Jones. The patient thinks for a minute. "Oh, yes," he replies, "he was in my Company when we went out over the parapet. I remember seeing the poor chap scrapping with a crowd of Germans, and I suppose they took him prisoner."

Romance and strange happenings frequently come within the ken of the searchers. There was an inquiry for an Australian lad who was lost sight of in Gallipoli. A searcher discovered a man in one of the hospitals who was able to clear up the mystery of his disappearance conclusively. It was a heroic but sad story. In a certain action on the Peninsula it was imperative that a message should he sent to another Anzac Force on the other side of the gully. Sending a man with it was out of the question, and exposure to anybody meant drawing the enemy fire in a second. But a lad volunteered to flag wave (semaphore) the vital message. He jumped up, got his message over and then immediately his task was finished was blown to bits by a shell.

Then there was the case that happened in the Southmead Hospital. A certain north countryman was posted as missing and the searcher had the good fortune to find a comrade who knew him well. "Oh. yes," he replied to the first inquiry, "I know where Jack is: he came over from France with me and you'll find him in Ward 3". And Jack was found, and his sorrowing friends were apprised of the glad news at once.

It often happens, as has already been said, that the homes of soldiers who come to the Bristol Hospital are a long way off. If the relatives are poor, it is of course a hard, and often impossible matter, for them to come to Bristol to see son or husband. But the Bureau removes difficulties by paying whatever is necessary in the matter of railway fares, and also finds the mother or his wife food and lodging while she is here. Some wonderfully happy meetings have

The nurses football match at Southmead.

been brought about in this way. There was the case of a lad whose condition was marked serious. His mother lived hundreds of miles away but the Bureau brought her to her boy's cot side. The end was expected soon and the mother stayed. Day after day passed and the boy did not die: he began to mend and his mother stayed on the guest all the while of the bureau. I think it was matter of weeks before she went back to her home, and she left the laddie well on the road to a complete recovery.

A wonderful War Organisation – the Bristol Inquiry Bureau

The Editor.[169]

One of the most important features of the bureau's work is the provision of concerts, entertainments, and mental cheer in a variety of forms. There is no need to say what a dull place a military hospital would be if nothing was done to relieve the monotony of routine. Well, quite early in the war the Bureau established a special department, and a register was made of almost every lady or gentleman with entertaining talent in the district. Their co-operation was gladly given and now eighteen concerts are given each week in the recreation rooms of the various hospitals, as well as ward concerts for those unable to leave their beds. The pleasure these entertainments give cannot be overestimated. The programme without exception is a first-class one, and twice each week the professional artists from the theatres and music halls are called upon and gladly respond. Some very remarkable incidents have

A wounded soldiers outing to Downend cricket club.

occurred at these concerts. Men have recovered their speech in the hilarity of the assembly, and thus in a second music, or a joke have done that which the highest medical skill had failed to accomplish.

The entertainments side of the work include providing happy gatherings outside the hospitals. Throughout the summer wounded soldiers were the guests of the Bureau or prominent citizens, at the beautiful Clifton Zoo, while since the drear months have set in there have been regular gatherings at the Bristol Art Gallery. The Corporation provided a soldiers' room and here after the wonders of the Art Gallery and Museum have been inspected, the men sit down to a substantial tea and a fine concert follows. Groups of citizens, private individuals, and trade societies are the hosts, and the guests rarely number less than 350.

This phase of the work would, of course, be impossible, if the Bureau had not a perfectly organised system of transport. Once again the co-operation of the people of Bristol has been secured, and almost everybody with a car is called into service. When it is stated that some of the monster gatherings, like that on Boxing Day, have meant the fetching and returning of 2,000 wounded soldiers, it will be realised that, the transport is an important matter. But it has been well described as a triumph of organisation, and there is never any muddling of arrangements ; the cars draw up with clock-work precision, discharge their passengers, and make room for the next. The men are rarely a minute late in arriving or in returning to their hospitals. I have seen most of

Mr Lionel Saunders Secretary of the Concert Section.

Mrs Osterle Head of Transport Section.

the work, and it is simply wonderful.

And every bit of the Bureau's work is voluntary. From the start, no one has received a penny piece for work done. Some of the members put in practically the whole of their time at it; if you look in at the Bureau office during the forenoon, you will see a veritable hive of industry. One lady has the telephone receiver in her hand for hours on end, she is arranging transport details; in another room there are several young ladies — daughters of prominent citizens, including the Lord Mayor — hard at it typing. And the work goes on day after day, and indeed year after year, without a break, without a sign of staleness. The enthusiasm which prompted all the members to put every bit of their energy into the work, when all was fresh and new and novel, is as apparent now, and will be as long as the war lasts.

There is a department of the Bureau known as the PFD which takes up the case of the discharged soldier, tells him how to proceed to get his pension, assists him to get suitable employment, and befriends him in every way possible. Then again, many a soldier would never be able to write to his friends for lack of postage stamps, were it not that in all necessitous cases they are provided by the Bureau.

Competitions

Private E. H. Combe Robinson[170]

In the first issue of *"Coo-ee!"* several competitions were announced as follows

Two competitions;- For patients and one for the nursing staff at Bishop's Knoll have been announced. Paymaster William H. Cole RNVR, who is taking very generous interest in the hospital, offered three prizes as follows

(1) For the best letter, written by a patient to the Editor of "Coo-ee!" on "How I spent last Christmas."

(2) For the best letter on "What I think of English Girls" written by a patient.

(3) For the best letter on "What I think of the patients at Bishop's Knoll," written by one of the nursing staff.

The Commandant and the Editor will adjudicate, and the names of the prize winner will be published in the December number of "Coo-ee!". Perhaps our friends on Salisbury Plain or elsewhere would also like to say what they think of our English (including of course Scotch or Welsh) girls. If so just send along your views in a letter to the Editor and there will be a useful prize for the best letter.

The winning entry in each class of the competition was announced in Coo-ee! issue 4 and is given below.

1. How I spent last Christmas

Corporal J.A. Davis[171]

Allow me to go back to a few weeks before Christmas 1915. We were behind the trenches at ANZAC resting, wondering where we would spend Christmas day. The wind was blowing a gale across the Aegean seas and it had been raining for the last two days. Our blankets were wet and covered in mud and our clothes likewise when an order was passed along to the effect that we were to be ready to move off to Lemnos Island where we would camp for some time. That meant Christmas in some sort of comfort. Up to the time of this news we were feeling pretty miserable, but what a change when the order was read out! Everyone brightened up: away in the distance someone commenced cheering and gradually it extended along the whole line. Hooray! Hooray! Hooray! Jacko the Turk obviously thought there was an attack on, so he promptly opened fire and sent over a few extra shells.

A week before Christmas we were under canvas on Sarpi, Lemnos Island and parcels were beginning to arrive from Australia. As soon as a mail was announced there was a rush for the Post Office. Then the sergeant would read out the name "Brown?" "Here!" a voice would roar in the crowd, like the explosion of a bomb. "Hooray, the old girl's remembered me." So great was the excitement that it seemed an eternity until the next name was called out. The last parcel having been given out, we began to disperse, the unlucky ones mumbling all sorts of pleasant things about the army and the Post Office authorities.

On Christmas morning we awoke to the strains of "Yankee Doodle", played by the brigade band; in about half an hour the whole camp was up and doing. Everyone seemed merry and bright, even the sun decided to shine, a thing it had not done for some days. At eleven o'clock the "fall in" was sounded; all was excitement for we were to be given a billy (can) each, full of good things from Australia, a Christmas gift to her sons. The scene in our tent shortly afterwards was one that, could Australians at home have seen it, they would have been amply repaid for their kindness. We were not men fighting for their lives then, we were simply great big children. "Bill, look what I've got!" "Tom, what do you think of this?" "Look here, carrots!" "What a bonzer!" Everyone was speaking at once and as pleased as Punch with the contents of their respective billies. Then someone would take a nice neat little parcel from his billy and hold it up. All eyes would be turned on him while he carefully undid the tissue paper, and a small bottle would come to light. "What is it Jim?" Then there would be scream of laughter as he slowly read out "Dr Williams Pink Pills for pale people." Ha! Ha! Joy reigned supreme in the tent. Someone else would hold up a parcel wrapped in pink tissue paper bearing the inscription "May this be the means of your friends deserting you." We thought it rather strange, but when we saw the contents we understood: it was a tin of Insectobane. These billies contained everything you could name, from an alarm clock to a tin of herrings in tomato sauce.

For dinner we had roast mutton and potatoes, plum pudding with sauce, all sorts of tinned fish and fruits and to finish up with a bottle of BASS. During the afternoon three other chaps and myself hired a sailing boat and went out to a warship. After we had been shown all over the ship we were taken downstairs for tea. The mess room was decorated with flags, holly etc., I could hardly imagine I was on a warship. Everyone was trying to make everyone else laugh, so you can imagine the result. We had an excellent tea. I had been told that Jack always had a merry time on board his ship at Christmas and now I am sure of it. It was after a grand afternoon that I sailed back to Sarpi in the best of sprits, to curl myself up in the blankets and dream of one of the jolliest Christmas days I had ever spent. So ends my second Christmas with His Majesty's Forces.

2. What I think of English Girls

Private F.G.Hull[171]

What do I think of the English Girls. It is not very difficult for me to give an answer to this interesting question, as I have been associated with two for the best part of thirty years, namely my mother and sister, both typically English, although they have been living in Australia for nearly thirty years. Perhaps you will think I am wrong to include my mother as a girl but if she is not one in years I can assure you she still is in manners. Of course, you are bound to know what I think of my people, so I will give you my impressions of English girls in general. Their fresh, sweet faces instantly appeal to you, and are as refreshing as water is to a thirsty man. I have seen a great many different types of girls in the course of my travels, but there is always the brightness and individuality lacking in the faces of foreign girls. As for an index of character, you have only to study for a second or two the faces of the English girls. They say beauty is only "skin deep." Perhaps it is ; who knows?

But putting aside superficial beauty for the time being there is another form of beauty ever so much more than skin deep, and that is the beauty of good nature and kindness, which almost every English girl possesses. Rich girls or poor girls, pretty or plain, it is all the same, they each one possess this latter form of beauty, which makes the very plainest of faces good to look upon. English girls have come in for a lot of criticism at times which is wholly unwarranted, for are they not our sisters in every sense of the word? Jolly, charming, and full of fun, and I am sure that is what we would like our own sisters to be. The majority of these girls have relatives fighting at the front, and some have brothers there whom they wish to be treated the same as they are striving to treat you. Now these girls, though perhaps young in years, are old in the matter of commonsense, and have a very good idea of the strenuous time soldiers have in general, and it is to lighten their lot that they make the soldiers' acquaintance.

And now we come to the girl heroines, those who are engaged upon the most important and human of all work — the Red Cross workers. I'll wait for a few minutes until the Sister has finished pulling the sticking plaster off my leg. It is rather a painful procedure, and my thoughts just at present are not very pleasant. Oh, no! not of the Sister with the plaster. Oh thank goodness it is over at last, so I will continue. Not alone in England, but everywhere in the far corners of "the Empire upon which the sun never sets," they are to be found engaged upon this self-sacrificing work. I have nothing but the warmest praise for the treatment I have received at the hands of the English Red Cross workers, and they have the blessings I am sure of every person who has at any time been in their care. We Australians will be a long way from home this Christmas, and those of us who can spend Christmas in England will indeed be fortunate, for next to our own relations we love the English people best. And now to finish.

Although I could fill page after page with the praises of the English girls, and such girls too — mothers to be of a nation that has always stood for liberty and right. And it is by knowing that these brave girls will "keep the home fires burning" that we go forward to battle to show Germany "The Day" she so often boasted about is approaching and that a well-merited vengeance is at hand.

3. What I think of Australians

Sister Sylvia[171]

This being a most difficult subject on which to write, it is with fear and trembling that I submit my contribution. Owing to the personal nature of the matter, I feel my only safety is in a nom de plume. And hope I shall not be found out, as one has heard so many lurid tales of the fierce deeds of "Backwoodsmen" . I must say in my experience I have never found them fierce, wild or woolly; but still, I will not risk raising their anger.

> What can one say but praise for them individually, but collectively – well, by the end of the war they may well be on the way to perfection; in fact they have already greatly improved since the Gallipoli days, when they suffered much from swelled heads, and used to try us English women much by implying that no one could fight but Anzacs. Another failing is their lack of "esprit de corps" particularly in their disdain of all NCOs and officers; but perhaps we ought to make allowances for this as they have no regimental tradition to look back on and to maintain.
>
> As patients they are considerate and grateful, though it is quite clear that to try and rule them with a rod of iron is impossible, but when treated with a certain amount of leniency, no one could expect more kindness and help than we get from them. We have heard much of their great bravery on the field of battle, but perhaps even more striking is the pluck and patience with which they endure suffering in hospital, where there is not the sustaining influence of war. It strikes one very forcibly how men of every age have come forward to help the Mother Country – I can almost say that we have had patients varying in age from seventeen to seventy!
>
> Considering the free life to which most of our Colonials are accustomed, it is marvellous how well they conform to the rules and regulations of hospital life; but with such a kind and generous Commandant, who has made his house more of a home than a hospital for them, they could not well do otherwise. Mr Bush thoroughly understands Australians, and in this they are most fortunate.
>
> It has been a great pleasure to make so many friends from overseas and I hope I shall not make enemies owing to these few home truths. One of the few redeeming features of this terrible war is the closer binding together of the Mother Country and her colonies, which I hope will long outlive the war.

Throughout the 12 issues of "*Coo-ee!*" there are accounts of outside events which are often repeated by later inmates so only a few examples will be reproduced here. It is obvious that this regular programme was already in place well before November 1916 when "*Coo-ee!*" first appeared. It is also clear that some careful management was undertaken to ensure that the hosts were always suitably thanked. One suspects that Bush selected, and perhaps rehearsed, the chosen spokesman beforehand, but maybe I misjudge the natural talents of the

Australian volunteer speakers. This was written by Bush himself in February 1917, although under his usual nom de plume of "Dinkum".[172]

> Among the patients at the Knoll we have had a succession of capital speakers. The first of the line of silver-tongued orators was Private Bill Stumbles, whose eloquence as chairman on occasions when patients and staff combined in a musical offensive made full amends for any possible shortage in artistic ammunition. He reached the zenith of his fame when the boys on a memorable afternoon presented Commandant Bush and Mrs Bush with an illuminated address in album form.
>
> Then at a later epoch came Private Ackerley, whose talent was first revealed after we had spent a delightful afternoon at Mrs Charles Cowlin's house overlooking the Severn Sea, at Portishead.
>
> But it was in the old Roman Bath at Bath that Private Ackerley was heard to the fullest advantage. He and "Tiny" Ryan were taking tea with Lady Henniker Heaton, widow of the great postal reformer, when the message reached him to say a few words of thanks to our host, the ex-Mayor of Bath. So well, however, did Ackerley, with his deep, sonorous voice, quit himself of the task, that the ex-Mayor afterwards declared it to be one of the finest speeches he had heard.
>
> Then Sergeant Douglas Woods blossomed out, and made many neat little speeches during his three months' occupancy of the post. Private Combe-Robinson was spokesman-in-chief for a while, and now Sergt Murray is admirably filling the position.

Music Sports and Outings

Trooper J Lennox[173]

This appeared in November 1916.

> MUSIC
>
> During the month our musical gatherings have been sustained with undiminished enthusiasm. On Tuesdays Madame Marion Glass and Mrs

Bowls at Bishop's Knoll.

Christopher George have continued their exertions in a way that have added to our obligations to them, while on Saturday afternoons the parties sent out by the Inquiry Bureau have rendered splendid programmes.

These latter concerts were under the direction of Mr D.R.Thomas, Mr A. Gough and Mr Alf Parkman. The concert on November 25th was of special interest, for Mr Alf Parkman not only gave us a grand programme, but in conjunction with Mr David Crombie provided the prizes for the billiard and card tournaments. On Saturday November 18th Major Sir John McCall, Agent-General for Tasmania was in the chair.

SPORT

The games at Bishop's Knoll have taken a great place in the life of the men here from time to time. With the English Tommies here in past days it was hockey, football, cricket, clock-golf, and bowls. They were up as early as possible and a good game in the freshness of the morning before breakfast brought them in as hungry as hunters, only however, to return with renewed energy directly it was possible. With the Australians began the less energetic games. Bowls was still played, but the chief games for the last few months have been billiards and cards. Weekly tournaments, organised by Mr Powell, have been carried on for the last four months, and each week four prizes are given to the winners. Two prizes are for billiards and two for cards.

The billiards are played off in two classes, "A" and "B". In both classes a great amount of interest is taken in the games, and some very good and clever play results. Cards have been played chiefly amongst those in bed or unable to play billiards for some reason or other. These too have been played with great zest.

Here is a list of last month's prize-winners:—
Billiards: Gray, Brewer, Christie, Lennox, Baker, Bloor, Treloar, Lovett, and Hooper,
Cards: Bloor, Campbell, Read, Whyte, Thomas, Stuart, Christie, Davies, Moore.

OUTINGS.
During the past month we have had some fine outings. On November 2nd we had a very happy time at the Bristol Fine Art Gallery. This was arranged by Mr Sage.

On November 3rd we visited the Picture House in Clare Street, by the invitation of Mr Robertson, the Manager, who has always been a good friend to soldiers. Tea was served for us at the Constitutional Club.

On November 23rd we were again at the Art Gallery, enjoying one of those wonderful soldiers' gatherings arranged by the Inquiry Bureau, while on November 24th we were the guests of the Bristol Cornish Society. Truly may it be said that Bristol folk are for ever looking about for some way in which they can show us hospitality and give us pleasure.

A main feature of the entertainment provided for the Australians were the regular concert parties organised by Mr Inman. In this he recounts how it all started:

With the Australians on the Plain

C.A. Inman.[174]

I propose in this article to tell the readers of "Coo-ee!" how I came to identify myself with the Australian forces. Although in the early days of the war it was my privilege to pay an occasional visit to one of the camps, it was not until December last that I was drawn into the Australian net for continuous service, from which I have never been able to extricate myself. It has been woven round me with the skill of the spider, and I believe there are very large spiders in Australia. Although I am the fly, I am still alive, despite buffetings and set-backs. In fact, my absorption by the boys from "down under" has been so complete that I almost feel like one of themselves. I recall a certain day in December 1916, I was suddenly roused from my forty winks (after dinner) by a stentorian voice : "Are you there, Charlie?" I knew immediately who my visitor was, and hastily pulled myself together. "Come down, Archibald," said I. (A.G.P. always had a knack of turning up at odd times.) Down he came, accompanied by a distinguished-looking officer.

"Let me introduce Captain ——, who has just come down from Codford. This is his first visit to Bristol, his instructions from the Commanding Officer being, "Try and find Mr Archibald Powell. Well, he has found me, and as his requirements are in your line I know you will see it through."

Well, thought I, that's the limit. Wanted a concert the next day for Codford, arranging transport and artists, auditor - what for? To give some boys going across the Channel a good sing-song before leaving. That decided me at once. The Captain returned with the assurance that I would be there the next afternoon.

How easy to promise, but how difficult it was to fulfill the trust. Every musician I 'phoned and interviewed "seemed" to be engaged. But I am glad to say the boys did have their concert, and it was contributed to by a party of the most prominent and versatile artists in Bristol. It was in every respect a triumph and being the first concert the Australians at this particular camp which had been provided with for months, naturally it whetted their appetite, and over the supper table my irresistible friend the Captain (now in France) made me promise

Mr Charles Inman.

to come again the next week, and I have been regularly each week since.

Here I would like to pay my sincere thanks to my many musical friends who have supported me in the most hearty way week by week, and without whose splendid services it would have been impossible to carry on. ***The services of the artistes have been voluntary and without any payment of any kind. I am making a very strong point of this fact, as it is likely to be overlooked by many people.***

Residents of a city cannot realise the winter conditions of motoring to the Plain, especially this past season. The fearful fogs, snow, mud, and intense cold experienced on the journeys I shall never forget; but the discomforts were momentarily forgotten on entering the regimental institutes, for each party is greeted with a fine Australian welcome. Hundreds of stalwart soldiers show their delight. They have perhaps been waiting there for an hour to get a seat.

The success of the Codford concerts travelled away to Tidworth, where the senior officer of the Australian YMCA is stationed, and at his request I devote every Saturday to the various YMCA huts at Larkhill, Perham Down and other districts, where the need for good, wholesome entertainment is great. My Saturday parties also are entirely voluntary, and receive no payment for their services and I think this makes them extremely popular with the boys. The concerts have given the greatest pleasure to thousands of Australians, who I am convinced are keen lovers of music, highly critical and appreciative. The thought has often occurred to me, do the men really want these entertainments, are they necessary? The answer was supplied the other week in the following convincing manner.

A Royal Review had taken place on the Plain and it meant a three days "stunt" (sic) for the Codford Battalion to the rendezvous. On the day the men returned I was due to give a concert as usual, but it was doubtful what sort of an audience would turn up. The boys had marched just about twenty miles a couple of hours previous to the time of commencing, and were tired out. Imagine with what surprise one looked upon a company of about 700 men. True enough, they were too tired to join in the preliminary chorus singing, but that they thoroughly enjoyed the relaxation and the music there was not the slightest doubt. Ask a man on the march whether a band is any help. Music is the greatest tonic to a weary body.

In all weathers.

I must touch on the present difficulties of motor transport. It may be my trouble will meet the eye of a prominent official, who in the goodness of his heart may be able to help in a solution of what is a great obstacle to the successful carrying on of this work. Matters approached a climax on the Friday before Whitsun. A message came on the 'phone late in the afternoon : "Is that you, Mr Inman? We cannot take you to the Plain to-morrow or Whit-Monday. All hired cars (except taxicabs) have been stopped under the new regulations."

The blow long expected had fallen. I had promised the boys a special treat on the two days, and expected huge audiences at Rollestone and Larkhill. What was to be done? I called on my trusty friend Leonard Rowe, and together we thought out various schemes, but all proved unworkable. I rang up private owners who did not come under the ban. I interviewed one excellent citizen late that night, and he said, "I'll take up the party if you can supply the petrol." He might as well have asked me for a potato.[175] (At this time almost impossible to buy!)

The next morning I called on a prominent official of a big company. I knew he had a soft spot in his heart for the boys. Well, I will not tell you how it was done, but through his kindness and that of another official I was able to carry on, and incidentally carry up and circulate quite a respectable number of copies of "Coo-ee!".

And now a word of genuine appreciation of the artistes for the last two or three concerts. Being an accompanist, and not a singer, I can speak without fear or favour. At the Rollestone hut boisterous applause greeted the songs of Miss Edith Barnard, one of the most popular singers I have ever taken with me. Miss Marion Ellen is an equal favourite, singing just the right songs — "Oh, John!" and kindred numbers — and gaining laurels at each appearance. The elocutionary efforts of Miss Ethel Rudman are listened to with rapt attention, her items are always given with true dramatic instinct and graceful charm. Amongst the men there is no greater favourite than Mr Leonard Rowe, with his bright and breezy songs. It is always "Come on, Leonard, we want more," the last three words being accented in terrific voice. Leonard Rowe always has some good stories for the boys. Another popular lady is Miss Margaret Edwards, a charming singer of the lighter songs which are so popular. This artiste is always sure of a great welcome, and is ever ready to sing again and again. Miss Evelyn Gore, Miss Alice Muir, and Miss Grace Troke, three delightful contraltos, are sure of a double, even triple encore from their friends.

I have "discovered" several clever performers in the Australian Force. Private Herbert Lee, of Durrington Camp, is a magnificent baritone, and has assisted me week by week, walking a considerable distance to a particular hut to take his share in the programme. His songs are always received with the greatest enthusiasm, and I am greatly indebted to Private Lee's Company Officer, Lieutenant Corry for making it possible for him to appear. Then I am indebted to Major Rowlands of the 12th TB (Training Battalion) Codford, for the services of Private Ernest Crosby and Lance-corporal J. Kirby two clever artistes who have delighted the patients at Bishop's Knoll Hospital.

Occasionally a visitor is invited to Codford as the guest of the Battalion Officers. I remember a very successful entertainment when Lieutenant J. Bowe-Brooks (Bristol) presided and gave a most inspiring address to the Australians, the excellence of which will long be remembered by those privileged to be present. Such is the work in which I have been engaged for many months. It is a severe tax on one's health. I feel physically I am not the person I was three years ago. Perhaps that is not to be wondered at for every moment of my spare time since the commencement of the war has been given to our splendid boys. An accompanist gets no rest; it is sheer hard work (especially on a camp piano).

I have been a member of the Inquiry Bureau since its formation, and under the auspices of that fine organisation have had the privilege of organising and performing at roughly 1,000 concerts to our wounded in the district, a record of which I am justly proud, and it one does feel somewhat "worn out", the thought occurs that it is better to have kept the flag flying to the end than to have attempted nothing.

One of the reasons why the YMCA featured so prominently in the entertainments provided for Australian soldiers on Salisbury plain was because the Australian military, with the agreement of the Commonwealth Authorities and British Ministry of Defence, had integrated men chosen by the National YMCA Committee of Australia into their forces. These were graded as officers and were of military age and although non-combatants, they carried on their work supporting the troops right into the fighting zone. As explained by E. Haddington Hunt in his account of the work of the Australian YMCA"*No one really understands the needs and wants of a fellow-being until one has learned - and no one can have learned so well as the fellow Australian - the nature of the Australian*".[176] There is no doubt that this underlying philosophy was the reason for the YMCA's success on Salisbury Plain. Many of those who had recuperated at Bishop's Knoll moved on to training brigades on to the Plain.

Performances at Bishop's Knoll

Marion Glass [177]

("*Coo-ee!*" February 1917)

I can't remember, writes Madame Marion Glass, the exact date of our first visit to Bishop's Knoll, but we have given eighty-five concerts there, so it must have been about eighteen months ago. If you do not get tired of us, I hope we shall come there every fortnight until the war is over.

Marion Glass.

My party consists chiefly of pupils (over a hundred), who have been splendid in coming to concerts and rehearsals whenever I have called upon them. One friend (and pupil), Miss Hughes-Garbett, has been to every concert with me. I expect the men will remember her best as the "boy" who has been the stage manager of all the "costume" concerts.

Mr Hubert Hunt (Organist of Bristol Cathedral) has been exceedingly kind in coming to very many concerts to give violin solos. Others who have helped are Miss Elsie Chester (the actress) and her daughter Miss Dolly Holmes-Gore, Mr Walter Francombe-Genee, Peggi and Bobbi Andrews, Miss Thelma Waldron, Miss Nancy Tricks, Miss Betty Shove, Miss Maude Wingate, and Mrs Cuthbert Hicks.

At the beginning of the war I was wondering whether it would be better to take up nursing instead of music. A friend said to me, "Oh, don't do that, its a pity to give up your singing and teaching, you can do that." So I took her advice and stuck to music.

Although we have motored so many thousands of miles to hospitals, we have had no adventures on the road, not even a broken tyre. We have only failed to put on one concert during the two and a half years of war, and that was the one at Bishop's Knoll, when the Commandant refused to let us come because the roads were not safe.

One day we arrived at a hospital where they did not expect us, through some mistake, so all the patients were out. We were getting ready to go home "sadder and wiser," when an audience of two arrived and begged for a "song". Of course we gave them a concert; but other men came in by degrees, and at the end of the programme the hall was crowded.

A few weeks ago I was staying in the country, so was asked to sing at the hospital there. After the concert was over one of the men said to me, "What a pity you don't live in Bristol, they would like to hear you sing at the hospital there." He came from about the only hospital in Bristol where I have never sung, although I hope to go there soon.

Our musical gatherings

Trooper EH Combe-Robinson [178]

(*"Coo-ee!"* November 1916)

As soon as the wounded warriors began to arrive in Bristol, the music and entertaining talent of the district was mobilised, and Bishop's Knoll, in company with the many other war hospitals, shared in the arrangements for providing regular concerts. Twice each week musical parties have crossed the Downs from the city, and have cheered the patients and staff with sweet harmony and skilful entertainment in various forms. Each Saturday the Bristol Inquiry Bureau, an organisation that has done unique war service in many directions, provides the artistes, whilst the Tuesday concerts have from the outset been under the direction of Mrs Christopher George and Madame Marion Glass.

The scene in the large ward, the ballroom of peace times, is a very interesting one on concert afternoons. As many of the patients from other wards as can be safely moved are brought in and tenderly placed in cots, whilst chairs are occupied by members of the staff, patients and visitors at either end of the ward and between the rows of cots. Usually the Commandant acts as Chairman, but now and then other well-known citizens take charge the Lord Mayor Sir Frank Wills, Alderman Frank Sheppard, Paymaster W. H. Cole RNVR, and Mr Harold Lowther being names which come to mind in this connection.

Old patients, as well as those who are now recovering from wounds or sickness, will have many happy memories of these musical gatherings. A very high standard of musical talent has been maintained, and enthusiasm is invariably the keynote of the proceedings. The concerts last as a rule an hour and a half; then comes the National Anthem, sung with fervour by all present, and the concert is wound up with a vote of thanks, proposed by one of the soldiers and seconded by the Commandant. During the past month the musical parties have been under the direction of Mrs Christopher George, Madame Marion Glass, Madam Eaves, Mr Fred Wiltshire, and Mr Alf Parkman.

EXCURSIONS.

Looking back over the past two years, one can recall some very delightful excursions and visits to Bristol entertainments, which by the generosity of friends the patients at Bishop's Knoll have been able to enjoy. To enumerate them all would occupy far more space than is available, but mention might be made of those which took place during the past month, and a few others :

October 9 — Berkeley Castle, by invitation of Lord Fitzhardinge.
October 13 — Animated Pictures, "The Birth of a Nation," at the Colston Hall. by invitation of Mrs Straehan.
October 19 — Matinee at the Bristol Hippodrome, when 2,500 wounded soldiers were present at the invitation of Mr Oswald Stoll.
October 26 — Matinee at the Prince's Theatre (later demolished during WW2 bombing), by invitation of the proprietors.
October 27 — Motor drive to Brockley Combe, tea at the Bristol Liberal Club and visit to Picture House.

Reference must also be made to the splendid trip to Bath when the ex-Mayor Mr G.T. Cooke, was the host. On this occasion tea was served in the old Roman Baths, which date from about the time of Christ. The delightful hospitality of Mr and Mrs Sidney Hill at Langford House, Somerset; Mr and Mrs Charles Cowlin, Portishead; Mrs Conrad Cowlin, Yatton; Mr Clayfield Ireland, Brislington; Mrs Scales, Bath. On several occasions the patients at Bishop's Knoll have been the guests of Mr Graham H. Wills and his friends associated with the Insurance profession, and similarly of the literary staff of the Western Daily Press and the old Sportsmen of Bristol. Mr Ivy M. Dunlop was responsible for a very pleasant excursion to Weston super Mare, a popular seaside resort on the Bristol Channel.

A very special treat was provided when the soldiers were invited to inspect the vast factories of the Imperial Tobacco Company. Bristol of course being the headquarters of this world famous firm. And the wonderful Inquiry

The visit to Bath.

Bureau have week in week out, provided splendid outings and entertainment in a great variety of forms, Bishop's Knoll being included in invitations that have been extended to all the hospitals in the Bristol district.

The social side at Bishop's Knoll.
The Australian Band and Pierrots visit

by Cobber [179]

During the past month the social side of hospital life at Bishop's Knoll has been well maintained, most entertaining concerts have been provided by our good friends Madame Marion Glass and Mr C.A. Inman and party.

THE BAND

And the fine band and Pierrot troupe of the [censored] Training Battalion AIF Codford. The latter event which took place on the 28th July was a noteworthy one. The Commandant had issued an open invitation to all friends of the Hospital, and there was a numerous response, the visitors including Sir W. Howell Davies M.P. and Lady Davies and many prominent citizens.

The Pierrot troupe on Bishop's Knoll Terrace.

THE PIERROT TROUPE

The concert took place on the terrace, which presented a charmingly picturesque scene in the brilliant sunshine. Bishop's Knoll is famous for its roses, and the bright-hued ramblers covering the pergolas and rustic arches made a vivid and charming contrast to the blue uniforms of the patients and the costumes of Sisters and visitors. The band and the pierrots proved an irresistible attraction, and the afternoon will remain one of the most pleasant of memories of Bishop's Knoll during war time.

Alderman E. H. Cook, during an interval, presented the prizes won in the tournaments, and took the opportunity of paying a warm tribute to the generous patriotism of the Commandant. Recent donors of prizes include Mr S. Bostock Smith, Mr Walter Reid Warton, the staff at Langford House, Miss Blanche Padden and Miss Agnes Rayson. To these good friends the thanks of the patients are due.

Our trip to Berkeley Castle

Private F.C. Ross[180]

Most of us who are having our first experience of the Motherland have longed for the opportunity to visit some of the famous old castles and institutions associated with bygone times.

It was, therefore, with more than ordinary pleasure that we set out from Bishop's Knoll on Friday, October 6th 1916 for Berkeley Castle, the ancestral home of Lord Fitzhardinge. All the patients who were well enough to travel were invited. Our party, which included several Sisters and the Editor of "Coo-ee!" to whom we were indebted for arranging the trip, were accommodated in two fine motor char-a-bancs.

A few days previously Mr F. A. Wilshire, barrister, had visited the hospital, and had given us a delightful lecture on the history of Berkeley Castle, and had also told us much about that part of Gloucestershire through which we should pass. Unfortunately, however, the weather met with on the way was violent, and rain storms marred the outlook. It cleared as we neared the old-world town of Berkeley, and we were able to catch a view of the monument to Tyndale, the translator of the Bible, and another to a son of one of the Dukes of Beaufort.

At Berkeley we were met and right heartily welcomed by Lord Fitzhardinge's agent, Mr J. Peter, and Mr George Clarke, and these gentlemen kindly acted as guides during the wonderfully interesting tour of inspection. We were fortunate in seeing very nearly all that was to be seen at the grand old place, and every one of us was fascinated by the experience of being amid scenes which had remained almost unchanged through the centuries.

Berkeley Castle was founded in the time of William the Conqueror, and it is one of the finest of the few remaining feudal strongholds in the country. From earliest times the castle has played an important part in all the civil wars in England, being frequently besieged and captured. Edward II was brought here from Bristol and murdered, and we visited the room above the doorway of the keep in which the deed was done. It remains, musty and mouldy, in much the same condition as when the monarch suffered his terrible death. We also saw the dungeon in which the king had spent some of his last days, a weird,

Berkeley Castle.

gloomy place, with only one opening from the top, through a trap-door.

The treasures of the house are beyond price: works of art by the great masters, beautiful tapestry, weapons and armour of the days of the Crusaders; and coming to later times, the cabin furniture from Sir Francis Drake's ship in which he made one of his famous voyages in the days of Good Queen Bess.

We had tea — a right royal feast — in the magnificent banqueting-hall, which has witnessed many a festive gathering of barons, knights and squires. It stands now practically unchanged from those far-away days, and it will no doubt stand for centuries yet to come, a splendid memorial to the skill of the old builders.

After tea Sergeant Woods expressed our thanks to Lord Fitzhardinge for his generous hospitality, and when Mr Peter had replied, we mounted our chara-a-bancs and proceeded to the kennels and stables. Here, as in the castle, a photograph of the party was taken by Mr Stevens, who had come out from Bristol for the purpose. It was a glorious trip, one that we shall never forget.

Our visit to Langford House

Private E Harris [181]

It will not do to single out one place where we have been entertained by hospitable hosts as being better than the others, yet to many of us who have been able to visit the beautiful home of Mr and Mrs Sidney Hill, at Langford, Somerset, the remembrance of our welcome will stand out as one of the happiest of many happy excursions we have made under the guidance of a good, well-tried friend. I was fortunate in being included in each party invited to Langford during the summer. The drive down was delightful. We went by motor char-a-banc, and created somewhat of a sensation as we passed over the Downs and through the southern district of the city, with our beloved flag of Australia gaily unfolded to the breeze.

About an hour's drive through typical English scenery — hill and dale, with the abundant foliage and the meadows in varying tints of green, through the gateway and up the drive and there on the lawn in front of the mansion Langford House — were our host and hostess with their children and a company of friends waiting to greet us. And what a cheery, hearty greeting it was. We felt at home at once. There was no preliminary shyness. We were made to feel we were welcome, and for the next few hours were completely happy.

First of all those of us who were able to move freely had a look round the gardens and through the glass-houses filled with the choicest of greenhouse plants, exotics and rare ferns. Then we spent half an hour or so on the rifle range, where the men belonging to our host's company of volunteers do their practice. Afterwards we took part in clock-golf competitions.

Tea was served on the lawn. A fine, bountiful repast it was, and the lady of the house and her friends attended to our wants as though we were the most honoured of guests. I am writing now more particularly of our second visit. On the former occasion Mr Hill had taken some photographs of our party. These we had had enlarged and framed, and when we had finished tea at our second visit Sergeant Lewis presented it to Mr and Mrs Hill. Few of us had regarded the Sergeant as an orator, but he made a jolly good speech for a soldier. A pressman was with us and he took it all down. This is what the Sergeant said:-

"Mr and Mrs Hill, I have been asked by my comrades to express to you

Langford House.

our sincere thanks for your hospitality to us today. Some of us have had the pleasure of visiting your beautiful home before, and others who have but recently come from the front have come here to-day for the first time. It is not easy for a soldier to say all he would like to say on an occasion like this, but I can assure you, Sir and Madame, that your kindness in inviting us here, and treating us so well, will never be forgotten. I should like to say on behalf of my comrades that the people of Bristol and those who live in the surrounding district, have shown such consideration for us soldiers as will make us think of them with gratitude all through our lives. Most of us came to the famous old city entire strangers, but from the start we have been made to feel we were among friends, and I am quite sure that many of us will leave with real regret.

When we were here a few weeks ago you were good enough, Mr Hill, to take our photograph. Well, Sir, we have had it enlarged and put in a frame, and we want you and Mrs Hill to accept it as a little memento of an occasion, which to us will be one of our happiest memories. It will perhaps serve to remind you and Mrs Hill and your dear children of a war-time gathering which made us soldiers, English born as well as Australians, forget our wounds and our troubles in the pleasures of your beautiful home and your great kindness."

Mrs Hill made a graceful little speech in accepting the gift. She said how proud they all were to have soldiers who had fought and had been wounded

Langford House tea.

in the great war, at their house, and she wished us all the best of luck in the future. Then our host and hostess, their children, friends and maids, cheered us, and we cheered them back as you may guess with right good will. Then, when most of us went back to the golf putting lawn, some of the boys stayed behind and returned the compliment by waiting on the maids when they had tea. Later, one of our crowd fancied his chance at billiards, and we all adjourned to the billiard room to see the sport. When the game was finished Mrs Hill distributed the prizes, and fine ones they were, which had been won for clock-golf.

You can guess that we were real sorry to come away and as we motored off laden with flowers and hearts full of thankfulness the welkin rang with our cheers. The drive back at the close of the summer day was just glorious.

Sidney Hill.

Mrs Hill.

Langford House departure.

Happy Days Our trips to Yatton

Sergeant Douglas Woods[182]

I suppose all of us Australian soldiers who have come wounded to the old city of Bristol, and have shared in the unbounded hospitality of the residents and those who live in the beautiful environment, will have one occasion in mind, or one series of occasions which will stick in the memory longer than any other.

Quite a number of us will remember Yatton for all time, and a beautiful old country house there, dating back I believe several hundred years. It was not a big place, or a show place, but it was a place of real homely hospitality. All through the summer of 1916, four names were chosen and put up on the notice board of the hospital, as the guests for Yatton and no notice was more eagerly scanned by the convalescent patients than this one.

On the day appointed, a car usually arrived at the hospital at half past one for the men who had probably been waiting half an hour on the doorstep and off we went, knowing full well that we were in for a few hours of real change and pleasure.

The drive to Yatton takes one through a glorious a piece of woodland scenery as could be met with in any part of Great Britain the famous Brockley Combe. It is a veritable fairy-land, and one could easily let the imagination rip, and conjure up visions of fairy elves, pursuing, whatever fairy elves are supposed to pursue, in this enchanted spot.

The run down usually occupied an hour and a quarter, so that we always had a few hours to spend with our hostess, Mrs Conrad Cowlin. Some of the earlier parties visited the old church, which is remarkable in many respects, and especially so as it being the burial place of a certain gipsy "king and queen" and their family: but in the later visits to Yatton the whole of the time was spent in the beautiful old-world garden of "The Ferns".

There was always a party of friends of our hostess to meet us, and from the time we arrived they just devoted themselves to the task of making us feel we were the most important people in the world, instead of being, as of course we were, negligible quantities in the vast army of the Empire.

We shall always remember the absolute sincerity of the welcome the unrestricted hospitality, the stroll round the flower and fruit gardens, and the game of bowls on the tennis lawn: but above all we shall find sweet remembrance in the fact that here we were; absolute strangers in a strange land, received into a typical English home as though we were old friends or even members of the family. I should like, and I am sure everyone of my comrades will re-echo this sentiment, to say how deeply we appreciated the kindness of our hostess and how much we will treasure the photographs she was good enough to take of the various parties.

Christmas at Bishop's Knoll

Members of staff.[183]

"Coo-ee!" January 1917

As this was the first Christmas most of our Australian patients had spent in England, it was decided that a real old-fashioned custom should be kept up—the singing of sweet old English carols. These were sung on Christmas eve by the choir boys of Stoke Bishop Church in the afternoon, and when the lights were lowered and the wards closed down, by the nursing staff in the evening. It was quite a pretty sight. All the nurses carried Japanese coloured lanterns, and as they went through the wards and along the corridors the words of the carols were caught up by the soldiers, and all joined in singing them together.

Everybody was awake early Christmas morning, and great was the excitement when it was found that each patient had his stocking filled by that wonderful old man, Father Christmas. Of course, the usual old jokes of refilling each other's stockings with brown paper, old slippers, etc., had to be carried through, but that only added to the fun of the whole thing.

A good many of the convalescent patients attended morning service, and from then until dinner-time they busied themselves with secret affairs, which later on in the day proved very wonderful and interesting. A most excellent arrangement had been made by the Commandant for one of the chief events of the day - the Christmas dinner. The oak-panelled hall and large conservatory were cleared and arranged to accommodate between sixty and seventy soldiers. The elaborate decorations and arrangement of the tables were most tastefully carried out by MissThornley, a very pretty and cheery scene she made of it too.

What a dinner it was! The finest and tenderest of turkeys, the richest of plum-puddings, more than enough of dessert, and just enough ale to drink, for, as Jerome says. "Thirst is a dangerous thing". Mr and Mrs Bush presided at one table and Mr Strachan very kindly took charge of another. All were kept very busy carving the turkeys and hams. The helpers were many and willing, and we must thank the scouts for their services that day too. The kitchen staff must be heartily congratulated on the cooking, for everything was done to a turn and served up piping hot. Crackers were pulled, jokes rattled off, and good-humour prevailed everywhere. But not a sound was heard when the Commandant called attention, and read aloud a stirring telegram sent by their Majesties to the Australian troops, and when it was ended cheer after cheer resounded through the building for King, Queen and Country.

Tables were cleared, a little rest taken by some of the less convalescent patients, and, to use an expression of one of the sisters : "Exit all nurses and patients and enter peoples of all nations and ages."

Then the scene was changed, and one met everywhere Indian chiefs, Elizabethan ladies and gentlemen with frills round ye necks, early Britons, black-a-moors, cavaliers, Quakers, college dons, and goodness knows what other characters dating from pre-historic times to the present day.

It would be almost impossible for me to describe all the costumes of the men, but I believe an abler pen has attempted it and succeeded. Ward I had been decorated and transformed into a scene of exceptional brilliance and beauty. Ordinary everyday beds had been moved and placed lengthways against the walls and covered with various coloured rugs, giving the appearance of oriental divans. Flags of all the Allies hung bravely, and holly and mistletoe adorned window sills and corners (Thanks are due to Messrs. Partridge & Love for so generously lending the decorations, and we wish them a very prosperous and happy New Year). In the centre of the ward a huge Christmas tree was erected, holding a present for every person in the hospital. This was the Christmas present to the patients from the nursing staff.

The ward itself is a work of art, with its lovely mirrors, magnificent organ, and beautiful hanging glass chandelier, so the scene may be imagined. Congratulations must again be offered, and this time to Privates Hooper, Flynn, Stuart and others for their untiring efforts of the morning to effect this remarkable change.

At 4.30 p.m. a Grand March Past of all in costume took place, and perhaps the simplest way to describe the sisters' costumes would be to recall them to my memory as they passed before me then.

Miss Bush and her small brothers and sisters entered into the spirit of the affair, and came very effectively attired as "Black and White Pierots and Pierettes (sic)", Mrs Herepath - Commandant of No. 12 Detachment—held her position well as a splendid "Oriental Lady," and a masked figure with side-curls, and dressed in a beautiful lavender and gold brocaded costume of a hundred years ago, eventually proved to be an "Ayah," the make-up was so real, even to the nose-ring, that her identity was not known until late in the evening. Although all the dresses were excellent, she deservedly took first prize. Sister Meck was "Powder and Puff," in yellow and white brocade, Sister Frické, "White and Black Pierette" and Sister Collen, with her dog "Billie," one of the best as "Mother Hubbard," Miss Haines "White and Red Pierette," Miss E. Swinton "Snow White," and Miss K. Swinton, an "Italian Girl," Miss Saville, "Norwegian Peasant," Miss C. M. Philp, a strapping "Cow-girl," Mrs Morris, "Nun," and Mrs Davis "Peace". This dress was particularly admired and ran

Christmas parade.

the winner very closely.) Miss Colthurst "Dawn", Miss Rudduck, "Black and White" (powder puff period). Miss B. Goss "Irish Colleen" and Miss O. Goss "A mermaid." Miss Ransford and Mrs Combe-Robinson (formerly Sister Richards, now married to a patient), "Dutch Girls", Miss Thornley "Coo-ee!" a suggestion that pleased the soldiers immensely. Mrs Rusby, "Italian peasant", Miss E. Holman "Spanish dancer", Miss Laing "Night", Miss Bernard "Italian lady", and Miss Ennis "Indian Girl". Special mention must be made of Miss Were, who was quite disguised as a "Snow Man" and Miss Bertish, who very cleverly represented a "Thermometer". These two also took a great number of marks in the ballot.

The tree was stripped, presents handed round, and seats taken for the evening concert given by the patients of the hospital. Privates Hooper, Hull, Owen and Flynn again being the leading lights. The items were splendid and thoroughly enjoyed by the audience. A remarkably good turn was by Private Hull, who sketched lightning pictures, and caused cheer after cheer with his illuminated "Happy Christmas" a very delightful compliment to Mr and Mrs Bush.

All good things must come to and end though, and after a few speeches and a hearty supper of cold turkey, ham and ale, all felt ready to sing "Auld

Nurses Fancy Dress.

Lang Syne", resume normal conditions and tuck into bed.

The whole day was a very happy and successful one, the only regret being that the Editor of "Coo-ee!", who owing to illness, was not present to share the frolic and fun. Although absent he was by no means forgotten and warmest wishes were sent to him from Bishop's Knoll.

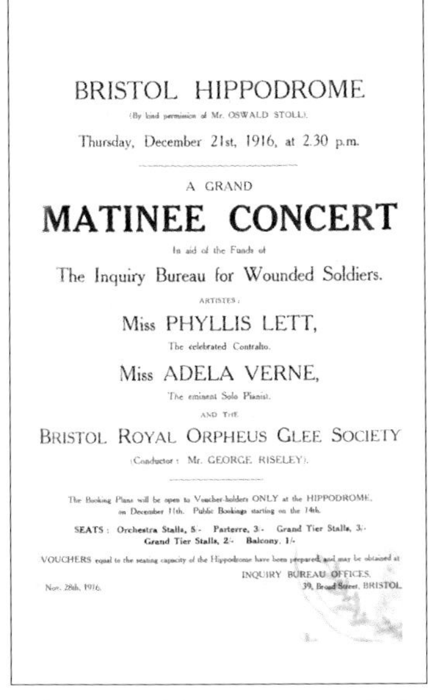

BRISTOL HIPPODROME

(By kind permission of Mr. OSWALD STOLL).

Thursday, December 21st, 1916, at 2.30 p.m.

A GRAND

MATINEE CONCERT

In aid of the Funds of

The Inquiry Bureau for Wounded Soldiers.

ARTISTES:

Miss PHYLLIS LETT,

The celebrated Contralto.

Miss ADELA VERNE,

The eminent Solo Pianist.

AND THE

BRISTOL ROYAL ORPHEUS GLEE SOCIETY

(Conductor: Mr. GEORGE RISELEY).

The Booking Plans will be open to Voucher-holders ONLY at the HIPPODROME, on December 11th. Public Bookings starting on the 14th.

SEATS: Orchestra Stalls, 5/- Parterre, 3/- Grand Tier Stalls, 3/- Grand Tier Stalls, 2/- Balcony, 1/-

VOUCHERS equal to the seating capacity of the Hippodrome have been prepared, and may be obtained at

INQUIRY BUREAU OFFICES,
39, Broad Street, BRISTOL.

Nov. 28th, 1916.

The 1916 pre Christmas Concert organised by the Inquiry Bureau.

Just as in 1915 the Christmas programme of 1916 was well filled. There had been a pre Christmas concert at the Hippodrome and On Boxing Day the Bishop's Knoll soldiers were part of a group of 2000 who were entertained by the Mayor and citizens of Bristol at the Drill Hall. Then on December 28 there was another of the many visits to Langford House as guests of Mr and Mrs Hill.

The Drill Hall December 26, 1916.

The lighter side of Hospital life

by Cobber[184]

"*Coo-ee!*" June 1917

During the month we have again been favoured with visits from the following ladies with their talented concert parties : Madame Glass, Mrs Percy Smith, Miss Thomas, Mrs Brooks and the Clifton Mummers Dramatic Party. The applause meted out to the various artistes is some indication of the pleasure with which these concerts are looked forward to. Especially is this so during the past few weeks, when practically all the beds in the hospital have been occupied, those able to sit up making way for bed patients from the other wards.

Even with old patients there is always sincere praise for the manner in which both old and new songs, recitations, dances, etc., are given and with so many recently wounded men constantly arriving there is always a big welcome and an unstinted cheer of thanks for the kindness of the many ladies and

Billiard Competition.

gentlemen (never forgetting the little ladies) that ungrudgingly give up their time to help break the monotony of hospital life.

Through the kindness of the Misses Clarke an invitation to a matinee of "The Maid of the Mountains" found us at the Prince's Theatre enjoying the splendid performance. On the 10th quite a number of us were among the party who were the guests of the members of the Constitutional Club. A most enjoyable concert was given, followed by a substantial tea, and the usual acceptable gifts of smokes.

The wind-up of the month, and this time we were appreciating the hospitality of the lady munition makers in Bristol. The weather unfortunately turned out rather cold, nevertheless we had quite an interesting time and our appetites certainly never suffered through the climatic conditions. To the many ladies and gentlemen responsible for the expense, time and trouble incurred at these most enjoyable outings we tender our sincere thanks for their great kindness extended to us.

SPORT.

We have again had some good card and billiard tournaments, and the following

Playing cards in the Winter Garden.

list of winners are recipients of treasured souvenirs of a very pleasant stay at the hospital:

Billiards — Sergeant McConnell, Corporal Guest, Privates Love, Harford, Halliday, O'Reilly, C. W. Smith and Jackson.
Cards — Corporals Guest and Kinger, Privates V. Mitchell, Evans, Thompson, Julian, Love and Halliday.

As the prizes usually are of useful and durable nature, such as cigarette cases, tobacco boxes, shaving outfits, wallets, purses, etc., in years to come they will be a pleasant reminder of the kindness of the Sisters and the ladies and gentlemen in Bristol responsible for the kindly thought and cost of these gifts, never forgetting our good friend Mr A. G. Powell, who since these weekly games were inaugurated has called upon the purses of most Bristol sportsmen and sportswomen, who when hearing of the purpose readily respond. Lieutenant Tom Richards, Gunner Whitrow, Officers of the 1st Batt. AIF, Mr Fred Burris, and Mr P. Burris, Junior, are recent contributors to the prize fund.

Gallipoli Day 1917

AGP (Powell with his other nom de plume)

Just over a year ago, a young officer who had on more than one occasion contributed to Coo-ee! (*this must have been Powell's son Leslie*) reminded his father in a letter of the near approach of the first anniversary of the landing at Gallipoli. "That day," he stated, "ought to be kept up in England as well as in Australia, for there were achievements by our navy and home forces, as well as the Anzacs, that are not likely to be excelled in this or any other war." The Lord Mayor (Dr Barclay Baron) was spoken to on the subject, and took up the suggestion with enthusiasm. He gave an open invitation to a gathering at the Mansion House, and though we had little more than a week to make the arrangements and find the men, we were able to get together 250 veterans of Gallipoli representing 83 different naval and military units.

This year with more time at our disposal, we were able to celebrate Gallipoli Day in a more public manner, and the event will be remembered by those who took part and the thousands of citizens who turned out to give the lads a cheer as they marched or rode through Bristol as one of the most impressive spectacular scenes of the war. Through the Press and at the hospitals 300 men were found who had taken part in the Gallipoli campaign. Each received a card of invitation from the Lord Mayor to join in the celebration. They assembled at the Council House and a procession was formed. It was headed by the Chief Constable with a body of mounted police. Then came the Lord Mayor and Lady Mayoress in the state carriage with the Sheriff (Colonel J.B. Butler) and Mrs Butler following. Gallipoli Officers and veterans of the Crimea and Indian Mutiny, Gallipoli men from the hospitals, discharged sailors, sailors on the active list, Australians, New Zealanders, and men from English, Irish, Scotch (sic) and Welsh regiments were also in the procession, while the band of the Bristol Volunteer Regiment (1st Battalion) provided music.

At the fine Art Gallery, the veterans were received by the Lord Mayor and Lady Mayoress and the roll of honour was signed by every man. This roll of honour by the by is a real work of art and has been handed over to the city authorities as a civic possession.

Despite the food restrictions, the Committee was able to supply a good

Gallipoli Day April 25, 1917.

repast, and afterwards came the Lord Mayor's address, an oration that thrilled everyone present. His Lordship, who has a fine gift of expression, recalled some of the outstanding incidents of the landing and the subsequent campaign. He dealt upon the glorious heroism of the navy, and the superb devotion to duty by the soldiers, and he spoke too of the magnificent courage and determination of the Australians at Lone Pine,[185] and the Gloucesters who fought on at Suvla Bay from midday till sunset after every officer and non-commissioned officer had been killed or wounded.

Captain Reeves (Leicesters) for the guests of the day acknowledged the Lord Mayor's remarks, and Sergeant W. Stumbles, AIF jumping to his feet, called for three cheers for his Lordship and the Lady Mayoress. These were given with rare enthusiasm, and the company settled themselves down to enjoy a particularly fine musical programme, five of the artistes - all first class. At six o'clock coffee and sandwiches were served and then the men were assembled again, and headed by the bugle band of the Boy Scouts proceeded to the Hippodrome, where they were guests of the management. The arrangements for this memorable gathering were made by the Bristol Inquiry Bureau, an organisation which has existed since the outbreak of the war, and has done wonderful work for the wounded.

Navy and military personnel involved in the Gallipoli campaign gather in Corn Street ahead of the ceremony.

The scene outside The Guildhall as the Gallipoli veterans set off on their march to the Museum and Art Gallery.

Anzac Day 1917 was a holiday in all army camps and at Codford a highly successful sports day was held. This included events such as the Anzac Sprint and the Gallipoli Gallup for all those who have been present at the landing there. At the end of the days there was another YMCA concert with Blanche Padden and her team.[186]

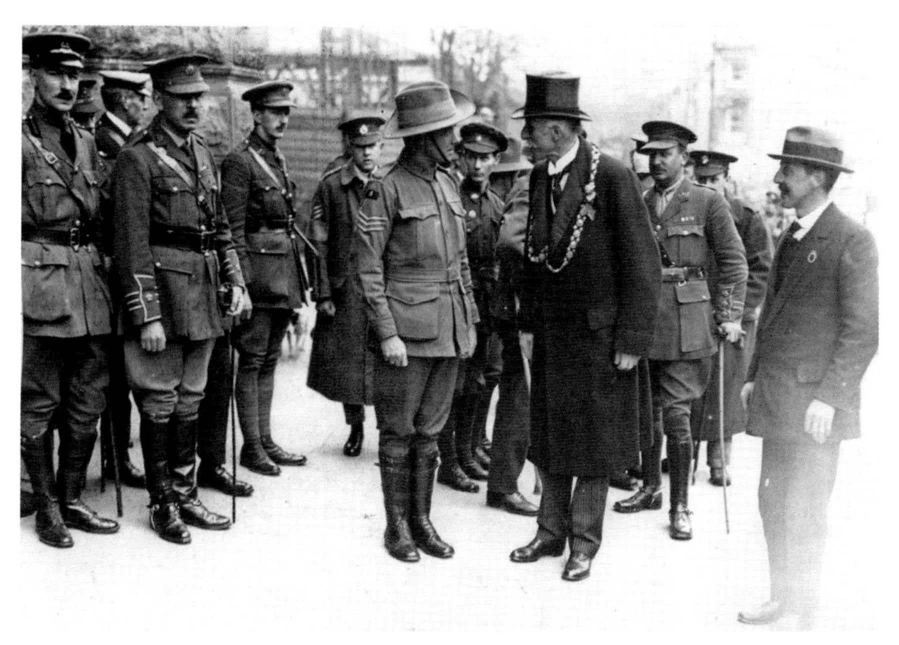

Archibald Powell, extreme right, introducing Sergeant W Stumbles of the AIF to the Lord Mayor. William Stumbles was one of the first wounded Australians to come to Bishop's Knoll, and was discharged and sent back to Australia. He then re-enlisted and suddenly appeared to help celebrate "Gallipoli Day," 1917 much to everyone's delight!

ANZACS signing the Roll of Honour at the Art Gallery, April 25, 1917.

CHAPTER 9

NEWS OF FORMER PATIENTS RECEIVED AT BISHOP'S KNOLL

INCLUDED HERE ARE mainly letters and news published in *"Coo-ee!"*. Other letters of news and thanks from soldiers, their parents and relatives were sent to Mr and Mrs Bush, many of which appear in the Bishop's Knoll records currently kept in the Bristol Reference Library.[187]

Private Fleming to Robert Edwin Bush, October 10, 1916 [188]

Twelve months ago today I got my first sight of England at Plymouth, and same day was admitted to your hospital. The memory of that day is a most pleasant recollection to me. First the train journey through Devon which was an eye-opener to me, the reception given us at Temple Meads on arrival, by the Red Cross members, and lastly the run to Bishop's Knoll, and my subsequent happy stay under your hospitable roof, are memories that will always be bright in my mind.

Since leaving England last March I have been back to Egypt, where I stayed for three weeks. From there I went to Marseilles, had a short stay in that city and then travelled right across France to these parts, where after a few weeks in a Details Camp I was fortunate enough to be sent on to rejoin my old unit, and am still with them.

Since that time I have had some thrilling experiences. Was at [censored] when our boys made their first charge, worked hard for three days and nights stretcher-bearing, was relieved and had a spell from the trenches for a couple of weeks, during which time I was doing nursing duties at different hospitals near the front. Went back with the Division, and did a further eight days' stretcher-bearing at the trenches. I had several close calls, but finally got through without a scratch. We were unfortunate in losing a number of bearers, killed and wounded. I wasn't sorry when we were relieved and left those parts.

At present I am in a much quieter part of the line, and the Ambulance is conducting a Rest Station. It is a comfortable place and close to a large town, which I have visited on several occasions. Attached to the hospital are a library, sports ground, and hot baths, which we chaps have the use of, football and cricket matches are played, weather permitting, two or three times a week. It is not hard to get a match on, as there are plenty of units about, Canadian, English, Scotch, and Australian, all anxious to play with us. At both games we have some of the best of players.

One of our chaps, Tom Richards,[189] will probably be known to you. He represented Australia with one of our last teams that visited England before the war. Prior to going to Australia he played for some time with Bristol, and I understand was a 'top notcher' in the team. Richards is on leave at present, and will no doubt be visiting Bristol, as he is a great friend of Mr Powell.

A few of us who are musically inclined recently started a Glee Club in connection with the unit, our object being to provide some recreation for ourselves during the coming winter months, and also some entertainment for the patients. We obtained music from London, and have made a good start with a choir of over twenty voices, among them being some first-rate singers. Our only handicap is that we have to borrow an organ for practices, but we hope to overcome that difficulty by procuring a dulcetone which being small, can lie easily transported with us to wherever we may move to.[190]

During the last few months I have met a number of the old Bishop's Knoll boys. Up at the trenches I met Adams, Kidman and Vincent. It was during the first few days that I met Vincent. He was on his way down to the ambulance, and told me that he was slightly wounded, a few small shell splinters in his thigh. I have since heard that he was afterwards killed, so presume he went back to firing line when the Division went in the second time.

I also heard from Bristol that Alexander was killed. They were both fine chaps, and I regret very much to hear of their deaths. Adams and Vincent got through alright. In these parts I met Angus, Barnes and White all looking their best. I saw several others of the old lads whose names I can't recollect. Stumbles did not come out this way at all.

In a letter I had from my father a few days ago he said that Stumbles had called to see them at Sydney, and had a long chat with them. He was then on two weeks' leave, so I presume he will be coming back here.

Please convey my regards to Mrs Bush and family Mrs Strachan, Sister Prout and staff, and accept same yourself.[191]

Private Jim Dolin, writing from Durban on his way to Australia the same month[192]

We arrive in Durban tonight about 9 p.m. and expect to all go ashore tomorrow to spend the day as guest of some kind Durban folks. I believe they are giving us a spread in the Town Hall. Then the Colonel informed us this morning that we will have the next day (Wednesday) to ourselves to visit the sights of Durban.

A man travelling home on one of these hospital ships does feel grateful to the Red Cross Society for the comforts they have procured for the returning troops. I do not think a man would receive more had he paid a first-class fare to Australia than what we are receiving now. Officers, NCO's and the totally crippled all have deck cabins, the rest of us below. Other comforts the same as a hospital exactly, blue uniforms, etc."

P.S. Please remember me to the Commandant, Sisters and all friends.

Private E. Harris, now on Salisbury Plain, to the Editor:

Just a few lines, hoping they will find you and all the boys, not forgetting Mr and Mrs Bush and the sisters, in the best of health. It is now a month since I

Advertising one of Mr Rowlands concerts at Bhurtpore Barracks, Tidworth, in May 1916 (the Rev J Goodlet is on the left).

left the Knoll and although I have had a real good time, you have never been absent from my mind.

Whenever I hear the boys here talking of their different hospitals, I always chip in and ask them if they have been to Bristol. I can tell you that quite a lot of them have heard about the reception we received from the Bristol people. Never mind. We had a delightful reminder of Bristol when Miss Muir turned up at a concert in our YMCA Hut. She was the star of the evening and had encore after encore. The boys sitting round kept saying. "She's the sort to cheer a man up," and I reminded them we had dozens like her giving up nearly all their time to the boys of Bishop's Knoll and the other hospitals in Bristol. They said I was silly to leave, but all good things come to an end.

Since writing the foregoing letter. A postcard has been received from Private Harris stating he is in a permanent job at Bhurtpore Barracks Salisbury Plain, and is going to see to it that the circulation of the magazine is maintained in his sphere of influence. Ed.

December 1916

Should auld acquaintance

News of former patients by Sister A[193]

This early article was written before Bush had obtained permission for only Australians to be treated at Bishop's Knoll and so is mainly about British patients.

We had an unexpected visit from Private Lorthrop, who was with us for a while, and he gave us news of several of the "old boys" whom we have not heard of just lately. Private Lorthrop himself is now on the Senior Medical Officers' Staff, so is frequently coming across men from Bishop's Knoll. C. Purchase and E. Parish have rejoined their units. Driver Baker is now doing Government work in London in the Post Office. Hargreaves, who it will be remembered got his Military Cross before leaving hospital, is on the staff in London. Another surprise visit was from Lance-Corporal Ryan, who has joined the Military Police Force. Owing to his visit to Bristol being one of "duty," it was unfortunately very brief.

Private Tom Robinson writing from Perham Down, says that he "has had two trips to Bonny Scotland". He also unkindly remarks, "Private Horn is still here. He is employed at the YMCA hut serving out cakes, and I suppose eats a few as he always did have a good appetite."

Private C. Gruff, who was in hospital at the same time was killed in July and Private Thew states, "He was shot in July and my division relieved his, that was on the Somme."

Private E. O. Thew has again been sent back wounded from France, but unfortunately this time did not reach Bishop's Knoll. He had a piece of shrapnel in his lung, and in writing says, "It is a nasty place to carry ammunition about with you, I would prefer it in my pack."

Sergeant George Lewis, who was an inmate of Bishop's Knoll for so many months, and who eventually got his discharge from the army, has been presented with a self-propelling chair from the Kitchener Memorial Fund. He was very delighted with it, and in writing says: "I thought you would like to

Sergeant Lewis and his new chair.

hear the news of my chair. I have got it and it is a great help to me".

Private Peck, in a letter to one of the Sisters says: "The weather is getting very cold here, and we are having a fair amount of rain, which makes things very uncomfortable. The mud is up to one's waist in places. I am spending a week at a machine gun school but shall be back with my unit at the end of the week. My word you make me long to be back in Bristol, writing of the grand time we all had at the Hippodrome. It must have been an excellent turn out if like the ones I have been to. But I do not begrudge the men the times they are having; they have fully earned them. We had some good news this week concerning this front, and still hope for better. Remember me to all at the hospital."

Private Gaynor and Private P. Harper are back again in the fighting line.

We are sorry to hear that Private Kunkley who was transferred to St. Marylebone Schools, Southall, is to have an operation, and hope we shall soon hear of his speedy recovery. Trooper G. Lukin, who helped us spend Christmas here last year but who was obliged to go back to Australia on account of his rheumatism, writes from Toogay "One never knows but I might be going back after the summer, as I think things will be alright for me by that time. Anyway I would very much like to go out to France and have a go out there as things are very slow at home while the war is on."

We are delighted to hear from Angus McLeod of the 2nd Black Watch, one of the earliest patients at Bishop's Knoll, that he has been promoted Corporal and at the time of writing was in charge of the Pipers, the Pipe-Major being on leave. "I am getting on famously," he writes, "and might finish up a General!" We wish him luck and hope he will. He is now in Mesopotamia, where he has been some time. He says: "The heat is not so bad now, but we have had a dreadful summer. This is the worst country in the world, really it is a proper No Man's Land only fit for Arabs to live in, and they even won't give us peace but come sniping at us all night."

February 1917

W. Stumbles writing to the Editor of "Coo-ee!" from his home in Australia,[194]

William Stumbles was one of the first Australians to come to Bishop's Knoll, and was discharged wounded and sent back to Australia. This was the usual procedure if an Australian was considered to need more than six months recovery. This letter was written after he arrived back in Australia at the end of 1916. However he subsequently recovered sufficiently to re-enlist and suddenly appeared back in Bristol in 1917 in time to help celebrate "Gallipoli Day," much to everyone's delight! (See page 196)

"I am once more a civilian, having received my discharge from the forces on the 7th September, and since that date have been holiday making in the different States. At present I am down home at the seaside having a quiet time, and am supposed to resume my civil occupation on the 16th inst., but am hoping to be back in khaki before that date, as I am seeking a commission in the Field Artillery, and given a chance should "make good". I am horribly discontented since getting about as a civilian, and feel I should be back with my mates again, now that I am getting so well, and I sincerely hope that my efforts will not be in vain.

I had a letter from Bristol this last mail, and it reminds me that just twelve months ago to-day I was in hospital in Bristol, and little did I think then that I was going to have some of the happiest days and times in my life in the months that were to follow, and many of these I owe my thanks to you for I only wish I were near you to grip you by the hand. If ever a young chap named Sergeant [censored] should call upon you, you can rest assured that he is a good, genuine fellow; he's just about to leave Australia for Salisbury Plain, and I told him to be sure and take a trip to Bristol and not under any circumstance fail to call upon the Australians' "godfather" in Bristol. I boost Bristol to every soldier I know who is leaving for the front, so reckon too that quite a number will visit the grand old city.

April 1917

Should auld acquaintance

News of Former patients by GYP[195]

It is with the deepest regret that we learn that Private Shawcroft, who was a patient at this hospital for over eight months, died at Brodsworth on March 7th from wounds received in the Dardanelles campaign.[196] Our sympathies are with his widow. We have been hearing very cheering accounts from the front, in spite of the heavy fighting our troops are encountering. Lieut. Adams in writing says: "Very strenuous times over here, but all are merry and bright, hoping that the war will come to an end in the near future."

Lance-Corporal Ryan in a letter from France:

"We have been pretty busy over here lately, plenty of work and fighting. We have them on the move at present, but expect they will make a stand shortly in strong lines. We had a fairly hot hand-to-hand fight last time, and struck some of the Reserve Prussian Guards. It was a see-saw battle for a few hours, mostly bombing, but it ended by us holding the trench we had taken the previous night. I am sorry to say that I lost several of my best mates, as the battalion bombers to which I belong bore the brunt of the encounter. I was fortunate enough to come out of it with a few scratches, though I was stunned for a while by the explosion of a Fritz grenade, and visions of Bishop's Knoll flashed through my brain."

We are glad to hear that Private Warrender has got a job on the staff at Worgret Camp.

Private Hooper, we are pleased to learn, has quite recovered from the "measles" and is now back on Perham Downs.[197]

Private F. Andersen, Private D. Hay, and Private D. Corderoy have all returned to the firing-line, and we wish them the best of luck.

We are sorry to hear that Driver F. Williams is back in hospital again at Lark Hill.[198] Corporal F. Peck writes to say that he is back in England, in hospital at Northampton, with trench fever. We wish he could have managed to get back to the Knoll.

Privates Cranfield, Flemming and Price are all back at the front, and write very cheerfully from there.

Private T. Lament, we are sorry to hear, is in hospital at Stratford-on-Avon, with a bullet wound in the thigh.

Private Hooper has, we regret to learn, had to have a further operation to his elbow. He is getting on very satisfactorily, however, and hopes soon to pay us a visit.

Lieutenant Baness called at Bishop's Knoll the other day, looking very fit and well. To his great regret he has had to leave the service, on account of the loss of his eye.

May 1917

Should Auld acquaintance

News of Former patients by GYP [199]

It is with very real pleasure that we learn that two of our old patients have been awarded the Military Medal, an honour we feel sure they richly deserve. The one is Lance-Corporal Ryan, now Sergeant Ryan, who with true soldier's reticence says he is being awarded the medal for work done on the night of

Sergeant Ryan in centre.

Private Cady.

March 1st and 2nd, "nothing much, just a bit of hard going such as is happening every day now." The other is Private Cady, who is receiving his for work done before his arrival at Bishop's Knoll.

Our heartiest congratulations and best of good wishes to Private Angus, who we hear has just been married. Private Cranfield has, we hear, been wounded again, but we trust not seriously. He is now in hospital at Birmingham.

Our excellent correspondent Private Bert Gaynor, still keeps us as well informed as he can of his doings in France. He says he has been meeting a few of the "Dug-out Kings" lately, and that one(of them) is hoping to be over visiting the Knoll shortly. We wonder which of their majesties it will be.

We are sorry to hear that Private Dawson has been wounded in the head, and is now in hospital at Birmingham.

Corporal F. Peck is in hospital in Northampton but is expecting to be going to a convalescent home shortly.

Private F. K. Anderson is back again in the trenches, and writes from there asking that his old bed in Ward 3 may be reserved for him if he has the luck to get back to Bishop's Knoll.

Lieutenant Adams and Private D. Hay also send very cheery letters from "somewhere in France".

Private Yates, Private E. Brooks, and Private M. Campbell are all expecting to go back to Australia very shortly for six months. We wish them a good trip over and a speedy recovery. Private Gilberthorpe is also going back to Australia, having got his discharge, and we wish him the best of luck.

Private Kunkler has got as far as Durban on his homeward trip, and in writing to one of the Sisters says: "We have had a splendid trip so far". He found to his surprise that Private Hulme was on the same boat, and says: "He looks splendid," which is excellent news.

Driver F. Williams, in writing from Larkhill Camp, says: "We are very busy here in this camp digging up the spare ground and planting all kinds of vegetables."

Private B. Rowston seems to be having a very good time in London. He writes to say that he met Private D. Davies at the Anzac Buffet, and that he was looking splendid.

We are sorry to hear that Private N. Fedorovich is ill again and back in hospital at Southall, and hope that it is nothing very serious. We had a delightful surprise visit from Driver Nisbet, who is now at Hurdcott, near Salisbury, and gave us news of several old "Bishop's Knollites" who went there too, including Hollis, Bale, Francis, McNabb, and Burgess.

We also had an even more unexpected visit from Sergeant Bill Stumble, who was one of the first Australians to come to Bishop's Knoll, and was discharged and sent back to Australia. He re-enlisted, however, and suddenly appeared to help celebrate "Gallipoli Day," much to everyone's delight.

It is with the deepest regret that we hear that Lieutenant Cooney is reported missing, and trust that we may yet hear news of him.

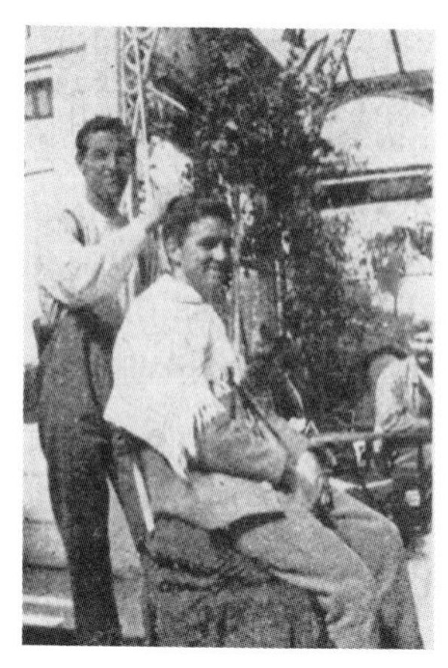

Pte Martin having his hair cut by Pte Smith in the Winter Garden.

Pte Rogers and Pte McNabb.

RSM Old (seated) and Pte Smith.

June 1917

Should Auld Acquaintance

News of Former patients by Sister A[200]

It has been a great pleasure to have had visits from several of our old patients during this month. Amongst them Private Cranfield, who came back to England again with a wound in the back, but has now quite recovered; Private Ross, who is still on Headquarters Staff in London; Corporal Matthews, who is at Larkhill; and Privates Downie, Reid and Whitrow.

We are very pleased to have at last had news of Lieutenant Cooney though we wish it were better than it is. He is now a prisoner of war in Germany and writes to say that he has seventeen wounds, two of them bad but that up to the time of writing he had not had them dressed, though it was nine days since his capture.

We hope that the news that Private Fischer has been drowned on his way to Australia is not correct.

Private J. T. Martin has been wounded again, but we are sorry to say that this time he has not come to Bishop's Knoll. He is at No.6 General Hospital. France, with a wound in the head, and writes to say: "When we got relieved to go back along the trenches a bit for a spell a shell burst about five yards from me and got me in the forehead over the right eye."

Private McNabb is still at Weymouth but is expecting to leave shortly for Australia. Our best wishes go with him.

Private F. Burgess writes from Hurdcott (where he is one of the Public Guard), and tells us that Private Rogers is there too, and that Private Baird is now at Wareham in the Military Police.

We are sorry to hear that Lieutenant Macleod, or Sergeant Macleod as he was when at Bishop's Knoll, has been wounded in the shoulder and head, but we hope not severely. He is now at the 3rd London General Hospital, Wandsworth.

Corporal Basford, writing from Gullewa says that "he happened to be in Geraldton, and there ran across Private W. Kidd." Both Corporal Basford and Private Kidd have their discharge from the army.

We have had a letter from RSM Old, who seems to be enjoying his furlough (leave of absence), and hopes to pay Bishop's Knoll a visit before he returns to the front.

We are glad to learn that Sergeant Robinson and Privates Marshall, Bankier, Roberts and O'Keefe have all arrived safely at Southall.

In a letter from Townsville, Queensland received by the Commandant, the parents of former patient of Bishop's Knoll write :

"We received the copy of "Coo-ee!" which we appreciate very much. It is very interesting, and I am sure in years to come young Australians will cherish this excellent hospital magazine. We trust "Coo-ee!" will be a great success."

An old 1914 patient also writes from Salonica, saying what pleasure he derived from seeing a copy of "Coo-ee!".

We have received kindly letter of appreciation and thanks for the treatment their sons and husbands have received during the time they were inmates of our hospital from Mr and Mrs Hooper, Woonibye, Queensland ; Mr and Mrs Yapp, Townsville, Queensland ; Mr and Mrs Stuart, Blue Mountains, N.S.W; Mrs Mathews, Gundagar, N.S.W.; and Mrs Loyentzen, Sydney, N.S.W

Pte Jeffcote.

Corporal Allen.

Pte E Parish.

July 1917

Should auld acquaintance

News of former patients - Sister A [201]

It is so nice to find that no matter whether they are in France, Mesopotamia, Australia, or England, so many of our old patients keep a place in their memory for Bishop's Knoll, and let us know how they are getting on from time to time.

Sergeant Ryan, writing from France, says, "We had a visit from Andrew Fisher, our High Commissioner, with General Birdwood, when about 150 of us were presented with our colours. Johnson has also received the Military Medal." He goes on to say that he met Private Jeffcote, who was looking very fit, and wished to be remembered to all.

Private Johnson, to whom we send our sincere congratulations for the decoration he has received. Corporal McLeod still writes very cheerfully from Mesopotamia, in spite of the heat, which he says is very severe. He is hoping to get a furlough in India shortly, which I am sure will be well deserved.

Private J.F. Martin, who has been wounded in the head, has arrived safely in England though unfortunately not in Bristol. He is at Tooting Military Hospital, but hopes soon to be on furlough, when perhaps we may see him again.

Corporal Allen is again back in France and we wish him the best of luck.

Private Ludick writes from the trenches to let us know that "so far things

Pte J.P. Davis.

are going on very well." Long may they so continue.

We are glad to hear that Privates Brooks, Read and Campbell are safely on their way home. Private Brooks in a very heavily censored letter says they are two days off their first port of call. He gives very good accounts of all except Signaller Read who we are very sorry to hear has lost the use of his arm altogether and can only move two of his fingers. We are glad to hear that Sergeant Robinson and Private Marshall, who are still at Southall, are getting on well. Private Marshall is expecting to go back to Australia shortly. Private E. Parish is still in France, where he has met Private W. Fallon. He says, "We are away from the line now having a rest. It is quiet time too, as we have been having a pretty rough time all through the winter."

Private J. P. Davies writes from Heaton Park Manchester. He says, "After being shifted about for ever so long I think that at last I have settled down for a little while. So far I have been unable to do hardly any walking, as I cannot put any weight on my heel, in fact, it has been worse ever since I left Bishop's Knoll."

He also adds, "They are awfully strict here, I do not think Australians would like it a bit." We are sorry his news is not better.

We are sorry that Private Dale may have to have another operation. He also is still at Southall.

It was a great pleasure to have had visits from Corporal Lorentzen, Signaller Cooper, and Privates Mahoney, McAlister, Taylor, and Cunnington.

Corporal Lorentzen, together with Privates Jackson and Mitchell, are expecting to go back to Australia quite soon. We wish them the best of luck.

"GONE WEST"

There were only a few deaths among those treated at Bishop's Knoll. In an era before the use of antibiotics this was truly remarkable. Twenty Australians are buried in the Arnos Vale Cemetery and 7 in the Roman Catholic cemetery (Holy Souls) next door. One Australian rests in Greenbank Cemetery Easton, and another in the Avonview Cemetery, St George. Not all of these were from Bishop's Knoll but those who were known to have been are Privates Dwan, Jess, Jack Roach, Frederick G Robinson, J.J. Simpson, and W.A. Ham.

August 4, 1916

Private J.J. Simpson

Bristol Daily Press

"An Australian soldier, Private J.J. Simpson who had given his life for the Empire was buried yesterday at Arnos Vale Cemetery. Only on Saturday last he was brought to Bristol from France and received at Bishop's Knoll Hospital. He had been grievously wounded and despite the best medical skill and the tenderest nursing, his life could not be saved. The funeral was semi-military in character and sympathetic interest was evinced as the cortège move slowly through the city. The coffin, coverage with the Australian flag and beautiful wreathes of flowers was borne on an open car and it was followed by Commandant R.E Bush, Bishop Clifford, Sister Prout (a matron of the Bishop's Knoll Hospital) and members of the nursing staff; Mr A.G.Powell, representing the Inquiry Bureau and upwards of 60 wounded men who were conveyed to the cemetery by char-a-banc..."

September 1917

The passing of Pte F.G. Robinson

"Coo-ee!" unattributed[213]

A splendid example of Australian manhood –

Pte F.G. Robinson.

> We very greatly regret to have to record the death of Private Frederick George Robinson XX Battalion AIF, who died from septicemia and pneumonia. He was admitted last April suffering from serious gun-shot wounds in the leg. The staff were fairly satisfied with his progress for the first three months but the septic condition gradually spread and eventually settled in the lung and in spite of devoted medical and nursing attention he passed away quite peacefully and without pain in the early morning of the 17th August. He was a splendid example of Australian manhood who by his brave patience and cheerfulness endeared himself to his mates and to the staff. Our profound sympathy goes out to his wife and children at Mount Gambier in South Australia.
>
> The funeral took place at Arno's Vale Cemetery on the 29th August. The Hospital was represented by the Commandant, several members of the staff and all the patients who were well enough to attend. A beautiful cross from the patients lay on the Australian flag which draped the coffin, and wreaths from the Commandant and Mrs Bush, the Bristol Branch of the Red Cross Society, the Staff, from Red Cross Nurse O. M. Goss and Mrs and Miss Stafford Jones were arranged about the gun carriage which carried the mortal remains of this brave Australian, who made the supreme sacrifice for the sake of the Empire and the liberty of the world.
>
> Regimental Sergeant-Major Yeomans represented the AIF at the funeral.

Two months later a fuller report appeared in the Border Watch a regional newspaper based at Mount Gambier which served the South East of South Australia.[214] This reproduced in full the 560 word letter which Robert Edwin Bush had written to Pte Robinson's widow explaining the circumstances of his death and giving the details of the funeral. The article also reveals that Nurse Hall-Houghton had written the Mrs Robinson in August soon after the soldier's admission to Bishop's Knoll and again two weeks later to inform her of his death. In the interim Pte Robinson had been able to dictate a letter to his wife and also have a reply read to him shortly before he died. It is clear from the nurse's first letter that here was one of the soldiers who had not been able to benefit from the immediate wound excision which would later save many lives (see page 52). In due course Mrs Robinson wrote to both Mrs Bush and Nurse Philps.

Mil Lel
Gambier
S.Australia

Dear Mrs Bush,
For a long time now I have been going to write to you but some how I don't seem to get time for I am kept very busy for there is always plenty to do on a farm and my eldest son who helps me has had a bit of illness, he is now laid up with a broken collar bone, he had a bad fall. I wish to thank you and Mr Bush for that very nice card you sent me some time ago and the newspaper and photo of the ANZAC Memorial. I do appreciate your kind thoughts very much. You cannot think what a comfort it has been to me that my dear husband was among such kind friends. I am sending you some views of Gambier I don't know if you have been to the area it is a very pretty spot. I will close with my very kind regards.

Your sincere friend,
M.Robinson

Mil Lel
20th September

Dear Miss Philps,
I am writing to thank you very much for your kind thought in sending me the photographs of my dear husband's grave. It is such a comfort to me to know his grave is well cared for. I do so long to go to his grave. If feel if I could go to it I could bear up better. You know how dear we were to him and how dearly

he was loved at home, the children will never forget him. They are so often talking about him. Will you please thank Mr Bush for his kind thoughts of us. You have all been so kind to me. I often think I would not have lived through it if I had not had such kind letters from the hospital very few of my friends thought I would get over it but it helped me such a lot to know he was so well cared for and had such good friends with him at the last. Now I will close by thanking you all for your great kindness to me.
I am your sincere friend

M Robinson

Two other funeral reports are included in the Bishop's Knoll scrapbooks as undated Bristol Press reports but one, that of William H Watts (3304) proved to be an ex AIF soldier who just happened to die in Bristol in 1927. Typically Bush saw to it had a proper burial and joined his comrades in Arnos Vale.[215] The other funeral report is shown below.

Private W.A.Ham

Private W.A. Ham of the Australian Imperial Force, who died suddenly at Bishop's Knoll on Thursday evening was buried yesterday at Arnos Vale Cemetery. It is only recently that he came wounded from France and seemed to be making good progress but the best of medical skill and the most careful nursing failed to avert the heart trouble which came suddenly and proved fatal. The first part of the service was at the chapel of the Royal Infirmary. It was a simple but deeply impressive service. The Commandant Mr R.E. Bush was there and so were several of the nursing staff while one side of the chapel was filled with comrades...

Far more soldiers who had recovered fully at Bishop's Knoll and returned to active service were subsequently lost in combat. Eight of these are recorded in various articles in "*Coo-ee!*". Usually the news came from their comrades at Bishop's Knoll but many more must have gone unrecorded as seldom were two Bishop's Knoll friends from the same unit. Here are just three that were fully reported.

October 1916

GONE WEST. LIEUT. T. L. RYAN AND PTE J. DOLIN

A.G.P.[216]

Jim Dolin.

Tiny Ryan.

Sad indeed is the task I am set to record the grief of all at Bishop's Knoll at the passing of two old patients, Jim Dolin and "Tiny" Ryan. The former was with us in the first year of the war, and came from Gallipoli. Poor Jim! Always it was known that, when his wounds were healed, there would be for him a hopeless struggle against a disease which, alas medical science has striven in vain. He died in Australia, having returned home a year or so ago. Jim had a rough exterior and an easy-going disposition, which made it so hard for him to keep out of trouble. But those of us who knew him well can bear testimony to his cheery spirit, his faithful comradeship, and his boundless pluck. Once he showed me a signature in his pay-book ; it was the name of a distinguished officer revered by every Australian soldier, and it was there as an earnest of reward for heroic conduct.

It needed a deal of persuasion, but the story associated with the signature was told in outline, and imagination easily filled in the details. There had been an attack on a Turkish position, and it had failed. But the boys could not bring in all the wounded, and some lay in their agony out in No Man's Land, close up to the enemy trenches. Some of their comrades resolved that when darkness fell they would go out and bring them in. Word of the affair was, however, taken to the company officer, and stringent orders were issued forbidding the hazard. But they did go out, and they did get back with the stricken lads, and it was for this that Jim and the others were recommended. I remember asking Jim if he had received his award, but sadly he pointed to various entries, all little petty offences, which in the aggregate, as I understood it, prevented the recommendation from going forward. Jim Dolin has gone, but he will not be forgotten. We shall remember him with many a kindly thought long after the greater names and events of the war have passed out of recollection.

Lieutenant J. Ryan, or "Tiny" Ryan as he will ever be known at Bishop's Knoll, was here during the summer of 1916, and of all the lads who have come broken from the war, and have passed out into the world again to take up the thread of duty, none will give happier memories than he. To a magnificent physique — he stood, I believe, 6 ft. 4 in. in height —was added a strong, manly character, and a charm of disposition that made him liked by everybody. I can recall many a delightful association with the free soldier of the Empire. Particularly I recall our visit to Bath as guests of Dr and Mrs Scales, and the wonderful exhibition which "Tiny" gave on the lawn with the Australian stock-whip. I have been looking over his letters to me since he returned to France. "I shall always," he wrote in December last, "look back on my stay in England as a very happy part of my life, and next to seeing Australia, it is my greatest wish to see the old country again, and renew the happy acquaintance made whilst at Bishop's Knoll." In another letter he tells of his work at the Officers' Training School in France, and the satisfaction with which he contemplates his commission. And now "Tiny" has fallen, and there will be sad, sad hearts at far-off Roebourne, West Australia. Aye, and sad hearts here at the Knoll, too, for this splendid man was some thing more than a patient to those whose skill and infinite gentleness help so much to assuage the pain of wounds and sickness. "I have sad news for you," said a sister as I entered a ward on Saturday, "Tiny Ryan is - killed!" and the catch in the voice told more than words could convey of sorrow for the passing of her old patient. In the ward too lay a patient who had served under Lieutenant Ryan. "A fine officer and a true man," were his words.

December 1916

Arthur Fleming

The Editor[217]

Arthur Fleming.

Arthur Fleming, good soldier, good patriot, true friend has Gone West. I had the news in a letter from Lieut. Tom Richards* just as I was writing the last few lines on the famous Australian footballer's wanderings. He was shot dead," writes Tom, "while collecting wounded on 'No Man's Land, in daylight, with a white flag up. Both sides were doing this, and we think that it was more by accident than design that he met his cruel end."

Arthur Fleming, was one of the best liked of all the Australian boys who have come wounded to Bishop's Knoll, and departed completely restored to physical well-being. His last night in Bristol was spent with his bosom pal, Bill Stumbles, at my house. Fleming had a glorious baritone voice, and he and other musical friends had charmed us with their gift of song. And now the voice is silent for ever. The sturdy, manly figure rests in a soldier's grave out yonder, and somewhere under the Southern Cross a mother and a sweet-heart will be heart-broken when they learn the sad tidings. Some of us who knew Arthur Fleming will share their grief, and extend to them sympathy which is so very, very difficult to express.

THE EDITOR.

*Thomas James "Rusty" Richards MC (April 29, 1882 – September 25, 1935) was an early volunteer and a veteran of Anzac Cove. He was the only rugby football player to ever play for both Australia and the British Lions, thus, the Tom Richards Trophy is named in his honour.

CHAPTER 10

SUNDRY ACCOUNTS

Private John Hamilton VC at Berkeley Castle in 1916.

Bishop's Knoll's VC

Private John Patrick Hamilton was an early patient at Bishop's Knoll and while there he learnt he had been awarded the Victoria Cross for his bravery at Gallipoli. He had enlisted as a Private in the Australian Imperial Force on September 15, 1914. After training in Egypt his battalion sailed for Gallipoli and took part in the landing at Anzac Cove on April 25, 1915 - his battalion coming ashore in the 2nd and 3rd waves. He was 19 years old, and still a private when fighting at Sasse's Sap during the Battle of Lone Pine on the Gallipoli Peninsula. His citation read

> "For most conspicuous bravery on 9th August, 1915, in the Gallipoli Peninsula. During a heavy bomb attack by the enemy on the newly captured position at Lone Pine, Private Hamilton, with utter disregard to personal safety, exposed himself under heavy fire on the parados, in order to secure a better fire position against the enemy's bomb throwers. His coolness and daring example had an immediate effect. The defence was encouraged, and the enemy driven off with heavy loss" (*Commonwealth Gazette No. 28 February 24, 1916*)

He was told the news of his award while he was hospitalised in Ward 4 at

Bishop's Knoll and not quite 21. He was described as a nice quiet fellow who seemed rather surprised by the award.

Hamilton was promoted to corporal on May 3, 1916 and fought at the Battle of Pozières in July, the Battle of Mouquet Farm in August and Flers in November. He was promoted to sergeant in May 1917 and that year his battalion served at Passchendale. He then received officer cadet training at Cambridge, and was commissioned as Second Lieutenant in January 1919 and promoted to Lieutenant in April 1919. After the War he returned to Australia and eventually died on February 27, 1961. He is buried at Woronora Cemetery, Sydney.

November 1916

Sister Eliza

a member of staff[202]

Sister ELIZA! What would we do without her? There is no one so much thought of, and all are willing to wait upon her, to see that she has all she needs. It isn't the size of her that is so awe-inspiring, but just her manner. She is able to become so heated if the slightest neglect is shown her, and when this is so patients and fellow-sisters suffer together.

Her chief function is to attend to all materials for dressings and operations, and if her temper has been disarranged, then for a little while dressings are cut short, and operations are almost an impossibility, until Sister Eliza once more is appeased. The only way to keep her cool is to allow her to let off steam whenever she becomes too heated, and then everyone all over the hospital can hear the noise she makes. It is only for a short time, and then she lifts up her head above such trivial things, and again gives out the dressings all ready for use.

Sister Eliza's face is most expressive of her feelings. When it is bright and clear all is well, but when it is dull and gloomy then there is trouble brewing for someone. This very often proves to be somebody who has neglected the task of polishing. There are some who live in great fear of her. One particularly so, whose duty generally lies upstairs at night-time, and she thanks her lucky stars that she, at least, never has anything to do with this Sister, who always works on the ground floor, and likes to keep her room so hot, that often anyone visiting her gets a Turkish bath for nothing. Lately she has endeared herself to those in Ward 3, having made herself responsible for giving out a hot-pack blanket for a nephritic patient every four hours.

She seems to have an iron constitution, so long as her great thirst is satisfied. She never drinks anything but water, but on this simple beverage is willing to work night and day. Sister Eliza has one very vulgar habit. She has a rooted objection to the use of a pocket-handkerchief, and having a very long nose, has to be supplied with a jam-jar for her permanent cold. Sister Eliza's office is conveniently situated just near the front door, and here she receives bishops, doctors, colonels, and others of high degree; for in her room is the telephone and other useful things. Although she keeps all the delicacies for the patients in her room. Sister Eliza is never tempted to sample any of them, being quite content with her diet of Aqua Distilata. And there she is year in year out, for the duration of the war, always content, never taking a holiday, not even her Sundays off. Who is Sister Eliza?

The steam autoclave was invented by Charles Chamberland in 1879.

December 1916

From Ward Gossip

Dinkum (i.e. Robert Edwin Bush)[203]

Edward Combe- Robinson.

Frances Richards.

In the local papers during the past few days appeared an announcement of the marriage of Edward Hey Cleveland Combe-Robinson and Frances Mary Ellen Richards. There was nothing in this notice to indicate a wedding out of the ordinary, but as a matter of fact, this particular happy event was a romance in real life, for Trooper Combe-Robinson and Sister Richards were until quite recently associated with Bishop's Knoll Hospital, one as wounded soldier and the other as nurse.

It was on 11th November 1915 that the gallant trooper arrived in Bristol from Gallipoli. His hurt was a serious one: a smashed leg which kept him in his cot for more than 8 months and involved an operation of a peculiarly hazardous character. All the while Sister Richards was working in the same ward, and helping with the other members of the nursing staff to win back to health and strength the fellows who had suffered from the havoc of war. The secret of mutual attachment, between one particular patient and a particular sister was, however, well kept, and the announcement was a surprise — a happy surprise — for all but those intimately concerned with the hospital.

The wedding took place at Westbury Church, and Bishop Clifford officiated. The bride, who was charmingly attired in a gown of white crepe-de-chene, with tulle veil and orange blossom, carried a sheaf of Harrisi lilies, and was attended by her sister Miss M. L. Richards, and Sister D.M. Adlam as bridesmaids. The best man was a hospital comrade. Sergeant Douglas Woods, of the Australian Imperial Force, whilst four wounded soldiers, in the

> familiar blue uniform — Trooper Lennox (North of England), Private J. P. Davies (North Wales), and Private Brewer and Private Everett Norton (Australia) — were groomsmen. Her father, Captain J. Richards, gave the bride away. The service was choral, the organist playing the Bridal March from Lohengrin and Mendelssohn's Wedding March.
>
> There will be many good wishes for the happy pair, for the bride had won the hearts of hundreds of soldiers who had passed through the hospital for her quiet, tender care of her patients, while the bridegroom was the personal friend not only of the soldiers but of the staff and many visitors.

Thomas Haywood and Winifred Haines.

A further comment, four months later, was that Private Combe-Robinson would have to undergo another operation, quite where is not made clear,[204] but despite this both Edward and his wife survived the war and had three children. Frances died aged 64 but Edward lived on to 1968 dying at the age of 73 in Birmingham.

There was another wedding reported in passing in the Ward Gossip Column of the April 191 edition of "*Coo-ee!*"

> We do miss Miss Freda Haines but she had to go and be married to Mr T Haywood. However she took away with her some jolly table silver and an engraved silver spirit kettle!! (Needless to explain these were given to her by Mr and Mrs Bush and the staff respectively.) She also had several handsome presents from her numerous friends she had made at the hospital. We wish her all joy and happiness.[205]

This was the Miss Haines who had been the "Red and White Pierret" in the Christmas Show 1916. Her full name was Winifred Agnes Haines who was then

Conscientious Objector: "NOW I PUTS IT TO YER, SIR, DO I LOOK THE KIND O' BLOKE AS WOULD 'URT A FLY?"

aged 32 years. Thomas Haywood was 14 years her senior and so unlikely to have been in the services. They married in London on March 29, 1917 and both lived on till the 1940s.

January 1917

At the Tribunal - some impressions

Leigh Woods with sketches by Pte Holland.[206]

The Military Service Bill had been introduced in January 1916, providing for the conscription of all single men aged 18–41 years. An appeal could be successful on the grounds of work of national importance, business or domestic hardship, medical unfitness, or conscientious objection. Over half those called up in Bristol lodged an appeal which was heared at the local Military Service Tribunal. By the end of the first six months of conscription 748,587 British men had made appeals to local military tribunals.

It would seem that Powell was a member of the Bristol Appeals Panel and perhaps its secretary, and must have taken the cartoonist Private George C Holland to at least one of these. This was the result.

A Special Commissioner appointed by a pushful London newspaper, has

been having a high old time, up and down the country, trying to improve Tribunal morals. And he has been successful in many places in showing that exemptions have been worked on the "you scratch my back and I'll scratch yours" principle. But he has not yet come to Bristol. If he had he would have drawn blank, for the work has been done without fear or favour in the old western city. Daily attendance at the Tribunal has been an interesting experience, and has added rather considerably to one's experience of human nature.

Pathos, humour, tragedy, artifice, and even threats, have at one time or another been in evidence. I am not likely to forget the tearful eloquence of a young wife, soon to become a mother. "Cannot you," she said in a broken voice, "let my husband stay until I am over my trouble? This will be my first baby, and he is to be called up just when I am expecting. What will I do if he has to go?"

Who could resist such a plea? Not the members of the Tribunal, or the military representative, Capt. Reeves, who to his honour comforted the distressed young lady with an assurance that he would himself see that her husband was not called up until she was safely through her trouble.

Then there was the sister who begged with all her might that the last of her six brothers should be allowed to stay and help her keep the little home intact. "I have brought them up since they were little ones," she said, "I have sacrificed my life to them: I might have been married, but I thought it my duty to look after the orphan boys. One of them is dead, and the other four are in the Army. And if the last one goes it will break my heart." This was another appeal that did not fall on deaf ears.

In quite different strain was the request made one day by a young woman who appeared before the Tribunal carrying a baby. She wanted to know why her husband was exempted while so many better men had had to go "The great lout," she exclaimed with unconcealed wrath, "he's going about swanking that he has been able to square the tribunal."

There was another woman before the members one day, a real English woman. Seven of her boys were fighting and she wanted to know if it was quite necessary that her eighth who had just come of military age should have to go. She knew her duty to her country, she said and was ready to let her youngest go if it was absolutely necessary. Alas it was. The boy didn't appear: brave lad, he didn't want to get off.

One slim youth who urged a conscientious objection, was formerly an outside broker in the bookie line. I knew him well and he guessed rightly that I regarded his conscience as a very loose end sort of affair, for at every opportunity he winked at me prodigiously.

It was in the early days that the anti-war cranks were so much in evidence. They came by the dozen, and with much hustle and show of self-importance. A wise and benevolent Government ordained that the Tribunals should be open to the public, but nothing was said about providing facilities to hear what happened at the tables. Thus the seats were placed as far away as possible, and all the Tribunal talk was carried on in whispers.

It was a knock-out blow for the anti-everything brigade, who in the main had to be content with the Chairman's concluding remark, "That will do, Mr Brown : you will hear from us in the morning". Some of their frantic efforts

to hear more resulted in some unique examples of facial contortion. They have vanished long ago. As Longfellow says, "They folded their tents like the Arabs and silently stole away."

I must not forget the young gentleman who constituted the first case in which work of national importance was offered. But he would have none of it. Being the first case I took a verbatim shorthand note of it. Lucky I did so. A few weeks later, the same patriot (sic), came up again. He had a lawyer with him who complained that while his client was willing to do work of national importance it had not been offered to him. As a consequence, said the lawyer his unfortunate client had been hauled before the magistrates.

"Really," said the Chairman, "just listen to this transcript of what actually took place."

The Chairman: "Would you be willing to do work of national importance?"

Applicant: "I refuse to do anything to help sustain the war."

The Chairman: "But you would be working on a farm helping to grow food for your fellow countrymen. Won't you do that?"

Applicant: "No."

All the man with the convenient memory could do was mumble some feeble excuse while his solicitor looked thoroughly disgusted.

Then there was the naive youth of the "bulldog breed", who when told he would have to join the army exclaimed, "What me enlist? Who's going to look after my pigeons?"

May 1917

"Coo-ee!" turns up in Egypt

The Editor[207]

MR. ERNEST J. TAYLOR, of Bristol, a very good friend of the lads at Bishop's Knoll, forwards a letter he has received from a former member of his staff. This letter includes the following:—

"Many thanks for sending me the Bishop's Knoll Magazine, Coo-ee. I passed it on, after reading it, to an Australian, when at Zietown, near Cairo, and strange to say, he had been at Bishop's Knoll himself. We had quite a long chat together about Bristol. He said he had spent some very happy days there before being sent out here, and asked me if I should ever get any further copies of Coo-ee to send them to him, so I'm sending on the one I received two months ago. They are splendid books, and I fully enjoy reading about dear old Bristol."

It is interesting to learn that Coo-ee is giving a little pleasure to our lads far away from home. Years hence our modest little magazine will be a much prized souvenir of this stirring wartime, and those who possess the complete set of issues will be much envied by others who neglected to have them sent home month by month for safe keeping. — EDITOR.

July 1917

Beaufort War Hospital

Notes by W.L.F.P[208]

By the time this article was written (June 1917) the Beaufort War Hospital, formerly the Bristol Asylum, had became a hospital housing more than 1500 patients.[209] The Hospital was requisitioned by the War Office and became part of the 4th Southern Hospital, (the reasons for which are unclear) but as it was in Bristol its patients enjoyed the social programme, organised by the Inquiry Bureau. The hospital later became the specialist orthopaedic unit for the region. Perhaps because of its origin, 30 beds were reserved for mental cases among local troops, and a ward of ten beds was established for sick German prisoners of war from local labour camps. After the war it reverted back to the Bristol Asylum. The artist Stanley Spencer enlisted in the Royal Army Medical Corps in 1915 and was posted to Beaufort War Hospital same year. One of his paintings is "A Convoy of Wounded Soldiers Arriving at Beaufort War Hospital Gates" which was painted in 1927. The author of this account "WLFP" wrote five articles for "*Coo-ee!*" with the same title covering various aspects of life at the Beaufort.

> Only ten Australians are now domiciled in this hospital. The last batch to leave were some who had been bedridden for many months. These were transferred under special instructions from headquarters to one of their own hospitals near London, in readiness for return to their own country. Naturally they were highly elated at the thought of once again seeing their homeland and those near and dear to them, but at the same time seemed somewhat loathe to leave Beaufort behind, which one described as his "English home." All of these poor fellows had either lost a limb or been rendered totally unfit for further military service — such are the fortunes of war. Another lad said he should always remember the thoughtful care and many acts of kindness received from the staff and Bristol friends. Such expressions as these, spoken direct from the heart, are ample recompense, if such were needed, for anything done to soothe the sufferings and brighten the lives of those who have forfeited so much, yea, loyally given their all to come so many miles to fight for the Motherland.
>
> During the month a large convoy of sick and wounded from Salonica came into Bristol: half were sent to this hospital and the other half to the 2nd Southern. From all accounts very exciting experiences were encountered on the voyage. Their ship was torpedoed in the Mediterranean, the torpedo penetrating the coal bunkers, killing six stokers. Other vessels immediately came alongside and took all aboard, and made for a French port. No sooner had they once again set foot on terra firma, all joined in singing "When you come to the end of a perfect day." Can you imagine anything more humorous after what had happened? So near the jaws of death, everything they

possessed gone, and yet so merry and bright. Such traits as these are typical of the British soldier and sailor, and have made our nation what she is to-day, and please God will keep her so. After a six days' sojourn, housed in a French prison, fed on Arabian delicacies (sic), a transport arrived and brought them safely back to Old England without further incident.

Once again the bright month of June brings with it the dawn of another summer, when Nature's floral colouring unbosoms itself in all its varied beauty. Then it is that our wounded heroes appreciate to the full this Isle of Isles, and is it any wonder that they sing, when far away in some foreign clime : "Take me back to dear old Blighty"? During the month the first of a series of open-air concerts was given on a recent Sunday evening, and what an impressive picture presented itself — some five or six hundred patients clad in their hospital blue, with here and there one wearing a bright scarlet coat ; sisters and nurses in their attractive uniforms, all sitting or lying around listening intently to the delightful strains of music coming from a well-trained orchestra of thirty talented instrumentalists, under the able conductorship of Mr Louis Watts. These open-air concerts are given two or three times a week, and how the boys look forward to them.

Saturday afternoons see another summer attraction in the shape of cricket matches, and great is the enjoyment and merriment, especially when the ball happens to land amongst a bunch of the boys. The writer well remembers a remark he overheard last season at the finish of a game. The home team had compiled a big total, but the visitors were dismissed for a very small score. When the last man went in and was promptly bowled first ball one of the boys shouted out in a rather sarcastic tone, "Don't go yet, mate, isn't there any other game you know?"

Prime Minister's son

Another patient of note was Driver E. M. Hughes MM - son of the Australian Prime Minister, William Morris Hughes. In June 1918 shortly after returning to London from an audience with President Wilson in the United States, Hughes had a telegram sent to Bishop's Knoll from AIF headquarters in London asking for Driver Hughes to be granted temporary leave in order to meet his father whilst he was in London.

STRANGER THAN FICTION

Many heart warming tales were related under this heading in various issues of "*Coo-ee!*". Here are a few.

February 1917

A few years ago I was a delegate for the I.L.P. (International Labour Party) at the International Socialist Congress at Stuttgart, and stayed at the house of a German, Hans Woesachhoeft by name. After the Battle of Marne I was with a force pursuing the Germans, and one day engaged in bayonet fighting a German cavalryman. Looking at him closer, I recognized my host of happier days. He recognized me, and we had not the heart to fight further. He saved the situation by surrendering.

Corp. HAYHURST, Shropshire Light Infantry.[210]

This one, on the same page, is particularly interesting as it is another story of Powell's son Leslie.

When my son came home from the East, he accompanied me to the Beaufort War Hospital. I had promised to preside at one of the concerts there, and the room was already full when we arrived there. We stood at the door a few minutes' looking at the great gathering, when a wounded soldier seated in the centre of the hall, stood up and shouted "Sieda". My son looked hard for a second or two, then nodded to the soldier and made his way towards him.

All through the performance I saw them yarning away, and when the show was over, and we were leaving the hospital, I asked my son who the other chap was. "Oh," he replied, "Funny that I should have met him, wasn't it? He belonged to an Australian battery posted near us on Gallipoli, and used to spend a lot of time in our dug-out. One day a shell landed among the battery, and I lost sight of my friend until we met today."

EDITOR

And here is another in the same issue written from Bishop's Knoll

Four of us reached a German trench together, but I went back to fetch some more bombs. When I returned the other three had vanished, and of course I thought they had been wiped out. Then I came up against something the Germans had sent over, and was detailed for Blighty. While lying on a stretcher at Bristol Station I heard somebody shout, "Hullo, Spud!" It was Private Harrison, one of the three I thought had "gone West."

Spud Murphy*

* Private W.E. Murphy of 50th Battalion of the AIF who was at Bishop's Knoll in October and November 1916.

April 1917

We were on Gallipoli, and were pretty well fed-up with things, especially in the grubbing line, when one day an Australian artilleryman who often slung the hatchet in our dug-out, said he was getting a spell with a crowd from his unit, at Alexandria. He expected to be back in a few weeks, so several of us gave him commissions to buy what he could to make life worth living and bring us back. I gave him a sovereign, and a slip of paper on which was written the things I particularly wanted. Less than a week after our contribution to the Naval Brigade kicked the mud of Gallipoli off our boots, and went over to Lemnos, preparatory to taking a hand in the Suvla Bay affair. Only once did I give a thought to the pound I had parted with, and that was when a unique opportunity for a snap-shot came and I had no films.

It was, I think, about twelve months later, when I was having a lemonade at the bar of a music hall in London. Half a dozen Australians were engaged in the same peaceful pursuit. I didn't take particular notice of them — they're fairly common round London way; but just as I was finishing up the lemonade, one of the crowd tapped me on the shoulder, and then pulled out his wallet and found a pound note,

"That's yours," said he.

"You be —," said, and then stopped short, for I recognised the chap.

"Sorry I couldn't let you have those things ; our crowd didn't get back to the Peninsula, and I couldn't send the pound on because I didn't know your name."

I've got that pound note still, and hope to keep it as a souvenir.[211]

May 1917

I know of nothing more strange in the way of coincidence than the sequence of events which befell a Belgium family named Frere. They lived, I believe, at Brussels, and until the war-clouds began to gather were happy and prosperous. When the German army began their march of invasion two of the sons responded to the call to arms, and with their units fought bravely in the early battles, Charles in the infantry and his elder brother in the artillery. Both were wounded on the same day, and both were dispatched in the same train to the same base hospital. But neither knew of the other's proximity. The same hospital ship brought them both to England, and the ambulance train took Charles as well as Frederick to the 2nd Southern General Hospital at Bristol.

As is probably well known, there are many military hospitals in and near the great City of Bristol, and when the wounded arrive they are in most instances distributed, some to the Royal Infirmary, some to Southmead, some to Beaufort, and so on. But fate willed it that the two brothers should go to the same hospital, although they were placed in different wards. It was I think Charles who was the first to reach the convalescent stage. One day he took it into his head to visit another ward, and to his amazement and joy he beheld his brother reclining in one of the cots.

The happy reunion hastened the recovery of both, and they were almost completely restored to health when Dame Fortune served up another surprise. The good folk of Bristol, like others all over the country, gave hospitality freely to the unfortunate refugees from Belgium, and homes were set up and maintained by collective effort all over the city. From one of these homes one day there was a party of visitors to the Hospital where the Frere boys were patients. They passed from ward to ward until they came to one where most of the patients were able to be up and about. Suddenly one of the visitors uttered a cry and ran forward. It was the mother Frere, who had recognised her boys, and the father too was soon hastening toward the group of convalescent soldiers. The joy and the excitement of the occasion can be imagined, perhaps, but not described.

EDITOR[212]

CHAPTER 11

SOLDIERS POETRY

It is remarkable how many soldiers appear to have been moved to write poetry during their time at Bishop's Knoll. One had thought that this was restricted to the well known English "war poets" like Sassoon, Owen, Brookes, Graves etc but perhaps Australian soldiers were similarly affected by their experiences. This is only a small selection from the pages of "*Coo-ee!*"

"Coo-ee!"

Private T.B.Cole[218]

Coo-ee, Coo-ee, 'tis a far coo-ee
To the fair Australian shores,
Where we left our homes and loved ones
To engage in Britain's wars,
We have come from far off Queensland,
And from all the other States ;
But victory still awaits us,
We wait at victory's gates.

Coo-ee, Coo-ee, 'tis a far coo-ee
To the whitening wheaten field,
Where the mountains rise from the valleys wide
And valleys their harvest yield.
Could we but look from the mountain crests
On those fields of billowy grain,
And know that fateful war had ceased
And earth was calm again.

Coo-ee, Coo-ee, 'tis a far coo-ee
To the golden wattle rows,
Where we used to breathe the fragrance
Of the sweetest flower that grows.
We are longing for the music
To fill our hearts with song,
The song our spirits sigh for,
The song of peace how long?

Coo-ee, Coo-ee, 'tis a far coo-ee
But the echo carries back
Crossing the waves of the ocean blue
To the farthest country track.
We are waiting for you in Australia -
'Tis the freest land on earth,
To welcome your homeward footsteps
With gladness and with mirth.

In Exile

Gunner Frank E Westbrook[219]

Australia, my Australia, should e'er it be my lot
To live in distant exile in lands that love thee not,
Through all the days that follow the dreary, yearning years
The music of thy melodies will echo in my ears,
The voice of bushlands whispering, the glimpse of moss-strewn dell,
The flowers on thy mountain-side, more dear than asphodel,
The bowers of tern and heather by which the springtime waits,
And sets her myriad gems ashine within thy wave-washed gates,
The flashing fire of wattle trees in league-long rows will rise,
The glory of thy hill and plain will spring to cheer my eyes,
Their rosaries of blossom, the incense of its fire,
The perfume of its yellow beads, the breath of my desire.

September o'er your kindly face will strew the gifts of spring
With sweet baronia scent and flower and wild clematis fling
With lavish hand. On sunlit slopes the trembling, dew-kissed leaves
Will steal the tints from sunset clouds and red gold from the sheaves;
Will fill your ears with melodies and twittering songs of birds,
Soft rippling of the water pools where drink the milking herds,
Ah! I will see thee ever, September at its best,
Thy songs and melodies of spring in flowery verdure drest.
O keep thy kiss, my country, thy smiling mother face,
For those who love and leave thee and find no better place,
For those in distant exile who dare the hand of Fate,
To keep thy well-loved honour and homes inviolate.
I ask no more, Australia, my dear-loved native isle,
Than this my longing hallows, the welcoming of thy smile.

Binks

Cuthbert Hicks[220]

For endless days and months and years
    Had Binks sat on his office stool.
He always added figures up,
    The sort of work he did at school.
Routine had swamped his tiny mind
    Till he became grotesque and droll;
No big idea ever came
    To stir his grimy little soul.
At last one morning looking through
    The curtained windows to the street,
He saw a glaring poster there,
    Of Justice on her judgment-seat.
Her ample figure caught his eye,
    Broad bosomed she and fine of limb,
Binks wondered what her eyes were like;

But noted that her mouth was grim.
And underneath, in words of flame,
A message from a blood-red pen,
Binks read his country's call to arms:
"This is our flag we want more men."
And like a sudden splash of sun
Upon a rainy April day,
The Big Idea came to him
And lifted him from common clay.
His soul rose up and faced the light,
And Binks cast off the care of years,
And looking back on wasted chance
His eyes filled up with scalding tears.
He tried to pay attention to
The items in his ledger-book,
But through the blur the flag was there,
It seemed to beckon as it shook.
All down the columns of each page
His figures stood in neat array,
But as he looked they turned to men-
Fine men, equipped to march away.
Rank upon rank they stood so still,
With bright eyes waiting for the word,
And Binks saw how they stared at him;
Their scorn cut through him like a sword.
Binks closed his ledger, got his hat;
His soul had orders to advance.
He left, his useless time behind
And now he fights "Somewhere in France."

To the VADs

Gunner W. Matthew [176]

Of D.C.Ms and D.S.O's
The papers write in plenty,
But what of the girls who work and strain,
Whose days are never empty?

Day in day out, they're on the go
Morning, noon, and night,
With eyes a flame and cheeks a glow,
Doing with all their might.

To them our hearts go out in thanks,
These girls of the VAD,
Who make us well, and send us back,
To homes across the sea.

A soldier's anthem

Author unknown [221]

Only just one more Reveille,
Only one more Night Parade,
Only one more Kit Inspection,
Then we 're marching home again.

When we get our civil clothes on,
Oh! how happy shall we be,
When this gory war is over,
No more soldiering for me.

Compliments will then be fewer,
Guards, fatigues, will be no more,

We'll be spooning with the wenches,
As we did in days of yore.

NCO's will then be navvies,
Privates own their motor cars,
No more "siring" and"saluting,"
No more tea in two pound jars.

No more marching, no more doubling,
In the mire at six-fifteen,
No more pushing blooming barrows,
On the range at Wormwald Green.

No more "smarter men, now smarter,"
No more bread like granite rock,
No more rising at five-thirty,
And "Lights out," at ten o'clock.

No more asking when we're marching,
"Please Sir, may we have a drink?"
Or because we drop a shovel,
No more putting in the "clink."

No more "shunning" "as you wer'ing,"
No more working for a bob a day.
When next this country has a war on,
We'll find a job that brings more pay.

People told us when we 'listed,
Fame and medals we should win,
But the fame is in the Guard Room,
And the medals are of tin.

When we're finished with the Kaiser,
At the Empire we shall sing,
This Battalion National Anthem,
Twice a night, God save the King.

Australia

A.M.E

Clear o'er the land as a silver trumpet's call
A message rang that echoed far and wide,
Simple its words, it bade them leave their all
And fight for freedom, nor in vain it cried.
Swift in reply they sacrificed the best
They had to offer. By a distant sea,
Some at their post of duty lie at rest
Who fought and died in far Gallipoli.
Per ardua ad astra* – still the gleam
Of what sad radiance shines upon our way,
That lead them onward. Still with us today,
Australia strives for Freedom's golden dream.
And still shall we, for whom their blood was shed,
Honour the living and the unconquered dead.

*This was already the motto of Royal Flying Corps which had been formed in 1912.

ANZAC

BY T. H. ROWNTREE.[222]

Parliament has decreed that the name of Anzac "shall not be used for purposes of trade."—Daily Press.

Oh, sacred and beloved name,
    Immortal, 'graved on memory's screed,
Imperishable midst deeds of fame,
    That unborn nations yet may read.
With pride and joy this glorious prize
    Henceforth no jargon may command
For petty gains of merchandize.
    The memory of this gallant band,
And this fair land—this England ours,
    Will guard with reverence and with pride.
This precious symbol that endures,
    The name of "Anzac" sanctified.

"Allies" in Wilhelms land

JGRH (1914)[223]

"You are old. Father William," the young man said,
"And your hair has been ruffled of late,
Don't you think you have been long enough at the head
Of affairs and might now abdicate?"

"In my youth," Father William replied to his son,
"I decided on 'Dropping the Pilot',
Your claim would suggest that a place in the sun
Is not so essentially MY lot."

"You are old," said the youth, "as I mentioned before,
And have grown most uncommonly wilful,
And you rattle your sabre at everyone's door;
Do you think that such tactics are skilful?"

"In my youth," said the Sage, as he curled his moustache,
"I promoted the Triple Alliance;

The accompanying cartoon.

Uncle Edward reduced my designs to a hash,
His Entente proves a Triple Defiance."

"You are old," said the youth, "yet the title you claim
Is High Admiral of the Atlantic.
As no ships fill the picture to add to your fame,
Pray, is not the title pedantic?"

"In my youth," said his father, "I took to the sea,
Which in due time became an obsession ;
But I find now that Jellicoe's waiting for me,*
The best part of Valour—Discretion."

"You are old," said the vouth, "one would hardly suppose
That your head was as steady as ever;

The impression is growing wherever one goes,
You are not so remarkably clever."

"I have answered three questions, you can't pull my leg,"
Said his father, "please, no more instruction
On how to extract the contents of an egg,
By the primitive method of suction."

* The British naval blockage of Germany led by Admiral Jellicoe began in August 1914

English Scenery

Pte E. J. Sherman[224]

Shrewton Downs is on Salisbury Plain which suggests that this contribution by Pte Sherman was sent to the Editor of "*Coo-ee!*" while he was based in one of the Camps there.

Tonight I walked o'er Shrewton Downs.
My soul! 'twas like I dreamed
That earth reflected Paradise,
The glory perfect seemed.

The sun, hot-passioned, low to west
(Emboldened seemed he grew),
Caused blushes like to living gold
In kissing earth adieu.

"Terestra" loveliest garb had donned,
Eye dazzling in its sheen,
Were not her mantle strangely soft,
Resplendent shades of green.

Wild flowers everywhere exhaled
Sense soothing, sweet perfume,
Gay tints that glad the artist eye
Were blended in their bloom.

Fit land to key our Empire,
The grandest 'neath His sky,
Bright star of human freedom,
God keep thy prestige high.

CHAPTER 12

PUBLIC COMMENT

IT SEEMS VERY likely that the comments below, received from colonial administrators were to some extent engineered by the editor sending copies of the first edition of *"Coo-ee!"* to those agencies.

A New Zealand Appreciation [225]

The following is an extract from the Chronicles of the N.Z.E.F., a journal which is admirably edited by Mr Clutha Mackenzie, a son of Sir Thomas Mackenzie, who is so well known and esteemed in Bristol:—

"The Editor has received from Bishop's Knoll Hospital, Bristol, a copy of the first number of "Coo-ee!" a very jolly paper edited at the hospital by Mr A. G. Powell.

It is not the first time that Bishop's Knoll has been heard of, for many New Zealanders have been there in the past, who get ecstatic stutterings when they attempt to describe its glories. The hospital, and everything to do with it, has been given for Australasian wounded by a generous Australian(!), who has made this his bit in the war. He personally looks after it, and with the warm assistance of the good people of Bristol, nothing is left undone which might give pleasure to those whose good fortune it is to find their way to Bishop's Knoll. "Coo-ee!" brightly reflects the spirit of the place, and promises to be a record which will be greatly valued by the fellows from down under, especially those who know Bristol and Bishop's Knoll. Materially it is a fine production, printed well on good paper."

An Australian Appreciation 1

OFFICE OF THE AGENT-GENERAL FOR SOUTH AUSTRALIA
112 STRAND, LONDON WC2
OCTOBER 4th 1916

TO THE EDTIOR OF "COO-EE!"

You, Mr Editor, have assumed a great responsibility your magazine must be equal to the reputation of the Bishop's Knoll Hospital and to the patriotism of Mr and Mrs Bush and family. I wish it every success.

The patients of this hospital are very fortunate in their surroundings. Apart from the comforts they enjoy at Bishop's Knoll itself, they are privileged to see a very beautiful and very interesting part of dear old England.

To me, as an Australian, the maritime ports of England, are of special interest. We Australians appreciate perhaps more fully the word "Empire" than do the people in these islands, and in my opinion "Our Empire" is very largely the creation of the brave seafaring people who in the historic past sailed from these ports, opening up new lands and establishing British rule and British ideals. Not only were the long voyages of those days tedious and dangerous, but the colonizers of old did not always receive much support or assistance from the ruling authorities. The part played in the discovery of the outer portions of the world by those who sailed from Bristol was worthy of that great city, and we owe to the character and sturdiness of its venturesome people most of the qualities in the people overseas which have been gloriously exhibited on the field of battle and glory by your readers.

FRED W. YOUNG
Agent-General for South Australia

...and from General Birdwood, General Officer Commanding Australian and New Zealand Forces 1914 –1918.

2nd December 1916

My Dear Mr Bush,

Just a line to thank you so much for sending me a copy of Coo-ee which is I think not only a very excellent journal to have been produced in your hospital but is a real indication of the feelings and happiness of the men, whom you and Mrs Bush are so kindly and so hospitably looking after. As I wrote to the Australian Government after seeing your place, my only feeling was that you perhaps made them feel so completely at home there that many men might be too ready to stay on, instead of coming back to us when fit!..............

.........Will you please give my kind regards to Mrs Bush and again with so many thanks to you on behalf of the AIF.

Yours very sincerely,

W.R. Birdwood [226]

Now one might wonder why General Birdwood had visited Bishop's Knoll but he was another Old Cliftonian, though 10 years Bush's junior, who had already been Military Secretary to Field Marshal Lord Kitchener before the War and like Field Marshal Earl Haig, another old Cliftonian, maintained close links with Bristol and the College.

Clifton College had a remarkable input to the armed forces of the First World War. The College had a tradition of encouraging military service, doubtless supported by Robert Edwin Bush's father who served on the School Council from 1860 (the year in which it was founded) until he died. By 1912 the Clifton Register could show that of the 7394 boys who had passed through the school by this date 16% (1180) had gone on to military careers.[227] During the First World War 23 Major-Generals and 52 Brigadier-Generals were old Cliftonians. A total of 578 Old Cliftonians lost their lives in the conflict and are remembered on the school's war memorial.

An Australian Appreciation 2 [228]

THE AGENT-GENERAL FOR VICTORIA, AUSTRALIA,
LONDON, W.C.,
9th January, 1917.

DEAR MR. EDITOR,

I have perused with very great interest and pleasure the two excellent numbers of "Coo-ee!" which have been published as journals of the Bishop's Knoll Hospital at Bristol, and both of these productions reflect the highest credit upon all who have been associated with their publication.

The number and variety of the subjects dealt with in these publications, together with the highly creditable reproductions of photographs and views contained therein, will make these papers most pleasant mementoes to the Australian Troops who have had the good luck to be quartered during the terms of their convalescence in the delightful country home of Mr and Mrs Bush. The sketch of "Our Commandant" by Mr F. G. Lewin is most able and natural, and is a very clever piece of work.

I have had the pleasure of a recent visit to Bishop's Knoll. There can be few country residences which surpass it and its grounds in scenery and restfulness, and one cannot conceive a more congenial place for convalescence for our wounded boys. I have already met a number who have been accommodated there, and all alike are profoundly grateful for the great care and attention bestowed upon them by their hosts, the medical men, and the nurses. Mr and Mrs Bush have placed Australia under a great debt of gratitude by their generous entertainment of the troops, and their names will unquestionably be household words in the Island Continent.

Sincerely yours,

PETER MOBBIDE.

An Appreciation from Western Australia [229]

It is an encouragement to those who are concerned with the issue of "Coo-ee! to receive from time to time letters from high quarters indicating appreciation of our magazine. The following letter has just come to hand :—

THE EDITOR, Coo-ee.

SIR,—I have received three copies of your little paper from a friend in England, and wish to congratulate you upon the splendid idea of issuing such a publication. It will certainly be read with interest by all who have been through Bishop's Knoll. I shall not soon forget a visit one Sunday morning in August, 1915, and I have often spoken at meetings of the hospital and the great work Mr Bush is doing. My wife, who visits the base hospital at Freemantle, met an old patient from Bishop's Knoll last week. He spoke very highly of the institution, and told her he had received a copy of "Coo-ee!" from one of the transports. The beautiful grounds, residence, and purpose the place is now serving will always remain a pleasant memory to us.

I am,

Yours faithfully,

J. E. DODD.

Mr Dodd is a member of the Legislative Council, Western Australia.

Letters of appreciation from former patients

Those received at Bishop's Knoll from former patients, parents and other members of the services are far more numerous unsolicited and heartfelt. Dozens were sent to Bush,[230] some to Powell and others to members of the nursing staff. Only a small number of these were published in "*Coo-ee!*".

OUR COMMANDANT.

"DYRABBA,"
ADDISON ROAD,
MARRICKVILLE,
April 3rd 1917.

No doubt you will be surprised to hear from me after such a long time. I have received a couple of the copies of the "Knoll" paper under your capable editorship, and was so delighted with same that I could not help dropping you a line of congratulation on the success of the publication. After having spent such a splendid time at "The Knoll," the articles in the paper were very interesting, and makes ones thoughts fly straight back to dear old Bristol. By the time you receive this letter I will be back in civilian life, as I receive my discharge on the 13th instant. I am improving rapidly, although I will not be fit for any further service. I have met several of the patients from the "Knoll," and all are doing first rate. I thought so much of the sketch of Our Commandant" that I have had it framed.

E. R. BENTLEY.[231]

SIGNAL SCHOOL,
LARKHILL,
14th June, 1917.

To the Editor
As I was walking out of my hut to-night, I happened to glance at one of the lads here reading, and to my surprise I found he was reading "Coo-ee!". Well, to cut a long story short, I wasn't long before I had this wonderful little magazine in my own hands, and to see, although it was of a very late date, a number of

familiar names, namely Jackson, Flynn, Love, Lorentzen, Sievwright, gave me the greatest pleasure, as it recalled the good times we have had together — the pillow fights and the tricks played on each others beds. Then there was the arguments we had about who had pushed the most perambulators on the Downs during the afternoon, and I think our old friend Fletcher always won. Then there was the tips flying round as to who would win the billiard tourneys, and this always turned out to be a very hard problem, as the players were always very well handicapped, thanks to the handicapper.

Well, Mr Editor, I will never forget Bishop's Knoll Hospital as long as I live, as the kindness bestowed upon us Ausies there could not be excelled. I can just imagine with what pride and pleasure your magazine will be received by our people at home in far off Australia.

Well, in conclusion, Mr Editor, I will ask you to remember me to all at Bishop's Knoll, and to thank them once again for all they did for me. At the earliest date you will receive from me my subscription for a year's issue of Coo-ee.

L. G. BROWNFIELD.[232]

The next three are taken from letters written to Bush and now held in Bristol Reference Library in the two Bishop's Knoll scrapbooks (Ref BLS B28421/SR37)

Sergeant Flindell, 32nd Btn. AIF

"The doctors here were very satisfied with my leg and shoulder. Before closing I must thank yourself and Mrs Bush for your wonderful kindness and unfailing attention to me whilst I was with you. Not once did I feel that I wanted for anything, and I felt I was looked upon, not as a patient, but as a son. I shall always remember very kindly everyone who was so good to me, especially the good Sisters, who were always so untiring in their efforts to do everything that was possible to make me comfortable.......

...........People often remarked how happy I seemed and the only answer was, that one could not help but be happy amongst such good friends. You yourselves, by your wonderful work, are not only earning the gratitude of the boys that pass through your home, but you are earning the prayers and thanks of our dear ones, who rest contented knowing full well that we are receiving the best of care and attention. Myself I feel I owe you a life-long gratitude, and I shall always remember you with pride."

Private George Tracy AAMC

"...the great work you have done and are still doing for the Commonwealth soldiers whilst in England, wounded or sick, all have received the best of attention. Having had my training in the Perth Public Hospital whilst in camp on Blackboy Hill and also done duty in our own Brigade Hospital in Egypt and France, and being a patient in the Second Imperial Hospital in France, I can speak and write with authority. Your hospital is conducted on far better lines than Dartford (where I was also a patient), or Harefield, or this place, in fact I found it a model Military Hospital, far better conducted, and the patients better cared for than any I know of. What struck me amongst other things I noticed, was the love and personal interest taken in all the patients by your very excellent nursing staff, no "from hot – from cold," but genuine until the patient was discharged. Also, generally speaking, the veneration which yourself as Commandant and Mrs Bush and the nursing staff in general were held by the boys. I am a close observer of these little things, which count for much, where all classes and types of Australians congregate. You sir have won the admiration of everyone I have met who has passed through the portals of your hospitable house. Personally I feel I am under a debt of obligation for all that was done for me – for the very fine skilful operation which, I was warned by a celebrated Harley Street man in France, was a most difficult operation. Our own Australian Doctors told me the same. To Dr Ormerod I wish you to tender my sincere and best thanks, also to Sister Hall-Houghton, who had the looking after me until she went away for a short holiday, also to Sister Lambert, for the interest she took whilst under her care."

Newlyn,
Weybridge,
Surrey,
11/1/17

To Mr Bush

Dear Sir,

Not seeing you when I left Bishop's Knoll I feel it is my duty to drop a line thanking yourself and staff for their kindness to me. The Sisters are the jolliest girls I have ever been amongst and Bishop's Knoll shall always remind me as one of the happiest homes I have even been in.

I am enclosing a £1 towards next week's tournament prizes. Hoping you are all well.

With kind remembrances to all at Bishop's Knoll.

I remain yours very sincerely,

Pte H. Percy Blake

There were also comments left in the visitors' book from which Archibald Powell chose the following for inclusion in his book.[233]

Gunner R.P., 37th Battery, 10th Brigade

"It hurts me muchly to leave Bishop's Knoll. It would take little persuasion to make me stay here 'for the duration' and three months after. Could say heaps of nice things but I feel sure Mr Bush and his excellent staff know how much I appreciate their work."

Corporal J.D.

"Men come and men go like ships that pass in the night but memory still remains with us, and through all time and change, I shall look back on Bishop's Knoll and its noble workers as a landmark of my life."

Private E.R.B.

"It is great pleasure to me to be able to commit to writing my sincerest thanks to the worthy Commandant (Mr Bush), Mrs Bush, the Sisters and Doctors of

Bishop's Knoll for the excellent treatment and kindness I have received whilst an inmate of the hospital. To leave such kind friends is like leaving one's own home."

Private T.T.H.

"No words of mine can adequately express my feelings of gratitude to the Sisters of Bishop's Knoll for their many kindnesses to me. Like good wine 'they need no bush,' but the 'Bush at Bishop's Knoll' enables them to utilize their splendid capabilities to the utmost advantage for the sick and wounded."

Letters of appreciation from parents

Linden Lodge,
Linden,
New South Wales
Sept. 3rd 1917

Dear Mr Bush,

Both my husband and I feel the deepest gratitude to you and Mrs Bush for all you have done for our son L/C Douglas Stuart, 20th Battalion who spent many months in your beautiful house getting every comfort and attention and thanks to that he has made D.V. a wonderful recovery.

Words seem to fail me to express how greatly we appreciate your noble work for our Australian soldiers who will look back with happy thankful hearts for their time of rest surrounded with the comfort and beauty of Bishop's Knoll. Without doubt great blessing will rest upon you and your dear ones having so loyally served your King Country and fellow man.

Yours sincerely,

Caroline Stuart

67, Samson Road,
Beaconsfield,
4/4/18

Dear Mr Bush,

Your very welcome letter of January 5th to hand, I wish to thank you personally for your kindness to my dear son who has been so grievously wounded.

It is a great relief to me to know that he is progressing so well in the hands of one who is able to give all the attention that can be afforded him. It is as though he is with a personal friend. Both my husband and myself remember your first wife's family very well when Mr Lochée was Manager of the West Australian Bank; and Dr Scott (his second wife's father) was our family doctor for some years and also a great friend of my husband's father...

...We wish you good luck in the very Christian and self sacrificing work you are engaged in... my husband joins with me in thanking you for all for your many kindnesses to our dear Walter.

Believe us to be yours gratefully,

Ellen Flindell

A letter from the widow of Private F.G Robinson, buried at Arnos Vale:

Mil Lel
(South Australia)
10/3/18

Dear Mr Bush.

Just a line to thank you for all your kindness to my dear husband. I am indeed very grateful for all you did for him and thank you very much for the ribbons and cards. I was so pleased to get them I did not expect such kindness and also for the magazines I gave one to my mother-in-law, she has been staying with me up until to a week ago. You will wonder I did not write before but I have been ill and even now I feel I cannot write about my dear husband. It was a dreadful blow I thought he would be sent home. If I had only known how ill he was I could have cabled a few loving words to him. It may have helped him to get better. His letters were always so bright and cheerful and never once hinted that he was not doing as well as he should, he always spoke so well of the nurses and said they were all so kind and good to him.

Again thanking you for all your kindness to my dear husband and myself.

Yours sincerely,

M.Robinson

CHAPTER 13

ROBERT EDWIN BUSH AND BISHOP'S KNOLL IN LATER YEARS

BY THE SUMMER of 1918 there were signs that the War was drawing to its close. On September 20, 1918 a lunch was held in Bristol for representatives of the overseas dominions and their journalists. During the speeches specific mention was made of the role of the Bishop's Knoll Hospital.[234]

The Red Cross Flag continued to fly on the tower of Bishop's Knoll until February 1919 when the last patient left. On March 31, 1919 General Sir William Birdwood, later to become Field Marshal Lord Birdwood of Anzac and Totnes (see Appendix 3), visited Bristol and after lunch at the Constitutional Club, revisited his old school and watched the Clifton College Officer Training Corps who were busily engaged on military engineering work. The week before on March 21 a complementary dinner was given at the Bristol Liberal Club for Robert Edwin Bush. At this General Birdwood praised Mr and Mrs Bush for their great service in caring for wounded Australian soldiers at Bishop's Knoll. It is likely that it was on one of these occasions that the plaque from the Australian War Contingent Association was presented to Mr and Mrs Bush. Mrs Birdwood was on the organising committee of the Association and would have accompanied her husband on these occasions. (See Appendix 4)

At the end of the War the emergency hospital services were closed down very rapidly. Between January 1, 1919, and the end of April all the patients were cleared from the 2nd Southern General Hospital, the remaining cases in the Bristol Royal Infirmary being distributed either to Bath or to the Red Maids'

The original plaque, now held by the Australian War Memorial in Canberra. It measures 900x 540mm.

Sections. By the beginning of May 1919, only a skeleton staff of the 2nd Southern General Hospital remained. This team consisted of the Commanding Officer J. Paul Bush, the Registrar and the Quartermaster, who finished the long and difficult winding-up process from temporary offices in Clifton.

Some accounts say Robert Edwin Bush attended the first International Red Cross meeting in Geneva in May 1919 as the Australian delegate. With his experiences with the British Red Cross during the War while still maintaining his contacts in Australia through Dalgety and Company Ltd, he was an obvious choice. However passenger lists show that he and his wife had left Liverpool for Sydney on April 3, 1919 on the SS *Lapland* and arrived at New York on April 12, 1919. They travelled to San Francisco via Paso Paso, and Honolulu, on the SS *Sonoma*, and arrived at Perth on May 27, 1919.[235] In fact he attended and spoke at the inaugural meeting of the council of the International Red Cross League held on March 2, 1920. As the leader of the Australian delegation he pointed out that the recent establishment of Red Cross branches in the states of Australia meant that that he and his colleagues had come to listen and learn.[236]

The formal end of the 2nd Southern General Hospital took place six weeks later on Thanksgiving Sunday July 6, 1919 when the laying up of its colours took place at the Cathedral. Doubtless J. Paul Bush was present as were detachments of the RAMC, nursing staff and 300 servicemen,[237] however it was likely that Robert Edwin was still on his way back from Australia.

Mrs Marjery Bush had received her OBE in the New Year honours of January 1, 1918. A number of Robert Bush's influential friends, notably Sir William Howell Davies and George Gibbs the 1st Lord Wraxall, were concerned at that time that he had as yet received no recognition for his considerable public service. As a result of their lobbying Bush received a letter dated January 10, 1920 from the Acting Secretary of the Order of the British Empire, then based at the Home Office in Whitehall, advising him that his name was about to be put forward for a CBE. On the January 14, Bush replied in the following terms:

> Sir,
> I beg to acknowledge the receipt of your letter of the 10th Inst.
> While I thank the Right Honourable Home Secretary, I pray that my name be not submitted to His Majesty the King for appointment as a Commander of the Order of the British Empire.
> I am sir, your obedient servant,
>
> Robert Bush[238]

The reasons for this are not given but family tradition holds that Bush declined the award because he felt he deserved a knighthood! Nine months later Lord

Westminster Abbey.

EASTER TUESDAY, APRIL 25, 1916—11.30 a.m.

AUSTRALIAN AND NEW ZEALAND ARMY CORPS.
FIRST LANDING IN GALLIPOLI
APRIL 25, 1915.

ADMIT ONE TO THE NAVE.

Entrance by Great West Door at 11.15 a.m.
(*No admission will be granted until after the entry of the Troops.*)

HERBERT E. RYLE.
Dean.

Birdwood wrote to Robert regretting that he would be unable to visit before his departure to India to take up command of the Northern Army there but his last paragraph is interesting.

> "I wish I could tell you all I feel about the want of recognition you have received, for to my mind, it is disgraceful, although I know that you do not personally worry about such things." [239]

Did he know Bush had declined the CBE?

Bush, who had already been Sheriff of Bristol in 1912, was appointed Deputy Lieutenant of the County of Gloucester and of the city of Gloucester and the city and county of Bristol in 1922,[240] and in 1923 was created a Knight of Grace of the Order of St John of Jerusalem by George V.

Anzac Day Services

The first anniversary of the landings at Gallipoli had been held in Bristol at

Bush's Knight of the Order of St John of Jerusalem medals. Awarded in 1923.

the Mansion House on April 25, 1916 when a number of veterans were present. Bush himself seems to have been attending the National Service of Remembrance in Westminster Abbey on this occasion.

In 1917 a much larger gathering was organised in Bristol when 300 men took part. In 1918 this took the form of a drumhead service on College Green attended by Sir Ian Hamilton who had been Commander of the Mediterranean Expeditionary Force. Sir Ian also attended in 1919 when "Gallipoli Day" was held on the April 26.[241] The day had been declared a public holiday in New Zealand in 1920, and in Australian states some form of public holiday was held from 1927 onward and at about this time the name changed from "Gallipoli Day" to "Anzac Day".

On Friday October 21, 1921 the Arnos Vale War Memorial was unveiled in front of three thousand people by Emily, Duchess of Beaufort, the President of the City and County of Bristol Branch of the British Red Cross Society. Those present included the Lord Mayor and Sheriff, and representatives of the Australian High Commission.[242] By that time 240 Commonwealth soldiers had been buried at Arnos Vale including the bodies of 20 Australians. From 1922 onward Bush was present at the annual Anzac Day Memorial service held there until 1939, the year in which he died.[243]

Under a change in the law which came into effect when all the old land leases in Western Australia expired in 1928, no single pastoral holding in the north west division of Western Australia could exceed 1,000,000 acres but by this time Bush's property exceeded 2,000,000 acres. So he split this holding into two companies: the western section being known as Landor and the eastern section retaining the name of Mount Clere. Both companies were nevertheless still owned by the Bush family! Bush sold Bidgemia (formerly "Lower Clifton Downs") in 1927 and Mount Clere was sold in 1951 some years

Robert Edwin Bush addressing the Downend Cricket Club, June 8, 1922.

after his death. For full details of changes of ownership after this period see McDonald, R., Winning the Gascoyne, Hesperian Press, Perth, 1991 and Battye J.S. (ed), The History of the North West of Australia, V.K. Jones & Co. Perth, 1915.

Robert Edwin became Chairman of Gloucestershire County Cricket Club in 1919 and remained so until 1922. It was during this period that the club bought back its present ground from the then owners J.S Fry and sons.[244] This would have pleased his former captain W.G. Grace who had originally bought the ground in 1889. Another pleasure for Bush was his attendance at the opening of the Downend Cricket Club pavilion erected as a memorial to Dr W. G. Grace, who was born in a house overlooking the ground.[245] (This was the first memorial to be erected to that great man, though at the time Lord's memorial gates were under construction.) In his address he said he was there because he considered it would be a great omission on the part of the Gloucestershire Cricket Club if it had not been represented on the occasion but that he was also there as an old friend of the Grace family, and as a representative of the older school of Gloucestershire county cricketers with whom he had the honour of playing in 1874. Those present were there to commemorate the name of the greatest cricketer that ever lived. He felt they

Anzac Day Service 1923. From left to right: Miss Philp, Mr R.E.Bush, Staff Sergeant Burrows A.I.F, Miss Hardy, the American Consul (Major Robert Honey) The Canadian Trade Commissioner (Mr Douglas Cole), Bishop Clifford, Mr E.C.Philp, Mrs Bush, Master Toby Bush, Miss Bush, Dr Omerod, Mr A.G. Powell (Hon Sec Bishop's Knoll Old Comrades Society), and an unknown lady. The Australian High Commissioner Sir Joseph Cook was also present on this occasion but does not appear in this photograph.

Arnos Vale 1925.

could not have selected any memorial more suitable to W. G. than that which his sister Mrs Gunn would unveil. He also regarded W.G. as one of the great Imperialists and one of the greatest ambassadors of the Empire who, through his great influence in the game, had helped to bind Australia to Britain.

Bush became President of Gloucestershire County Cricket Club the following year,[246] and continued to play an active role in other areas of Bristol public life. He was an accomplished artist and in 1929 became President of the Bristol Savages. In 1930 he was made President of the Old Cliftonian Society.

The Bishop's Knoll Old Comrades' Society

The Bishop's Knoll Old Comrades' Society was formed at Christmas 1917 to *"perpetuate friendships formed during those stirring war times and to keep alive associations with Bristol"* It also seems that all those who recovered at the hospital were given Bishop's Knoll Comrades' medals.[247]

The Honorary Secretary of the Society was Archibald Powell who does not seem to have ever visited Australia but with his help Bush remained in contact with many former patients and the families of those who had passed through Bishop's Knoll but not survived the War.

How Bush managed to maintain contact with former patients is unknown but he clearly did so. No evidence of any later news sheet has been found and in the days before the invention of the spirit duplicator this could only have been by typing and multiple carbon copies. The Bush's produced a Christmas card 1916-1918 but for how many years afterwards and how wide a circulation this had is unknown. It is clear from the replies he received that he wrote a great many letters to former patients. It is also possible that contact was maintained through correspondence with the Returned Soldiers and Sailors Imperial League of Australia which had been established in 1916 and which operated through branches in all Australian states.

Badge worn by members of the Bishop's Knoll Old Comrades' Society.

According to Archibald Powell, Bush visited Australia 13 times after the War, almost certainly this was partly business travel as a Director of Dalgety and Company but Bush took the opportunity to meet up with former patients who had by this time formed local reunion groups. The first visit was in June 1919 and while he was in Melbourne Bush received a letter inviting him to a lunch with a few Old Cliftonians.[248] This came from Arthur Jose, the former Australia Correspondent of the London Times who was now working in Royal Australian Naval Intelligence. Jose records in his letter to Bush that he was in the Clifton Junior School when Robert Edwin was Captain of the School's First XI.

By the time Robert Edwin was planning his visit to Australia in 1922 Archibald Powell was ahead of him and the Brisbane Courier carried a notice from him as the Hon Secretary of the Bishop's Knoll Old Comrades Society, giving dates in late March and early April when Bush hoped to meet members of the Society in Brisbane, Sydney, Melbourne, Adelaide and Perth.[249] Bush paid a similar visit to Australia in September 1926,[250] this time accompanied by Mrs Bush their two daughters and son John.[251] The impact of these can be assessed from this report of his reunion in Adelaide on November 4, quoted here in full from the South Australian Mail of Saturday November 6, 1926.

HOST OF BISHOP'S KNOLL

Mr R.E. Bush in Adelaide

MESSAGE TO OLD PATIENTS

"I want to send greeting and best wishes through 'The Mail' to all South Australian soldiers who were at Bishop's Knoll and who were unable to meet me at Dalgety & Company on Thursday," said Mr Robert Bush of Bristol.

"Mrs Bush and I are passing through Adelaide on our way back to England, and have been overjoyed at the reception given to us all over Australia. On some future occasion we hope to have the pleasure of shaking by the hand those men whose faces we have missed during our brief stay in Adelaide."

In the Board Room of Dalgety & Company Limited on Thursday a small band of returned men waited from noon to well after 1.00pm for a chance of greeting Mr and Mrs Robert E. Bush of Bishop's Knoll, Bristol. Lunch hour was spent in talking over old times in hospital during the war and the need for food was forgotten in the joy of reunion.

MANY FACES RECALLED

"I know your face well. You were at Bishop's Knoll in 1916 with trench feet."

"That's right, sir," A beaming smile accompanied the words.

"No, I just cannot remember your name. There were so many of you."

Mr R.E. Bush sat in the board room at Dalgety's looking eagerly into the no less eager face of the returned man.

There were many returned men in the room waiting an opportunity to speak to these English visitors, Mr and Mrs Bush who turned their beautiful home at Bishop's Knoll, Stoke Bishop, Bristol into a hospital for Australian soldiers during the Great War. Those patriotic Britishers converted their house into a 100 bedded hospital, equipped it, and ran it for four and a half years entirely at their own expense for the benefit of the Australian sick and wounded. Between two and three thousand men passed through the hospital, and both Mr and Mrs Bush are distinctly proud of the fact that it was the one general hospital in England which took only Australians direct from the front.

CALLING THE ROLL

Spread out in front of him on the table Mr Bush had a long list of the names and addresses of the South Australians who had been patients at Bishop's Knoll and as each man came up to him he ticked off the name on the list.

Many amusing incidents of hospital life were recalled and Mr Bush fired off a rapid series of questions to each man.

"Married now?" he asked one.

"Yes, sir."

"Any children?"

"Three, sir."

"Good lad. Boys or girls?"

"All boys."

"Splendid, Still at the same address?"

"No, that was my mother's address. I am at so and so."

"Run away from mother have you. Got a good job. Excellent".

"Wound all right now? That's fine." And with a hearty handshake the digger was passed on to pay his respects to Mrs Bush.

THAT LAMB CHOP

A general laugh was caused when one man coming in late rushed up to Mrs Bush and said excitedly as he grasped her hand and wrung it vigorously,

"You remember me, don't you. I was the man to whom you gave the first decent meal I had had for about a month. Don't you remember it? It was lamb chop and I had been living on nothing but milk foods."

"Remember the sister we called her Shrapnel and how she used to bully us. She would have done anything for the boys though."

DIGGERS WIVES TOO

There were women in the little congregation too. Some of them the wives and sisters of the men present, and they were taken up and proudly introduced. Blushingly they thanked the visitors for what they had done for the boys, and in most cases they presented Mrs Bush with a posy of flowers.

There were other women who had come with messages from men unable to be present, messages from men in hospital, still paying the dues of war. There were also one or two women folk of men who had passed out, women who had not forgotten stories of the kindness and great heartedness of Mr and Mrs Bush which had been brought home to Australia by grateful diggers.

Some proud fathers brought along chubby youngsters tightly clutching posies in their hands and the little ones lost all sense of shyness under the influence of kind words and smiles.

On all sides were heard references to the royal time at Bishop's Knoll, where sufferings were as nought, when compared with the magnificent treatment they had received.

Mr and Mrs Bush are taking back to England the knowledge that Australian diggers whom they have befriended have not forgotten. They have spent pleasant hours of reunion with old boys at Brisbane, Sydney and Melbourne and hope to meet Western Australian diggers in about a fortnight.

On this occasion when back in Western Australia Bush took the opportunity to present a cup for the winner of the Landor Races held by the East Gascoyne Race Club at Aurillia Creek.[252]

Bush's last visit to Australia was in late August 1938 when he was received by veterans in Dalgety's offices in Brisbane with the same enthusiasm.

> Mr Bush had a cheery word and time for an exchange of reminiscences with each of the 15 former inmates of Bishop's Knoll.
>
> "1916—Smith with the crooked arm."
>
> "I'm the one who helped the one-legged chap over the fence when he was late back one night to Bishop's Knoll."
>
> "Remember you, Mr Bush? Why you've never been out of my mind."
>
> Every one of the 15 had a memory to whisper to their old friend.
>
> Mrs R. Street entered; for a moment Mr Bush was puzzled and then remembered when she said she was Miss Clarrie Smith of Bristol who had sung for the soldiers, and in the assembly was Mr K.V. Gunn who had been her accompanist in many informal concerts for the Diggers.
>
> Former Inmates who met Mr Bush were Messrs. L.V. Roberts, D. J. Kennedy, A.N. Smith-Finkle, P.V. Ryan, L.N. Young, M. Bloom, E.J. Rule, R. A. Wightman, B. Francis, H.V. Barnes, W. Hilleard, C. Dorgan, S. Chapman, R. Sloman, and P.S. Smith.[253]

A further account of this occasion is given by Frederick William Gunning who had been introduced to Bush three years before through a mutual friend the Bishop of Bristol Clifford Woodward. Gunning had studied the early history of settlers in the Gascoyne and clearly had the highest regard for Bush.

> "...I took my last farewell of Bush on board the *Otranto*, surrounded by what seemed to be the whole staff of Dalgety Ltd. They were mostly young men and they had come to say farewell to their W.A. Chief who was going to take charge of things in London for a year. R.E. Bush had travelled by plane from the Eastern States in order to catch the boat and at Marylands had met his old friend Wittenoon.... I went to Mr Bush's suite of rooms and placed on his bed a bulky volume of manuscript in which figured so many of the men he had known 40, 50 and 60 years ago... his reply from Bishop's Knoll made me feel that it had been worthwhile." [254]

The Bush Family Memorial
Names included on it:
Major Robert Bush
(1809-1877)
Emily Aida Bush - his widow
(1822-1908)
Adria Georgina Bush -his daughter
(1861-1943)
Colonel James Paul Bush - his son
(1857-1930)
Prudence Cheney Bush - his daughter-in-law
(1890-1930)
Robert Edwin Bush
(1855-1939)
Brigadier Robert Francis Lochée Bush - his son
(1896-1955)

The following month Bush was in Adelaide where he had been invited to address the State Board of the Returning Sailors and Soldiers League of Australia. He also met more former patients there before returning home to England.

It is clear that in his later years Bush also found time to enjoy his grandchildren. John Sandes, this time writing for the Australian Press during his brief residency in England, describes how his visit to Bishop's Knoll in 1920 coincided with a children's party in which Robert Edwin participated fully, playing the piano while "gleeful bright eyed children romped through Sir Roger de Coverley".[255]

According to Bush's granddaughter June, who visited the house as a child just before he died, the Conservatory then contained two bronze cranes, large enough for a six year old to sit on. There were also two Australian birds: "George" a white cockatoo, and "Twenty-eight" a green parrot which were kept in a large cage.[256] At that time Robert Edwin was still wearing his Australian hat when he carved the lunch as he can be seen doing so in the

hospital photograph in 1917!

Bush died on December 28, 1939 and after his cremation at Arnos Vale Cemetery on January 1, 1940 there was a Memorial Service in Bristol Cathedral attended by members of the family and a large number of civic dignitaries.[257] His name was added to the foot of the family memorial in Arnos Vale where it can be seen today above that of his son, Brigadier Robert Francis Lochée Bush, who died in 1955.

The probate records give Bush's estate as £19,245 (worth £1,155,725 today) which was administered by his wife and his first cousin Rear Admiral (Rtd) James Tobin Bush.[258] Mrs Bush attended the Anzac service in 1940 and then moved away to spend the remainder of her life in comfort in Lyme Regis Dorset close to where her widowed daughter Diana Mary was living.[259] She died in September 1960.

On September 25, 1940 a disastrous daylight German air raid on the Filton works of the Bristol Aircraft Company (BAC) took place. Ninety two employees were killed and another 166 injured and the development of the new Beaufighter aircraft was seriously delayed. Bishop's Knoll was requisitioned as the BAC apprentice school. After the end of WWII the house was taken over by the Bristol Royal Infirmary as a hostel and school for preliminary

Trainees of the Bristol School of Nursing attending the official opening of 1949. L-R Back row: Joan Mason, Maureen Goatman, Front row: Dorothy Ross and Margaret Norton.

The Bristol School of Nursing

requests the pleasure of the Company of

Nurse Norton

on the occasion of the

Opening of the School

by

H. R. H. The Princess Margaret

on Monday, March 28th, 1949, at 12.30 o'clock.

Morning Dress.

Guests are requested to be in their places in the Ballroom at the School of Nursing, Bishop's Knoll, Sneyd Park, Bristol 9, not later than 12 noon.

A Buffet Lunch will be served at the School following the Opening Ceremony.

R.S.V.P. to: The Secretary to the Board, United Bristol Hospitals, Bristol Royal Infirmary, Bristol 2.

Invitation to the opening of Nursing School.

nurse training. The unit was formally opened by Princess Margaret in March 1949. It is reported that she signed the visitors' book using the pen which her grandmother Queen Mary had used when visiting with George V in 1915.[260, 261] However as far as is known the King and Queen never visited Bishop's Knoll but had met Mr and Mrs Bush at Southmead Hospital that year, so quite which visitors' book was signed is not clear.

Bishop's Knoll continued to be used for Preliminary Nurse training until the 1960s when nurse training in Bristol was reorganised and relocated. The house was then empty for some years before being bought in 1972 by the developers English and Continental Homes Ltd. They appointed MWT Architects of Bath to design a residential development on the site. After extended consultation, during which the design was commended by the Royal Fine Arts Commission experts Sir Hugh Casson and Lord Esher, Bristol City Council approved MWT's design and work was about to start when the 1973 oil crisis caused the scheme to be put on hold.

By this time the house had been demolished and the plaque which had

Princess Margaret signing the visitors book.

been removed in 1971 was in the possession of the Board of Governors of the United Bristol Hospitals. This was brought to the attention of the Australian High Commission in London who, appreciating the importance of the hospital to Australian troops during the war, asked if the plaque could be sent to Australia. This was agreed and it was received by the Australian War Memorial in July 1972 where it remains today.[262]

In 1981 the site was acquired by Benson Brothers, a local Bristol building firm who ignored the earlier plans and built the present three blocks of flats and donated part of the site, which had been Bishop's Knoll's garden and arboretum, to the Woodland Trust .

The restored walls and the terrace steps above the kitchen garden.

An original feature in need of restoration.

CHAPTER 14

BISHOP'S KNOLL TODAY

IN 1983 THE Woodland Trust undertook planting of broadleaf trees in the paddock area. Then, with the support of the Avon Gardens Trust, it successfully applied for matched funding from the Yanley and North Somerset Environmental Company to repair two hundred metres of stone walls which were becoming dangerous and to reinstate terrace steps, this at a total cost of £13000.

In 2013 a number of local Woodland Trust members under the leadership of Bev Knott formed a volunteer group – The Friends of Bishop's Knoll Wood - to care for the wood.

In 2014 the group applied successfully to the Overseas War Graves Fund of the Australian Department of Veteran Affairs for funding for a replica of the 1919 plaque which had been removed when the house was demolished. This has been placed at the entrance of the wood to inform visitors of this important link between England and Australia and the remarkable work of Mr and Mrs Robert Bush. Further work will be undertaken, as funding allows, to reinstate the railings and walls within the garden.

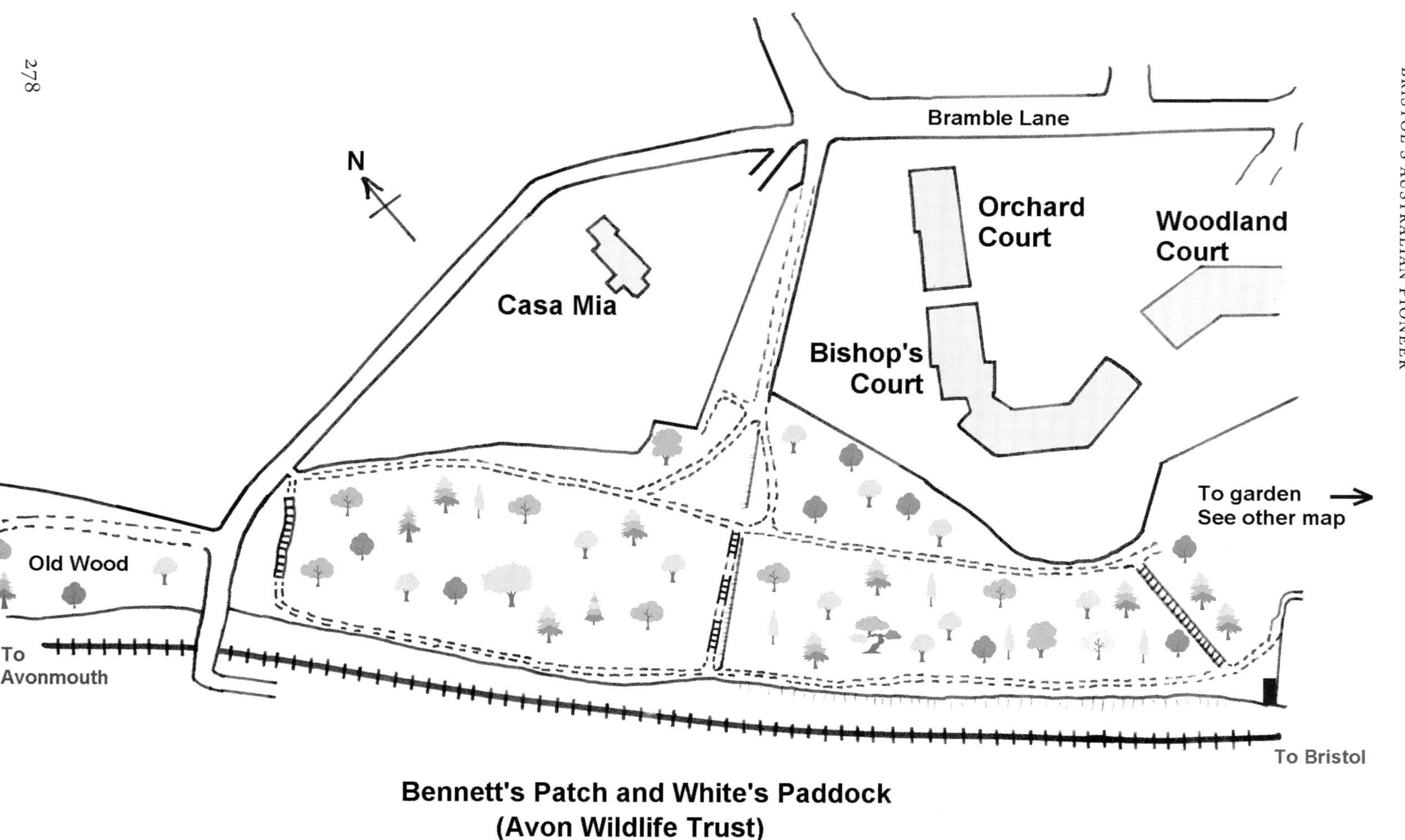

Bramble Lane
N
Casa Mia
Orchard Court
Woodland Court
Bishop's Court
To garden
See other map
Old Wood
To Avonmouth
To Bristol
Bennett's Patch and White's Paddock
(Avon Wildlife Trust)

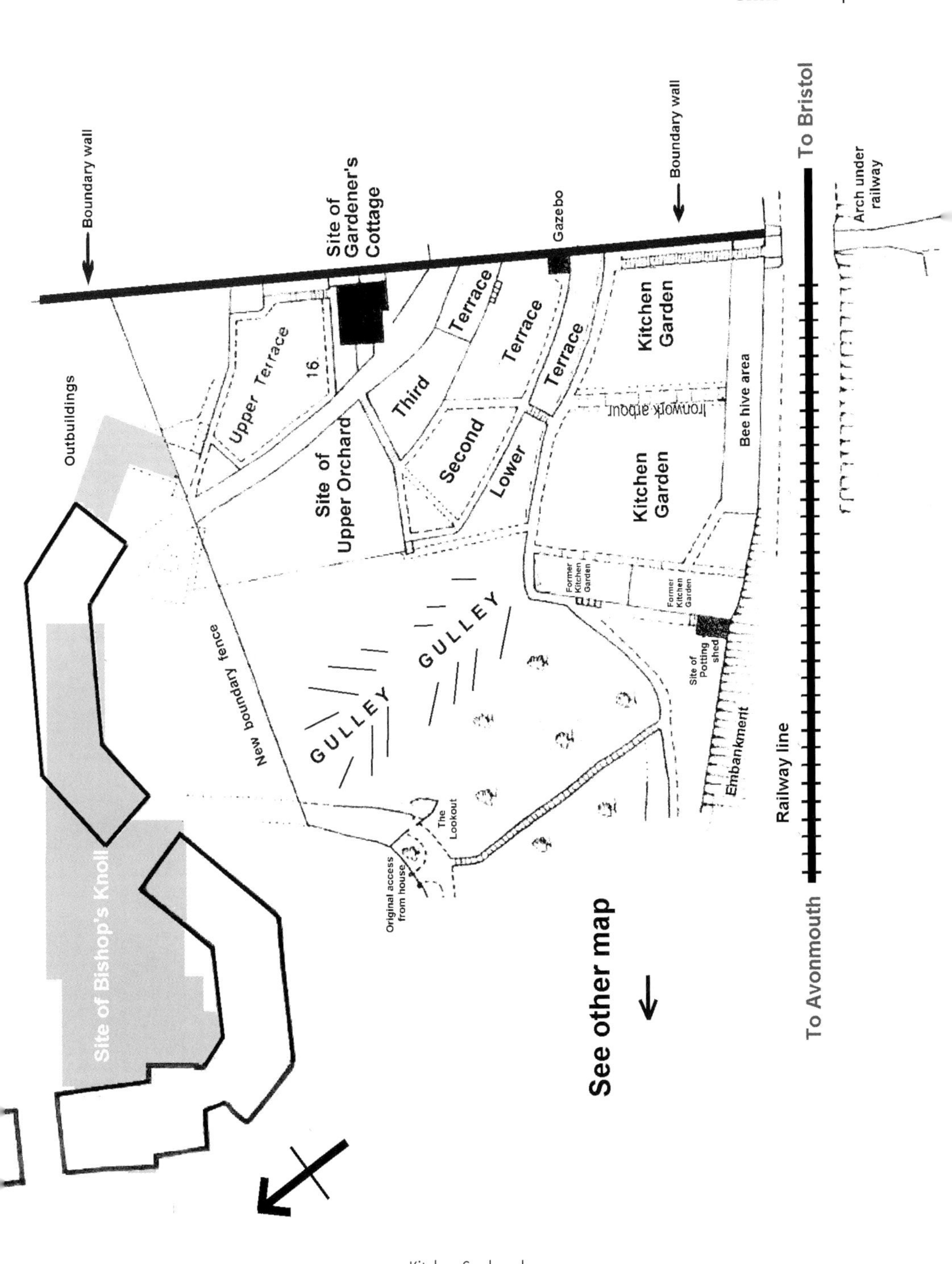

Kitchen Garden plan.

One of the restored garden walls.

Woodland Trust volunteers May 2016.

FURTHER READING

Battye, J.S. (ed), *The History of the North West of Australia*, V.K. Jones & Co., Perth, 1915.

Beckett, R., *The Australian soldier in Britain 1914-1918*. PhD Thesis, University of London, 2008.

Byrne, E., Burlton, C., *Bravo Bristol!* Redcliffe Press, Bristol, 2014.

Chapman, C., Jetzer, P., *An historic landscape survey of Bishop's Knoll Historic gardens*. Avon County Planning Department, 1995.

Cowan, P. (Ed). *A faithful picture - letters of Eliza and Thomas Brown at York in the Swan River Colony 1841-1852*.Freemantle Arts Press, Freemantle, Western Australia, 1977.

Hawkins, F.C., Seymour-Bell, E., *Fifty years of the Clifton Rugby Football Club*. J.W. Arrowsmith, Bristol, 1922.

McDonald, R., *Winning the Gascoyne*. Hesperian Press, Carlisle, Western Australia, 1991.

Powell, A.G., *A short history of Bishop's Knoll Hospital*, Van Dyke Printers, Bristol, 1930.

Tippett, W., *A survey and assessment of Bishop's Knoll Sneyd Park Bristol*. MSc Report, University of Bath, 2014.

Wells, C., Stone, G F., (Eds.)*Bristol and the Great War 1914-19*, J.W. Arrowsmith, Bristol. 1920.

Westbrook, F.E., *Anzac and after - a collection of poems*, Leopold Classic Library, Kiev, Ukraine. http://www.leopoldclassiclibrary.com (First published by Duckworth and Co. in 1916).

Withnell Taylor, N.E.,*Yeera-muk-a-doo. A social history of the settlement of North West Australia 1861-1890*, Freemantle Arts Centre Press, Freemantle, Western Australia, 1980.

REFERENCES

1 Planche, J. R., *The Conqueror and his Companions, Vol II,* Tinsley Brothers, London, 1874. p.25

2 He also recovered by law some of the former possessions of Westbury, and others by purchase, including the churches of Henbury and Stoke with all tithes.

3 Sadleir, S. F., *A memoir of the life and time of the Right Honorable Sir Ralph Sadleir,*Longmans Green and Co, London, 1877. Ch III

4 He had already been made knight 1540,the same year as he was made a privy councillor and principal secretary to Henry VIII.

5 William Jackson (born circa 1635), possibly his father was a Quaker, Master of the Merchant Venturers in 1680, Sheriff of Bristol (1678) and Mayor (1688/9).

6 It is perhaps of relevance that Joseph Jackson's daughter Catherine had married John Martin (1692-1767) of Overbury Park.

7 Rudder, S., *A new history of Gloucestershire* 1779, Republished by Alan Sutton Publishing, Stroud, 1977. p.801

8 Matthews, M., *Bristol and Clifton Directory and Almanack*, M. Matthews, Bristol, 1851. p66

9 Latimer, J., *The annals of Bristol in the nineteenth century,* WF Morgan, Bristol, 1887. p.343

10 Beeson, A. *North Bristol*, Amberley Publishing, Stroud, 2014. p.76

11 In 1882 Mr P. D. Prankerd gave £1,000 for the endowment of a bed in the Children's Ward of the Bristol Royal Infirmary. See Smith GM *History of the Bristol Royal Infirmary,* J.W. Arrowsmith, Bristol, 1917. p.390

12 Oxford University Alumni 1500-1886

13 His son Richard Percy Prankerd (i.e. P D Prankerd's grandson) died in 1918 and is recorded on the Memorial Lynch gate of St James Church, Tonbridge Wells.

14 Bettey, J.H., Paul Bushe the first Bishop of Bristol. *Transactions of the Bristol and Gloucestershire Archaeological Society,* 1988; 106: 169-172

15 See Davis, J.D., *Pewter at colonial Williamsburg.* Colonial Williamsburg Foundation, Williamsburg, 2003.

16 Burnside, A., *A Palladian Villa in Bristol,Clifton Hill House and the people who lived there,* Redcliffe Press, Bristol, 2009. p.24

17 National Archives Prob 11/1338/185

18 In 1824, the 96th regiment was reformed. Over the next half a century it would garrison a variety of territories around the world. It also provided detachments for convict ships sailing to New South Wales, Tasmania and Western Australia.

19 In 1849, the 96th arrived in Calcutta in India, where it was under control of the British East India Company. They left the subcontinent in 1854 and returned home to the UK.

20 A Bristol charity established in 1769 to provide for the poor and elderly.

21 Latimer, J., *The annals of Bristol in the nineteenth century,* W and F Morgan, Bristol, 1887. pp.363-4

22 This would lead ultimately to the Territorial and Reserve Forces Act of 1907.

23 Bush was appointed on September 13, 1859. The unit's name changed in 1881 to 1st (City of Bristol) Corps changing again in 1883 to 1st Volunteer Battalion, Gloucestershire Regiment. With the reorganisation of the Territorial Force in 1908 it became 4th (City of Bristol) Battalion of the Gloucestershire Regiment.

24 Westlake, R., *Tracing of the Rifle Volunteers 1859-1908,* Pen and Sword Books, Barnsley. 2010. p.97

25 Latimer, J., *The annals of Bristol in the*

nineteenth century. W. and F. Morgan, Bristol, 1887. pp. 363-365

26 The land on which Prince Street and Narrow Quay were built was purchased by Bristol Corporation from St. Augustine's Abbey in 1239. In 1725 building leases were issued to Henry Combe for two tenements in Prince Street and a warehouse behind on the Quay. By 1830-31 Messrs. Acraman had acquired the leases of the three houses at the south end of Prince Street on which the new warehouse was built. It was undoubtedly the most architecturally ambitious warehouse in Bristol, with the then huge rateable value of £540 a year.

27 The Bush company had been formed in 1833 or 1834 to take advantage of the removal of the East India Company's tea monopoly, although there is some confusion as to whether their warehouse was used to store tea, tobacco or both.

28 Curiously while the 1861 Census states Redland as his place of birth, the 1871 Census gives this as Westbury-on-Trym.

29 April 5, 1860

30 *Clifton College Register 1862-1912,* J.W. Arrowsmith, Bristol, 1912. p.XXV

31 It is highly likely that he provided some of the capital necessary to found the school.

32 Hawkins, F.C., Seymour-Bell, E., *Fifty years of the Clifton Rugby Football Club,* J.W. Arrowsmith, Bristol, 1922. pp. 7-20

33 Casey, P., Hale, H. I., *For College and Country- a History of Clifton Rugby Football Club.* MX Publishing, London, 2009. pp.212-3

34 Alcock C.W. (Ed), *James Lillywhite's Cricketers' Annual,* James Lillywhite, Frowd & Co., London, 1875.

35 He has a further place in Wisden in connection with a house match at the College – South Town v Brown's - which was regarded as a curiosity. South Town ran up the big total of 379, yet there was not one double figure contribution to the score. The explanation of this puzzle was that Bush scored 228, another batsman got over a century, and the others, including "Mr Extras," contributed 10 between them and was noted in Lillywhite's annual as the best public schoolboy of the year.

36 Clifton College provided not only the WW1 Commander-in-Chief (Douglas Haig) and an Army Commander (William Birdwood), but also 23 Major-Generals and 52 Brigadier-Generals.

37 Like James Paul Bush WG studied medicine at Bristol, enrolling there in 1868 at the age of 20 years.

38 WG Grace also played rugby on a few occasions, see Hawkins, FC, Semour-Bell, E., *Fifty years of the Clifton Rugby Football Club.* J.W. Arrowsmith, Bristol, 1922. p.20

39 Powell A.G.,*Bristol Evening World,* November 29, 1933

40 Casey, P., Hale, R.I., *For College, Club and Country,* MX Publishing, London, 2009. p.20

41 *Clifton College Register 1862-1947.* J. W. Arrowsmith, Bristol, 1948

42 Cameron, C.W.M., R.E. Bush Gascoyne explorer and pastoralist. *Journal of the Royal Western Australian Historical Society,* 1982; 8: 55-69

43 Probate records show his estate was valued at "less than £30,000".

44 State Library of Western Australia, 7285A/1

45 McDonald, R., *Winning the Gascoyne,* Hesperian Press, Carlisle, Western Australia, 2008. p.4

46 The Lady Elizabeth later sank off Rottnest Island Western Australia June 30, 1878.

47 Thomas Soutter Lodge, born in London 8th May 1852, and died at Cottisloe, Western Australia, 24th February 1938. He married Sarah Constance Leake (1860-1939), 4th daughter of George Walpole Leake QC who in 1883 was acting attorney-general and had a seat on the Legislative Council. In 1890-94 he was a nominee member of the first council under responsible government where he would have served with Robert Edwin Bush.

48 Gold had been found in Yilgarn the previous year.

49 Cameron C.W.M., R.E. Bush Gascoyne explorer and pastoralist. Lecture to the Royal Western Australian Historical Society, 1981

50 Cameron, C.W.M., R.E. Bush Gascoyne explorer and pastoralist. *Journal of the Royal Western Australian Historical Society,* 1982; **8:** p.56

51 This unusual spelling led Mrs Marjery Bush to later adopt the spelling of "Margery" for herself and that of "Marjorie" for her

eldest daughter.

52 A corroborie is an Aboriginal ceremony which is a dramatic representation, in mime and song, of the mythical history of the tribe. These ceremonies have many functions and take many forms. The death corroboree precedes the laying the dead member with their tribal forefathers usual in a limestone cave.

53 Cossack is now a ghost town, the pearling industry having moved away at the turn of the century.

54 McDonald, R. *Winning the Gascoyne.* Hesperian Press, Carlisle, Western Australia, 2008. pp 2-6

55 Taylor, N.E., *Yeera-muk-a-doo. A social history of the first settlement of Northwest Australia,* Freemantle Arts Centre Press, Freemantle, Western Australia,1980. pp.14-36

56 *History of Western Australia - Robert Edwin Bush* https://en.wikisoursce.org/wiki/History_of_Western_Australia/Robert_Edwin_Bush. Accessed 31/03/2016

57 Known also as the Itchy grub (Ochrogaster lunifer). these caterpillars migrate from a nursery 'tent' to a new location in the branches of a tree, where they create large cocoons before their metamorphosis into moths. These cocoons were formally used as bandages by native Australians

58 See Gunning, F.W., *Last of the Gascoyne pioneers* .Royal Western Australian History Society.

59 Bush's second wife's mother was Penelope Fanny Scott née Scholl.

60 Cameron C.W.M., R.E. Bush Gascoyne explorer and pastoralist. *Journal of the Royal Western Australian Historical Society*, 1982; 8: 64

61 Barker, A.J., *The WACA: An Australian Cricket Success Story,* Allen and Unwin, Sydney, 1998. pp.22-25

62 Bush, R.E., *Journals 1878 and 1879-80.* J.S. Battye Library of Western Australian History, Perth,.Western Australia.

63 Harte, C., *The History of Australian Cricket*, Carlton Books, London, 2008. pp.32-4 and p.58

64 Cricket and Football, *Western Mail Special Centenary Edition*, January 5, 1933. p.50

65 This may have been the younger brother of his future father-in-law Dr Edward Scott

66 *Northern Times,* Carnarvon, Western Australia, July 5, 1913.

67 In 1911 the National Census records them as living in Kensington, where Robert Edwin and his wife now had a flat but his wife's parents later lived in Stoke Bishop, only a few hundred yards from Bishop's Knoll. Her father is reported as practising medicine in Clifton for a few years before dying in Stoke Bishop in 1920.

68 Census of England and Wales,1911

69 In his obituary Powell says he served as a Director of Dalgety's for 27 years

70 Bristol Reference Library. Acquisition number B28421/ SR37, Vol. 1,2

71 When he demitted office the Council passed a formal a vote of thanks in recognition for the energy and diligence with which he had served.

72 Each battalion of fewer than 1000 men had a regimental medical officer and 16 stretcher bearers this increased to 32 during a major attack.

73 Scotland, R., The war on wounds. *Surgeons News,* Royal College of Surgeons of Edinburgh, June 2015, pp.30-33

74 By this time Robert Edwin Bush was living within sight of Sir George White's estate of Old Sneed Park.

75 The 1st Southern General was at Selly Oak Birmingham (See http://www.1914-1918.net/hospitals_uk.htm)

76 In November 1876 he played rugby as one of the two backs for the Medical School in their game against Clifton. The other back was Mungo Smith who was to go on to write the history of the Bristol Infirmary. In November 1885 these two applied for the vacant post of Assistant Surgeon at the Bristol Infirmary in which Bush was successful having had the advantage of previously serving as House Surgeon, House Physician and Senior Resident Medical Officer there. Mungo Smith was also a later a Lt Col. in the RAMC (T).

77 Smith, T.M., *A history of the Bristol Royal Infirmary,* J.W. Arrowsmith, Bristol, 1917. p.364, 405

78 This was funded by Mr Alfred Mosely C.M.G., LL.D, a wealthy philanthropist who had been born in Bristol. Having acquired a fortune from a claim in the South African diamond field, he was able

to retire at an early age and devote the rest of his life to the furtherance of progress in British education. He also funded the bust of Cecil Rhodes at 6, King Edward St, Oxford and the memorial on Plymouth Hoe to the West Country soldiers who fell in the South African War.

79 Smith, T.M., *A history of the Bristol Royal Infirmary*, J.W. Arrowsmith, Bristol, 1917. p.413

80 Ibid, p.459

81 It was not until April 1917 that Paul Bush joined the regular army when he accepted the post of Officer Commanding the 56th Southern General Hospital, B.E.F. and left for France taking with him a large number of medical officers, nurses and R.A.M.C. staff. He received the CBE in 1919.

82 This may have been the reason why his brother converted Bishop's Knoll so early in the War.

83 As has been mentioned Robert Edwin Bush had served on the fund raising committee.

84 Eventually Southmead hospital contained more than 1300 beds, a quarter of these in tented accommodation.

85 Butler, A.G., *Australian Dictionary of Biography,* Melbourne University Press, Melbourne,1966.

86 Booth, C., *ANZAC soldiers in Bristol* in Bristol and the First World War - The Great Reading Adventure 2014 Bristol Cultural Development Partnership for Bristol, 2014 (http://www.bristol2014.com/assets/files/reading-adventure/Great_Reading_Adventure_Book.pdf)

87 Two Australian divisions and one New Zealand Division.

88 *Adelaide Advertiser,* October 1, 1914, p.8

89 Programme of the Matinee in aid of the Australian wounded soldiers. His Majesty's Theatre, London, November 19th, 1915

90 Beckett, R. The Australian Solder in Britain, 1914-1918. in *Australians in Britain : The Twentieth Century Experience.* Bridge, C; Crawford, R; Dunstan, D. (Eds), Monash University ePress, 2009.

91 State Records Office of Western Australia http://www.sro.wa.gov.au/archive-collection/exhibitions-online/world-war-1-wa-tipsified-germany-glyphic. Accessed June 24, 2015

92 *"Coo-ee!"* Vol.1 No.1 p.14; (Leigh Woods was A.G.Powell its editor)

93 Almost certainly W.G. Grace and Bush's brother James Arthur who had been his best man and who had accompanied W.G to Australia in 1874.

94 Letter from War Office Ref. Medical 12127 (F4) dated 30/12/1914 to G.O.C., Southern Command, Salisbury

95 Powell, A.G., *A short history of Bishop's Knoll Hospital,* Van Dyke Printers, Bristol, 1930. p.7

96 Bishop's Knoll Hospital, *Bristol at War*, October 1915 p.3

97 *"Coo-ee!"* Vol.1 No.1 p.31

98 By the end of the War there were over 3,000 auxiliary hospitals in the UK administered by Red Cross.

99 Overall in Bristol,South Wales, Gloucestershire, Somerset and Wiltshire there were over 130 hospitals providing 18,000 beds

100 Sandes, J., Mr Robert Bush at Bishop's Knoll. *Sydney Morning Herald,* September 18, 1926, p.13

101 Friend of the wounded, *Melbourne Argus,* June 16, 1919

102 Postcard from Mrs Grieg of Sydney to Mr Bush, dated May 28, 1919. Bristol Reference Library. Acquisition number B28421/ SR37, Vol. 2

103 Powell, A.G., *A short history of Bishop's Knoll Hospital,* Van Dyke Printers, Bristol, 1930. p.10

104 *"Coo-ee!"* Vol.1 No.1 p.31

105 Powell, A.G., *A short history of Bishop's Knoll Hospital,* Van Dyke Printers, Bristol, 1930. p.8

106 Ibid p.26

107 *"Coo-ee!"* Vol. 1 No.10 p.15

108 London Gazette, October 28, 1927, Issue 33324, p.6807,

109 Letter August 14, 1914. held in the Bristol Reference Library. Acquisition number B28421/ SR37, Vol.1

110 *"Coo-ee!"* Vol. 1 No. 5 p.20

111 Sandes, J., Mr Robert Bush at Bishop's Knoll. *Sydney Morning Herald,* September 18, 1926, p.13

112 The Oak estate had been owned by Thomas Yandell Venn (1810-1882) a ship owner. When he died his unmarried daughter Sarah Jane lived on there till

1901; but died in Barton Regis later that year.

113 Chapman, M., Jetzer, P., *An historic landscape survey of Bishop's Knoll historic garden,* Avon County Planning Department, 1995, p.5

114 *"Coo-ee!"* Vol.1 No.4 p.25

115 See Carden-Coyne, A. *Politics of Wounds –Military Patients and Military Power in the First World War.* Oxford University Press, Oxford, 2014. pp.245-247

116 *"Coo-ee!"* Vol.1 No.4 p.27

117 *Western Daily Press* April 27, 1931. p.3

118 He not only played for hymn singing in the Ward but is recorded in the Grand Concert of November 30, 1915 as opening the programme with a Grand Organ Overture. It seems likely that he learned to play the organ at school where Mr Trimnell had become the first organist and choir master at Clifton College in 1864.

119 Letter from J.W. Arrowsmith Ltd., to J.A. Ferguson, February 25, 1920. Bristol Reference Library. Acquistion number B28421/ SR37, Vol. 1

120 See http://nla.gov.au/nla.obj-6935540/view#page/n29/mode/1u

121 Letter March 28th 1919, held in the Bristol Reference Library. Acquisition number B28421/ SR37, Vol. 1

122 Powell, A.G., *A short history of Bishop's Knoll Hospital,* Van Dyke Printers, Bristol, 1930. pp.52-3

123 *"Coo-ee!"* Vol.1 No.1 p.48

124 Meredith, J., *The Coo-ee March: Gilgandra – Sydney 1915.* Macquarie Publications, Dubbo, New South Wales, 1981.

125 The Bristol Chronicle of April 1915 reported that: "The hall (of Bristol Grammar School) was resplendently decorated, free of charge, by Messrs. Partridge & Love, Ltd." This firm would also publish the Wills Works Magazine and the Fry Works Magazine after the War.

126 *"Coo-ee!"* Vol.1 No.3 p.38

127 http://www.scoop-database.com/

128 The BUP would later take over the Bristol Evening World from Lord Rothermere and be responsible for publishing both the Western Daily Press and the Bristol Evening Post.

129 http://cricketarchive.com/Archive/Scorecards/265/265847.html . Accessed November 26, 2015

130 Powell, A.G., *The Graces (E.M., W.G., and G.F.),* Cedric Chivers, Portway, Bath, 1974. (First published 1948)

131 One of his sons born 1896.

132 *"Coo-ee!"* Vol.1 No. 2 p.15

133 *"Coo-ee!"* Vol.1 No. 11 p.13

134 *"Coo-ee!"* Vol.1 No. 1 p.21; Archibald Powell would write three articles on dogs for *"Coo-ee!"*, "Dogs Tails", "Village Scamp" and "Ratting".

135 *"Coo-ee!"* Vol.1 No.6 p.1

136 *"Coo-ee!"* Vol.1 No.12 p.1

137 Stone, G.F., Wells, C., *Bristol and the Great War 1914-1919,* J.W. Arrowsmith, Bristol, 1920. p.365

138 There are two soldiers of this name (6070 and 9947) but neither appears on the Australian War Memorial Roll of Honour so it would appear that he did survive the war.

139 *"Coo-ee!"* Vol.1 No.2 p.1

140 *"Coo-ee!"* Vol.1 No.2 p.1

141 See http://nla.gov.au/nla.obj-8447243/view#

142 *"Coo-ee!"* Vol.1 No.2 pp.10-12

143 *"Coo-ee!"* Vol.1 No.1 pp.30-31

144 Westbook, F.E., *Anzac and after, a collection of poems,* Duckworth and Co., London, 1916. p.47

145 He is now remembered as the Editor of the 12-volume *Official History of Australia in the War of 1914–1918*

146 i.e. Move into an area

147 *"Coo-ee!"* Vol.1 No.1 p.42

148 *"Coo-ee!"* Vol.1 No.9 pp.27-8

149 *"Coo-ee!"* Vol.1 No.1 pp.23-4

150 *"Coo-ee!"* Vol.1 No.3 p.3

151 *"Coo-ee!"* Vol.1 No.2 pp.7-8

152 *"Coo-ee!"* Vol.1 No.5 p.30

153 *"Coo-ee!"* Vol.1 No.2 pp.33-4

154 *"Coo-ee!"* Vol.1 No.1 p.31

155 *"Coo-ee!"* Vol.1 No.9 p.21

156 *"Coo-ee!"* Vol.1 No.7 pp.21-3

157 *"Coo-ee!"* Vol.1 No.7 p.23

158 *"Coo-ee!"* Vol.1 No.8 pp.24-5

159 Letter to R.E Bush dated July 15, 1915, Bristol Reference Library. Acquisition number B28421/ SR37, Vol. 1

160 *"Coo-ee!"* Vol.1 No.9 pp.6-8

161 *"Coo-ee!"* Vol.1 No.5 p.2

162 *"Coo-ee!"* Vol.1 No.8 p.36

163 *"Coo-ee!"* Vol.1 No.8 pp.20-3

164 *"Coo-ee!"* Vol.1 No.7 pp.32-3

165 *"Coo-ee!"* Vol.1 No.3 p.27
166 *"Coo-ee!"* Vol.1 No.3 pp.19-21
167 Lieutenant-Colonel Arthur John Bigge, 1st Baron Stamfordham (1849-1931) was a British soldier and was Private Secretary to George V during most of his reign.
168 Sir Frederick George Milner, (1849 –1931) was a British Conservative Party politician who sat in the House of Commons from 1883 to 1885, and from 1890 to 1906 In 1906 Milner retired from politics due to problems with his hearing, but continued with his work to help ex-servicemen.
169 *"Coo-ee!"* Vol.1 No.4 pp.16-7
170 *"Coo-ee!"* Vol.1 No.1 p.48.
171 *"Coo-ee!"* Vol.1 No.2 p.20-22
172 *"Coo-ee!"* Vol.1 No.4 p.31
173 *"Coo-ee!"* Vol.1 No.2 p.40
174 *"Coo-ee!"* Vol.1 No.8 pp.13-5
175 Potatoes at the time were in extremely short supply. Curiously while there were potato famines in Australia and Germany at this time none was reported in England.
176 *"Coo-ee!"* Vol.1 No.3 p.14
177 *"Coo-ee!"* Vol.1 No.4 pp.32-3
178 *"Coo-ee!"* Vol.1 No.1 pp.44-5
179 *"Coo-ee!"* Vol.1 No.10 p.14
180 *"Coo-ee!"* Vol.1 No.1 pp.12-3
181 *"Coo-ee!"* Vol.1 No.2 pp.4-6
182 *"Coo-ee!"* Vol.1 No.3 pp.4-5
183 *"Coo-ee!"* Vol.1 No.3 pp.31-33
184 *"Coo-ee!"* Vol.1 No.8 p.31
185 The Battle of Lone Pine, also known as the Battle of Kanli Sirt, was fought between Australian and Turkish forces between 6 and 10 August 1915. The battle was part of a diversionary attack to draw Ottoman attention away from the main Gallipoli assaults.
186 *"Coo-ee!"* Vol.1 No.7 p.30
187 Bristol Reference Library. Acquisition number B28421/ SR37, Vol. 1
188 *"Coo-ee!"* Vol.1 No.1 p.28
189 Thomas James "Rusty" Richards, of Cornish extraction, was the only Rugby Union player to represent both Australia and the British Lions. The Tom Richard Trophy, named in his honour, is an international rugby union trophy awarded to the winner of British and Irish Lions vs. Australia test series. It was commissioned for the 2001 British Lions tour to Australia. Richards fought in both Gallipoli and the Western Front and achieved the rank of Lieutenant and was awarded the Military Cross in August 1917.
190 This was late 19th century keyboard instrument in which a series of steel tuning forks were struck by hammers. It was superseded by the celesta.
191 Private Fleming later lost his life in action – see "Gone West"
192 *"Coo-ee!"* Vol.1 No.1 p.29
193 *"Coo-ee!"* Vol.1 No.2 p.34
194 *"Coo-ee!"* Vol.1 No.4 p.25
195 *"Coo-ee!"* Vol.1 No.6 p.19
196 Brodsworth Hall, near Doncaster, a Victorian Grade 1 listed house, was requisitioned as an auxiliary WW1 hospital.
197 Worget camp, Wareham became a muster point for territorial soldiers and Australian and New Zealand troops. Perham Down (nicknamed Perishing Down) between Tidworth & Ludgershall was one of the camps on Salisbury Plain.
198 A large camp on Salisbury Plain close to Stonehenge which was established 1899. Now a garrison town.
199 *"Coo-ee!"* Vol.1 No.7 pp.25-6
200 *"Coo-ee!"* Vol.1 No.8 pp.27-8
201 *"Coo-ee!"* Vol.1 No.9 pp.10-11
202 *"Coo-ee!"* Vol.1 No.1 p.25
203 *"Coo-ee!"* Vol.1 No.2 pp.36-7
204 *"Coo-ee!"* Vol.1 No.6 p.19
205 *"Coo-ee!"* Vol.1 No.6 p.30
206 *"Coo-ee!"* Vol.1 No.3 pp.6-9
207 *"Coo-ee!"* Vol.1 No.7 p.35
208 *"Coo-ee!"* Vol.1 No. 9 pp.29-30
209 Wells, C., Stone, G.F., (Eds.), *Bristol and the Great War 1914-19*, J.W. Arrowsmith, Bristol, 1920. p.151
210 *"Coo-ee!"* Vol.1 No.4 p.35
211 *"Coo-ee!"* Vol.1 No.6 p.34
212 *"Coo-ee!"* Vol.1 No.5 pp.7-8
213 *"Coo-ee!"* Vol.1 No.11 p.5
214 *Border Watch*, November 20, 1917. p 4
215 Bristol Reference Library. Acquisition number B28421/ SR37, Vol. 1
216 *"Coo-ee!"* Vol.1 No.12 pp.28-9
217 *"Coo-ee!"* Vol.1 No.2 p.12
218 *"Coo-ee!"* Vol.1 No.1 p.10
219 *"Coo-ee!"* Vol.1 No.1 p.33
220 *"Coo-ee!"* Vol.1 No.1 p.26
221 *"Coo-ee!"* Vol.1 No.3 p.5
222 *"Coo-ee!"* Vol.1 No.4 p.5

223 *"Coo-ee!"* Vol.1 No.8 p.30
224 *"Coo-ee!"* Vol.1 No.12 p.29
225 *"Coo-ee!"* Vol.1 No.3 p.34
226 *"Coo-ee!"* Vol.1 No.3 p.3
227 *Clifton College Register 1862-1912,* J.W. Arrowsmith, Bristol, 1912. p XV
228 *"Coo-ee!"* Vol.1 No.4 p.2
229 *"Coo-ee!"* Vol.1 No.7 p.36
230 Letters held by the Bristol Reference Library. Acquisition number B28421/ SR37, Vol. 1
231 *"Coo-ee!"* Vol.1 No.9 p.5
232 *"Coo-ee!"* Vol.1 No.9 p.5
233 Powell, A.G.,*A short history of Bishop's Knoll Hospital,* Van Dyke Printers, Bristol, 1930. pp.42-4
234 Stone, G.F., Wells, C., *Bristol and the Great War. 1914-1919,* J. W. Arrowsmith, Bristol, 1920. p.370
235 The "Lapland" sailed to New York and then they took the "Sonoma" from San Francisco
236 Bush, R.E., *Address to Red Cross March 2nd 1920,* Bristol Reference Library. Acquisition number B28421/ SR37, Vol.2
237 Stone, G.F., Wells, C., *Bristol and the Great War 1914-1919,* J. W. Arrowsmith, Bristol, 1920. p.382
238 Letter January 14, 1920 held in the Bristol Reference Library. Acquisition number B28421/ SR37, Vol.2
239 Letter dated September 14, 1920, Bristol Reference Library. Acquisition number B28421/ SR37, Vol.2
240 *The Times,* October 14, 1922.
241 Stone, G.F., Wells, C., *Bristol and the Great War 1914-1919,* J. W. Arrowsmith, Bristol, 1920. p.346, 355, 363, and 380
242 *Bristol Times & Mirror.* October 22, 1921
243 The last annual service of this era was attended by his widow in 1940 but in 2015 a Centenary Service was held there.
244 Nevertheless during the period of the Fry ownership the Gloucestershire Club had played 100 matches there.
245 Report, Western Daily Press, June 7, 1922
246 In 1872 his father had been elected to the Committee of the newly reformed club.
247 War-time memories, *Mackay Daily Mercury,* August 31, 1938. p.6
248 Letter 14th June 1919 held by the Bristol Reference Library. Acquisition number B28421/ SR37, Vol.1
249 *Brisbane Courier,* Friday March 3, 1922, p.6
250 *Sydney Morning Herald,* September 6, 1926, p.10
251 Passenger List, Orvieto, 4/9/26 and 5/10/26
252 McDonald, R., *Winning the Gascoyne,* Hesperian Press, Carlisle, Western Australia, 2008. pp.25-6
253 *MacKay Daily Mercury,* August 30, 1938.
254 Gunning, F.W., Robert Edward (sic) Bush, Last of the Gascoyne Pioneers, *Western Australian,* January 6, 1940. p 5. (Gunning's book *The Lure of the North - Seventy Years' Memoirs of George Joseph Gooch and his Pioneer Friends of Western Australia.* was published in 1952.)
255 An early English country dance, also known as *The Haymakers.*
256 These were given to the Bristol Zoo when he died.
257 *The Times,* January 2, 1940
258 Born France in 1874. The 1911 census records him as Commander R.N., living in Hampstead with his wife Antonia Harriet née Lander, born 1876 and a 4 year old daughter, Antonia Harriet Bush. He died in 1949
259 Diana had married a cousin Flt Lt Francis Colin Scott in Bristol in 1939 who died a year later in October 1940.
260 This would seem to imply that Mrs Bush left the visitors book in the house when she left.
261 See http://www.britishpathe.com/video/royal-visit-to-bristol-and-liverpool/query/LIVERPOOLS+OLD
262 Rutherford, D. (Australian War Memorial, Canberra.) Personal Communication, April 11, 2016
263 *"Coo-ee!"* Vol.1 No.3 p. 2
264 The Australian War Contingent Association. *The Advertiser,* Adelaide, Monday July 24, 1916
265 Powell, A.G., *A short history of Bishop's Knoll Hospital,* Van Dyke Printers, Bristol, 1930. pp.33-4
266 Ibid p. 59
267 *"Coo-ee!"* Vol.1 No.7 p.36
268 Bristol Reference Library. Acquisition number B28421/ SR37, Vol.1
269 Telegram from the War Office dated September 7, 1914 held by the Bristol Reference Library. Acquisition number B28421/ SR37, Vol.1

PICTURE CREDITS

KEY

BRO = Bristol Record Office

BLS = Bristol Library Service

p21 Ordnance Survey 1880
p22 Top: BRO 35893/29/b (4), bottom: BRO 35893/29/b (16)
p23 Clifton College Archive
p24 Chris Stephens
p25 BRO 43207/17/010
p27 Clifton Rugby Club Archive
p28 Tessa Kerry
p29 Chris Stephens
p33 Chris Stephens
p42 Tessa Kerry
p43 Tessa Kerry
p44 Top & bottom: Tessa Kerry
p45 Tessa Kerry
p47 Top: Western Daily Press of Australia 1930, bottom: BRO 35893/29/b (13)
p48 BLS B28421 Vol 1
p49 Chris Stephens
p50 BLS B28421 Vol 1
p54 BLS 100216-164/5
p55 BLS B28421
p56 BRO 43207/9/47/014
p57 Stone, G F, Wells, C. *Bristol and the Great War 1914-1919*, J W Arrowsmith, Bristol 1920
p59 BLS B28421
p60 Clive Burlton
p64 BLS B28421
p66 BLS B28421
p67 BLS B28421
p69 BRO 11176/1
p70 Top: Tessa Kerry (colour photo album), bottom: BRO 43207/9/49/31
p71 Top: Tessa Kerry (colour photo album), bottom: BRO PicBox/7A/WW1/3
p72 Top: BRO 35893/29/b (11), bottom: BLS B28421
p73 Top: BRO 35893/29/b (14), bottom: Tessa Kerry
p74 Top: BRO 35893/29/b (13), bottom: Tessa Kerry
p76 BRO 11176/1
p77 BLS B28421
p78 BLS B28421
p79 Top left: BLS B28421, top right: Coo-ee Vol 1 No 10, middle three: Tessa Kerry (colour photo album)
p80 Coo-ee Vol 1 No 8
p82 Top & bottom: BLS B28421
p83 Tessa Kerry
p84 Tozer collection - part of the archives of the Sneyd Park Local History Group
p88 & p89 BLS B28421
p90 Top: BLS B28421, middle: BLS B28421, bottom: BRO 43207/22/14/001
p91 Top: BLS B28421, middle: BRO 17563/1/0063, bottom: Tessa Kerry (colour photo album)
p93 Chris Stephens
p95 BLS B28421
p96 Coo-ee Vol 1 No 1
p98 Coo-ee Vol 1 No 11

p100 BLS B28421
p102 Coo-ee Vol 1 No 2
p109 BLS B28421
p111 Coo-ee Vol 1 No 1
p119 Coo-ee Vol 1
p127 BLS B28421
p129 BLS B28421
p131 BLS B28421
p133 BLS B28421
p137 Coo-ee Vol 1 No 8
p140 Coo-ee Vol 1 No 10
p141 BLS B28421
p146 Left & right: BLS B28421
p147 Left & right: BLS B28421
p149 Left & right: BLS B28421
p150 BLS B28421
p153 BLS B28421
p154 BLS B28421
p156 George Morley
p158 Coo-ee Vol 1 No 4
p159 BRO 43207/9/50/28
p160 Coo-ee Vol 1 No 4
p167 BLS B28421
p169 Coo-ee Vol 1 No 8
p171 Coo-ee Vol 1 No 1
p174 BLS B28421
p177 BLS B28421
p178 Coo-ee Vol 1 No 10
p180 BLS B28421
p182 BLS B28421
p183 Top: BLS B28421, bottom: Coo-ee Vol 1 No 1
p184 BLS B28421
p188 BLS B28421
p189 BLS B28421
p190 BRO 36819 (14)
p191 Tessa Kerry
p192 Tessa Kerry
p194 BRO 36819/7/p39
p195 Top - BRO 36819/7/p40
p195 Bottom - BRO 36819/7/p6
p196 Top: BRO 36819/7/p47, bottom: BLS B28421
p202 BLS B28421
p206 Coo-ee Vol 1 No 7
p208 Left: Coo-ee Vol 1 No 8, middle: Coo-ee Vol 1 No 8, right: Coo-ee Vol 1 No 8
p210 Left: Coo-ee Vol 1 No 9, middle: Coo-ee Vol 1 No 9, right: Coo-ee Vol 1 No 9
p211 Coo-ee Vol 1 No 9
p213 Coo-ee Vol 1 No 11
p216 Top: Coo-ee Vol 1 No 12, bottom: Coo-ee Vol 1 No 12
p218 Coo-ee Vol 1 No 2
p219 BLS B28421
p220 Coo-ee Vol 1 No 1
p222 Top: Coo-ee Vol 1 No 2, p222 Bottom: Coo-ee Vol 1 No 2
p223 Coo-ee Vol 1 No 6
p224 Coo-ee Vol 1 No 3
p225 Coo-ee Vol 1 No 3
p226 Coo-ee Vol 1 No 3
p227 Coo-ee Vol 1 No 3
p243 Coo-ee Vol 1 No 8
p252 Coo-ee Vol 1 No 1
p260 BLS B28421
p262 BLS B28421
p263 Chris Stephens
p264 BRO 43207/37/4/1/3
p265 Top: BLS B28421, bottom: BLS B28421
p271 Chris Stephens
p272 Chris Stephens
p273 Margaret Slade (nee Norton)
p274 Margaret Slade (nee Norton)
p275 George Morley
p276 Top & bottom: Chris Stephens
p280 Top & bottom: Chris Stephens

BRISTOL RECORD OFFICE AND BRISTOL REFERENCE LIBRARY ACKNOWLEDGEMENT

Bristol Books Community Interest Company and the author, Chris Stephens take this opportunity to thank the staff at both Bristol Record Office and Bristol Reference Library for their help throughout the research and production phases of *Bristol's Australian Pioneer*.

Authors, publishers and researchers would not be able to tell untold stories without the professionalism of archivists, curators and librarians who care for and make available the amazing collection of documents, photographs and objects that are held across the City's publicly funded institutions.

It is crucial to the cultural heritage and well-being of the City of Bristol that these institutions survive and are allowed to flourish and develop in the future.

APPENDICES

APPENDIX 1

The Children of Robert Edwin Bush

1. Of his first marriage to Constance Harper née Lochée (1893)

Charlotte Lochée Bush born April 2, 1894 in Perth died April 1993 in Bristol.

Robert Francis Lochée Bush was born May 15, 1896 in Perth and educated like other male members of the family at Clifton College. He left the College in 1914 and became a gentleman cadet in the Royal Military Academy Woolwich, passing out as a Second Lieutenant in the Royal Artillery in February 1915. He then served in France and Belgium, was wounded twice and mentioned in despatches in 1917. From June 1917 to March 1918 he served as observer in the Royal Flying Corps with the rank of acting Captain. (He took a pilots course but did not pass.) Between the wars he served in Palestine, Egypt and India with the rank of Major. In September 1939, now an Acting Lieutenant Colonel, he embarked for France with the BEF and was evacuated from Dunkirk. By 1940 he was the Commanding Officer of the 23rd Field Regiment Royal Artillery and finished up in Norway at the end of the war. He retired in June 1948 with the rank of Brigadier. He visited Australia in 1950 sailing on January 5 of that year and died November 21, 1955 in Salisbury, UK.

Of his second marriage to Marjorie Scott (1907)

Marjory Elizabeth (Betty) Bush Born April 1, 1908; died April 1990, Bullingdon, Oxfordshire.

Family in 1922. L-R): Mrs Marjery Bush, Richard Edwin Bush, Paul Tobin Bush (Tobin), John Edward Bush, Diana Mary Bush.

John Edward Scott Bush, was born on April 2, 1909 in Bristol. He was educated at Clifton College from 1922 to 1927. He married Patricia Marriott and became a Lieutenant Commander in the Navy. He died on HMS *Kipling* during the evacuation of Crete on May 23, 1941.

Diana Mary Bush, born in 1914. She married Francis Colin Scott on the November 13, 1939 and died suddenly at Overton, Lyme Regis on the March 5, 1959.

Paul Tobin Bush born on March 30, 1916 in Bristol. He was educated at Clifton College from 1929 to 1934. He went to Sandhurst and then joined the Royal Scots Fusiliers. In the Second World War he was a Captain in the RASC and then a Lieutenant in the Army Air Corps. He died in 1973.

Richard Edwin Bush born on April 17, 1921. He was educated at Clifton College from 1930 to 1934. He was then a Pilot Officer in the RAF and was reported missing, believed killed in April 1942. He is commemorated on the Runnymeade Memorial.

APPENDIX 2

The Census of England and Wales 1911

Flat 25 Kensington Court Mansions, London (a large 4 bedroom flat costing £3.7M in 2014)

Occupants

Robert Edwin Bush 55 yrs
Mrs Marjery Bush 26 yrs
Marjory Elizabeth Bush 3 yrs
John Edward Scott Bush 2 yrs
Rebecca Ann Ivory 54 yrs (Nurse/domestic)
Beatrice Florence Plowman 22 yrs (Housemaid)
Mary Ellen Hunt 29 yrs (Parlourmaid)

Bishop's Knoll, Bristol

Occupants

a) The House – none

b) The Lodge Bishop's Knoll 1*
William Charles Pidgeon 35 yrs (Gardener, Domestic)
Alice Pidgeon 32 yrs (Wife)
Edith Pidgeon 8 yrs (Daughter)

c) The Lodge Bishop's Knoll 2*
Charles Lapham 53yrs (Coachman)
Martha Lapham 59 yrs (wife)
Herbert Percy Lapham 20 yrs (Groom, domestic)
Frederick Pollard 21 yrs(Boarder, Chauffeur, domestic)

* As there is only one Lodge the term "The Lodge Bishops 2" is rather confusing since Lodge 1 appears to be the Gardeners Cottage

Occupants of The Oaks, Bristol

None

a) Oak Lodge

Henry Sweeting 52 yrs (Market gardener)

Mary Sweeting 49 yrs (Wife)

William Henry Sweeting 21 yrs (Son, gardener, domestic)

Beatrice Sweeting 20 yrs (Daughter, school teacher)

Elise Sweeting 18 yrs (Shop Assistant)

Walter Stanley Sweeting 15 yrs (Son, gardener assisting father)

APPENDIX 3

General William Riddell Birdwood GCB, GCSI, GCMG, GCVO, CIE, DSO

Quite apart form his remarkable military and later academic career as Master of Peterhouse, General Birdwood, later Field Marshal Lord Birdwood of ANZAC, was a man of great humanity. He was also another old Cliftonian though 10 years younger than Robert Edwin Bush.

In 1916 Archibald Powell wrote of him:

"It would not be easy to name another officer of high rank in the army of the Empire who is more beloved by all ranks than General W.R. Birdwood. In the great adventure on Gallipoli he was, to quote Sir Ian Hamilton's despatches, *"The soul of Anzac. Not for one day has he ever quitted his post. Cheery and full of human sympathy he had spent many hours in each twenty-four inspiring the defenders of the front trenches, and if he does not know every soldier in his force, at least every soldier in his force believes he is known to his chief"*. Only a day or two ago I was yarning after supper with one of non-commissioned rank who took a hand in some of the hottest of the early fighting on the Peninsula, and he assured me that the General, dressed like the rankers, in shorts and a khaki tunic, spent most of his time in the front trenches, and he had a word for almost every man. Once he paused for a moment, and watched a man overhauling his clothes, and putting out of action the hosts of his tormentors.

"Catch many?" asked the General. "Millions," said the soldier. "So do I," replied the General."[263]

APPENDIX 4

This notice appeared in the Adelaide Advertiser on Monday July 24, 1916

AUSTRALIAN WAR CONTINGENT ASSOCIATION.

We are asked to publish the following information concerning the Australian War Contingent Association, 50, Palace Street, London, England, which was formed at the commencement of the war at the instigation of the British Government:— Since its formation the association has spent over £15,000 in comforts, special provisions, tobacco, personal kit, clothing, souvenir chocolate at Christmas, social care, reading matter, excursions and entertainments, games, outfits, and in many other directions, for troops in the fighting areas and in England. It has also organised and carries on systematic visiting of hospitals and workrooms for ladies; has arranged visits of hundreds of officers and men to private homes throughout Great Britain; acted as Information Bureau and forwarding agents; and is now officially appointed to receive and forward exempted durtable (sic; likely to have meant those exempt from excise duty) gifts from Australia for Australians in British regiments stationed in Great Britain or in the British Navy; such gifts to be collected in Australia, where information is published thereon. The association wants more illustrated and other weeklies for troops and welcomes any work for the Australian troops or their relatives. The High Commissioner of the Commonwealth is the president. General Sir Newton Moore (Agent General for Western Australia) the chairman, and all the Agents General and their wives, Lady Birdwood and others are on the executive committee.[264]

APPENDIX 5

Qualification of the Doctors of Bishop's Knoll Hospital (Medical Register, 1919)

KYLE, Henry Greville MB BCh U Oxford. (1899) Later MD.
31, Westbury Road Bristol

LEES Edwin Leonard, MRCS Eng (1885); MBCM (1885), MD (1890) Edin.
Chesterfield House, Queens Road, Clifton

PARSONS Henry Francis MRCS London, LRCP Eng (1897).
The Heath, Snede Park, Bristol

ORMEROD Henry Lawrence LRCP London, MRCS Eng (1889); MBBS (1893), MD (1896) RU Ireland
Westbury on Trym, Bristol

MYLES George Thomas MRCS (1884), LRCP Edin (1884)
147 Whiteladies Road, Clifton.

APPENDIX 6

The complete list of staff who worked at Bishop's Knoll Hospital 1914-1918

Mr R.E. Bush Commandant
Mrs M. Bush Quartermaster
Bishop Clifford Chaplain

Nurses and VADs

Miss G. Prout (Sister in charge)
Miss A.M. Hall-Houghton
Miss M.M. Lambert
Miss E.K. Collen
Mrs Crawley
Miss E. Jenkins
Miss Masoli
Miss A. Moretti
Miss Haines
Miss H.C. Hardy
Mrs M.E. Herapath
Miss H.M.S. Allen
Miss J. Annandale
Mrs G. Green Armytage
Miss E. M. A. Atchley
Miss R. Atchley
Miss N. Austin
Mrs Bamberger
Miss B. Barnard
Miss T.M. Bayley
Miss A.E. Bertish
Miss Briggs
Miss H. Browne
Miss W. Browne
Miss D.M. Burt
Miss N.H. Burt
Mrs Burbey
Miss C. Bush
Mrs G.M. Carter
Mrs J. Chapman
Miss G. Coad
Miss C. Colthurst
Miss A.N. Cook
Mrs K. Cruddas
Miss H.M. D'Arcy
Mrs A.M. Davis
Miss Hart Dyke
Miss A.M. Ennis
Mrs Gibbs
Miss D. Goss
Miss Gouldsmith
Miss Gunter
Miss Holman
Miss Huddleston
Miss M. Jenkins
Miss L. Stafford Jones
Miss M.J. Laing
Mrs Lavington
Mrs Lecky
Mrs H. Morris
Miss Montague
Mrs D. Mortimer
Mrs D. Nicholls
Miss A. Parsons
Mrs M. Pascoe
Miss C.M. Philp,
Mrs A. Phillips
Miss R. Ransford
Mrs Richards
Miss E. H. Ruddock
Miss V.M. Savile
Mrs Skull.
Miss E. Bostock Smith
Miss D. Spofforth
Miss E. Spofforth
Miss N. Spofforth
Miss B. Stoddart
Miss D. K. Strachan
Miss A. Style
Miss K. Swinton
Miss M.E. Swinton
Miss F.J. Thornley
Miss Williamson
Miss D.J. Were
Mrs Lindrea
Mr Alway
Mr Boucher
Mr Forward
Mr D. Marshall Gay
Rev F. Norton
Mr Williams
Mr Crump
Mr Philp
Mr Morris

Doctors

Dr Nixon
Dr Myles
Dr Ormerod
Dr Parsons
Dr Leonard Lees
Dr Rendle Short
Captain Kyle

APPENDIX 7

Distinguished visitors to Bishop's Knoll Hospital 1914 - 1918[265]

After the War Archibald Powell was asked to produce a short history of the Bishop's Knoll Hospital by the Director of the Australian War Memorial for inclusion in its library at Melbourne.[266] Sadly this is only 59 pages long and reveals little more than that which had already been published in the "Coo-ee!" magazine's 12 issues. This is probably because Bush was always very reluctant for anything to be published about his personal role, as opposed to that of the Hospital which he always regarded as a team effort. However the book did include a list of "distinguished visitors". All these, like the patients, signed the Bishop's Knoll visitors book, but which sadly is now lost.

Commissioners and Agents General

The Rt Hon George Reid G.C.B., P.C., Australia's first High Commissioner in London.

Sir Thomas Mackenzie G.C.M.G., High Commissioner for New Zealand.

Sir Frederick Young, Agent General for South Australia.

Sir C.G. Wade, Agent General for New South Wales.

Sir Thomas Robinson G.B.F., K.C.M.G., Agent General for Queensland.

Sir B. R. Wise, Agent General for New South Wales.

Sir James Connolly, Agent General for West Australia.

Sir Peter McBride, Agent General for Victoria.

Sir John McCall, Agent General for Tasmania.

The Rt Hon Andrew Fisher, High Commissioner for Australia accompanied by a delegation of the Australian and New Zealand Press

George Fenwick, Dunedin, New Zealand.

R. D. Douglas Maclean, New Zealand.

M. I. Reading, Christchurch, New Zealand.

Frederick Fielding, New Zealand.

W. A. Whitehead, Victoria, Australia.

I. Mackintosh, Melbourne, Australia.

J. J. Knight, Brisbane, Australia.

Alfred Carson, Perth, Australia.

W. H. Simmonds, Hobart, Tasmania.

Military visitors

Major-General Sir George Younghusband K.C.I.F., C.B., K.C.M.G., Commander 7th (Meerut) Division (recently forced to relinquish this due to wounds).

General W.R. Birdwood G.C.B.,G.M.G., G.C.V.O., D.S.O., later Field Marshal Lord Birdwood.

Sir James Heath, Bt. Former M.P. for N Staffs and Captain in its Yeomanry was another old Cliftonian and had been another First XI cricketer there.

Rt Hon Sir Robert Borden, G.C.M.G.,P.C.

Sir Thomas Woodhouse, Southern Command.

Major-General Sir Newton Moore, K.C.M G General Officer Commanding AIF Depots, UK. would later become 8th Premier of Western Australia. [267] Sir Newton, who had been born in Freemantle in 1870, would have known Bush there.

Others

Mrs Hughes, wife of the Rt Hon W. Hughes, Prime Minister of Australia.

Sir James Carroll K.C.M.G., of New Zealand, Former Minister of Native Affairs.

Lord Morris, of Newfoundland, Prime Minister of Newfoundland's Wartime Government.

Another group of visitors to Bishop's Knoll, would have been unknown but for a letter from George H Clark, the Clifton Preparatory School's housemaster.[268]

40, College Road
Clifton, Bristol
21st June 1915

Dear Bush,

I am so grateful to you for letting the little chaps come over last night to Bishop's Knoll. Of course they are rather too young to realise unless they see: and I wanted them to see how close the War was to us and also (if you don't mind me saying it to your face) what a splendid use of his time and energy and money a public spirited man can make. After we went home to Prep I read them out what the Register had to say about the members of the Bush family. They won't forget and the visit will make a difference, though like ordinary healthy boys they won't say much. I wish I could have brought the whole 29 but a lot were out with their parents.

For myself I had the added delight of hearing so gifted a singer as M. Oumanoff. Many thanks for the opportunity, and I hope we weren't in the way.

Yours sincerely,

G.H. Clark

APPENDIX 8

Soldiers resident at Bishop's Knoll October 1916 - September 1917

Bush had been required to make daily returns to London of the numbers of sick officers and men.[269] It is not known if these still exist and what appeared in copies of "*Coo-ee!*" may well have been compiled from these.

It would seem that it was originally the intention to include in "*Coo-ee!*" the destination of those who had recovered sufficiently to return to active duty but this must have proved too much of a burden and was abandoned after the first month. There were still some British soldiers at Bishop's Knoll in the Autumn of 1916 but by the end of the year the residents were almost exclusively Australian.

The names of the men resident during each month between October 1916 and September 1917, together with their ranks, units and service numbers are shown in appendix 8.

OCTOBER 1916

TO LIGHT DUTY, October 3rd 1916

Dvr H. McAndrew	7th Bty., 3rd Bgd AFA	2289
W.H. Roberts	28th Bn	687
Pte S.S. Thomas	32nd att. 48th Bn AIF	2425

TO LIGHT DUTY, October 10th 1916

Pte B. Rowston	8th Bn AIF	3676
Pte W.H. Ball	32nd Bn AIF	440
Lce-Cpl N A. Hughes	53rd Bn AIF	3322
Spr J.Scott	7th Bn AIF	4343

TO LIGHT DUTY, OCTOBER 13th 1916

Cpl D. G. T. Woods	10th Bn AIF	145
Pte H. Jephcott	24th Bn AIF	2189
Pte R. Hardy	19th Bn A.I.F	2647
Pte J. Lyons	23rd att. 24th Bn AIF	3568
Gnr N. C. Hargreaves	15th Bty, 5th Bgd AFA	7592
Pte T. H. Whalen	18th Bn AIF	2837

TO DARTFORD, OCTOBER 13th 1916

Pte M. T. Davis	47th Bn, AIF	1647
Pte T. Brayshaw	27th Bn AIF	4047
Pte William Biggs	48th Bn AIF	3787
Pte A.J. Baker	12th Bn AIF	4757
Lce-Cpl J. Beale	60th Bn AIF	750
Spr J. McDonald	3rd Fld Co Aus Engrs	2523
Pte T. Cunnington	25th Bn AIF	2264
Pte J. Cranfield	17th Bn AIF	1682

TO LIGHT DUTY, OCTOBER, 23rd 1916

Lce-Cpl C.E. Clayton	12th Bn AIF	203
Pte S. Bennett	13th att. 45th Bn AIF	4732
Pte A. L. Gilberthorpe	53rd Bn AIF	4792

TO SOUTHALL, OCTOBER 23RD 1916

Pte A. E. Gell	24th Bn AIF	200
Pte R. A. Kolby	7th AMG Co.	646
Pte E. O'Neill	46th Bn AIF	4568
Pte C. F. Werner	AASC	1696
Pte F. V. Shepherd	2nd Bn AIF	4324
Pte W. H. O'Brien	18th Bn AIF	2517
Pte W. Way	45th Bn AIF	2976
Pte L. Bragg	17th Bn AIF	3768
Pte P. Cunneen	7th A.M.G. Co.	3073

Pte A. Walker	4th Bn AIF	2864
Pte G. W. Seamons	7th Bn AIF	4312
Pte J. Callow	24th att. 48th Bn AIF	3473
Pte N. Passmore	12th Bn AIF	4236
Pte G. F. Raffen	10th Bn AIF	5189
Pte W. J. Weekes	53rd Bn AIF	3648a
Pte W. Ichurn	45th Bn AIF	4209
Pte E. Salikis	5th Bn AIF	3545
Pte E. K. Payne	2nd Bn AIF	4571
Pte R. Rae	26th Bn AIF	4195

PATIENTS AT BISHOP'S KNOLL HOSPITAL DURING OCTOBER 1916.

Tpr J. Lennnox	N'thumberld Hussars Yeo	623
Tpr E. H. Combe- Robinson	3rd Co. Lond. Yeo	992
Pte J. P. Davies	RWF	1782
Pte C. J. Brewer	2nd A. Fld Ambulance AIF	4101
Pte M. Campbell	3rd Bn AIF	1924
Pte H. Hinkley	13th Bn AIF	4/3121
Pte F. G. Ross	18th Bn AIF	2197
Pte D. Davies	20th Bn AIF	410
Pte E. J. Brooks	1st Pioneer Bn	2787
Pte S. E. Baker	48th Bn AIF	5059
Pte J.W. Lovett	52nd Bn AIF	1680
Pte F. Jess	20th Bn AIF	3953
Pte R.C. Hooper	9th att. 47th Bn AIF	1779
Pte R. Wade	15th Bn AIF	3602
Lce-Cpl D. Stuart	20th Bn AIF	682
Pte R. Kay	12th Bn AIF	2712
Pte F. Flynn	19th Bn AIF	1185
Pte F.C. Moore	9th att. 49th Bn AIF	1867
Pte W. E. Murphy	10th att. 50th Bn AIF	1159
Sig C. Read	10th Bn AIF	2847b
Pte G. Wallace	21st Bn AIF	2832
Pte C. J. Kuntler	49th Bn AIF	1676
Pte J. Harrison	50th Bn AIF	3842
Pte H. Lamont	8th Bn AIF	3838
Pte B. J. Ashby	2nd Bn AIF	3684
Pte S. Hulme	4th Bgd H.Q.	4842
Pte B. F. Baird	23rd Bn AIF	3762
Pte D. W. Tullock	5th Bn AIF	4320
Driver J. Nisbet	4th Battery AFA	986
Pte F. Gray	22nd Bn AIF	2279
Pte H. Price	22nd Bn AIF	3901
Pte T. B. Pole	1st A. Field Ambulance	1828
Pte H. Buck	23rd Bn AIF	495
Pte C. Brown	4th Pioneer Bn	1816
Pte J. Walters	24th Bn AIF	754
Pte W. T. Fryer	9th att. 49th Bn AIF	3043
Pte S. Shaw	29th Bn AIF	936
Pte A. J. Hill	13th Bn AIF	4208
Pte F. Anderson	21st Bn AIF	4356
Cpl H. A. Allen	11th Bn AIF	2340

Pte T. de Raupak Ropenberg	22nd Bn AIF	4411
Pte V. P. Groom	AASC	1941
Gunner W. Matthew.	1st ADAC	11359
Pte D. A. Sheil	47th Bn AIF	4567
Pte J. K. Anderson	47th Bn AIF	5215
Cpl F. Bennett	1st A. Pioneers	3287
Pte H. W. Love	12th Bn AIF	1768
Pte E. W. Fraser	21st Bn AIF	4115
Pte C. Evans	12th Bn AIF	3135
CSM F. G. Turner	1st Bn AIF	213
Pte S. Downey	1st Bn AIF	5680
Pte A. H. Jcwell	24th Bn AIF	3850
Spr G. H. Bloor	1st Mining Co. AIF	498
Spr P. Dunn	1st Mining Co. AIF	989
Pte H. Wilson.	12th Bn AIF	4898
Tpr L. Taylor	4th ALH, 2nd Anzac Mtd. Reg.	1951
Pte L. Christie	32nd Bn AIF	2897
Pte E. Williams	10th Bn AIF	4633
Pte J. McNabb	8th Bn AIF	5412
Driver W. H. Smith	AASC	33
Driver B. Frank	AASC	6966
Pte H. G. Russon	5th att. 23rd Bn AIF	4481
Pte A.G. Winter	48th Bn AIF	1856
Pte F. T. White	13th Bn AIF	4341
Pte S. P. Brown	27th Bn AIF	1514
Pte C. Reay	22nd Bn AIF	526
Pte W. Goodall	2nd Canterb'y Inf.Bn N.Z.	6/1855
Pte E. Treloar	7th Bn AIF	35
Pte F. A. Thomas	2nd Bn AIF	3950
Pte S. A. Ellis	22nd Bn AIF	2458
Pte J. Barrett	20th Bn AIF	4364
Pte A. W. Higgins	28th Bn AIF	4131
Pte F. Jordan	10th Bn AIF	2391
Pte J. Ryan	28th Bn AIF	3252
Pte F. Jackson	24th Bn AIF	3995
Gunner E. Hayes	14th Battery AFA	7385
Pte J. Kerr	28th Bn AIF	462
Pte J. Orchard	2nd Pion'r Bn, late 5/9th Bn	2456
Pte G. Honey	24th Bn AIF	2150
Pte A. Clayton	56th Bn AIF	1630
Pte H. Holiday	56th Bn AIF	1671
Pte H. M. Power	6th Bn AIF	3425
Pte C. McKay	21st Bn AIF	2757
Pte H. Fisher	27th Bn AIF	4422
Pte G. E. Rowe	25th Bn AIF	3266
Cpl F. Lemmon	2nd Battery, 1st AFA	4617
Spr E. C. Stonehouse	5th att. 2nd A.Tunnelling Co.	4789
Pte S. N. Turner	19th Bn AIF	4256
Pte T. Delaney	25th Bn AIF	841
Pte J. White	25th Bn AIF	2016

NOVEMBER 1916

Pte M. Campbell	AIF	1924
Pte H. Hinkley	AIF	4/3121
Pte D. Davies	AIF	410
Pte E. J. Brooks	AIF	2787
Pte S. E. Baker	AIF	5059
Pte J. W. Lovett	AIF	1680
Pte F. Jess	AIF	3953
Pte R. C Hooper	AIF	1779
Pte W. J. Wade	AIF	3602
Lce-Cpl D. Stuart	AIF	682
Pte R. Karp	AIF	2712
Pte F. Flynn	AIF	1185
Pte F. C. Moore	AIF	1867
Pte W. E. Murphy	AIF	1159
Sig C. Read	AIF	2847b
Pte C. J. Kunkler	AIF	1676
Pte J. Harrison	AIF	3842
Pte H. Lamour	AIF	3838
Pte B. J. Ashby	AIF	3684
Bombr S. Hulme	AFA	2842
Pte B. F. Baird	AIF	3762
Pte D. W. Tulloch	AIF	4320
Dvr J. Nisbet	AFA	986
Cpl H. A. Allen	AIF	2340
Pte F. Gray	AIF	2279
Pte H. Price	AIF	3901
Pte T. B. Pole	AMB	1828
Pte H. Buck	AIF	495
Pte J. Walters	AIF	754
Pte W. T. Fryer	AIF	3043
Pte S. Shaw	AIF	936
Pte A. J. Hill	AIF	4208
Pte F. K. Anderson	AIF	4356
Pte J. R. de Ranpak	AIF	4411
Pte V. P. Groom	AASC	1941
Gnr W. Matthews	ADAC	11359
Pte D. Shiell	AIF	4567
Pte H. W. Love	AIF	1786
Pte E. W. Fraser	AIF	4115
Pte C. Evans	AIF	3135
CSM F. G. Turner	AIF	213
Pte S. Downey	AIF	5680
Pte A. H. Jewell	AIF	3850
Spr G. H. Bloor	AIF	408
Spr P. Dunn	AIF	989
Pte H. Wilson	AIF	4898
Tpr L. Taylor	ALH	1951
Pte L. Christie	AIF	2897
Pte E. Williams	AIF	4633
Pte J. McNabb	AIF	5412
Dvr W. H. Smith	AASC	33
Dvr B. Frank	AASC	6966
Pte H. G. Russon	AIF	4481
Pte A. G. Winter	AIF	1856
Pte F. T. White	AIF	4344
Pte S. P. Brown	AIF	1511
Pte C. Reay	AIF	526
Pte D. W. Goodall	Inf. BnN.Z.	6/1855
Pte C. J. Brewer	A.Field Amb.	4101
Pte E. Treloar	AIF	35
Pte F. A. Thomas	AIF	3950
Pte S. A. Ellis	AIF	2458
Pte J. Barrett	AIF	4364
Pte A. Higgins	AIF	4131
Pte F. Jordan	AIF	2391
Pte J. Ryan	AIF	3253
Pte F. Jackson	AIF	3995
Gnr E. Hayes	AFA	7385
Pte J. Kerr	AIF	462
Pte J. Orchard	AIF	2456
Pte G. A. Honey	AIF	2150
Pte A. Clayton	AIF	1630
Pte H. G. Holiday	AIF	1671
Pte H. M. Power	AIF	3425
Pte C. McKay	AIF	2757
Pte H. Fisher	AIF	4422
Pte G. E. Rowe	AIF	3206
Cpl F. Lemmon	AFA	4617
Spr E. C. Stonehouse	AFA	4789
Pte S. N. Turner	AIF	4256
Pte T. Delaney	AIF	841
Pte J. White	AIF	2016
Pte L. Everett-Norton	AIF	1808
Pte A. G. Davis	AIF	415
Pte J. H. Manwell	AIF	2898
Pte W. Clems	AIF	382
Pte W. J. Parker	AIF	2510
Pte J. Lee	AAMC	8814
Pte F. Lawler	AIF	1975
Pte W. A. Clifton	AIF	4391/180
Pte J. A. Kelly	AIF	1667
Pte T. Bell	AIF	2347
Pte P. L. Taylor	AIF	2460
Pte A. Reid	AIF	1722
Pte W. Gosling	AIF	4728
Pte W. H. Gifford	AIF	4105
Pte W. G. Hale	AIF	2694
Pte T. L. Hansen	AIF	1737
Sig D. K. Corderoy	AIF	4763
Pte H. C. Hollingsworth	AIF	2382
Pte P. S. Walker	AAMC	6118
Pte W. Warrender	AIF	3065
Pte E. L. Maguire	AIF	4168
Pte A. G. Whyte	AIF	4611

Pte A. Yapp	M.G. Co. AIF	92
Pte J. Symonds	AIF	1741
Pte J. Caffery	AIF	2607
Pte B. Francis	AAMC	1589
Sgt G. E. Bradshaw	AFA	1956
Cpl G. M. Udell	AIF	867
Pte H. W. Shean	AIF	4202
Cpl J. Davis	AIF	1207
Pte W. Trim	AIF	1736b
Pte J. O. Swift	AIF	2356
Pte F. G. Hull	AIF	4576
Pte W. Rogers	AIF	5485
Pte C. A. Wyndow	AIF	4790
Lce-Cpl C. W. Revell	AIF	2821
Pte H. Hollis	AIF	1551
Pte E. Blundell	AIF	2876
Pte A. O. Neill	AIF	4741
Pte G. Sterck	AIF	4776
Pte C. M. Smith	AIF	5765
Pte C. T. Smith	AIF	8183
Pte W. Fisher	AIF	2903
Pte N. K. Yeates	AIF	2486
Pte E. A. Plunkett	AIF	4509
Bombr. F. Corder	AFA	1736
Pte A. .J. E. Frewin	AIF	5393
Pte E. T. Bone	AIF	2294
Pte W. F. Ham	AIF	4452
Pte L. G. Hewitt	AIF	4449
Pte W. P. Price	AIF	1980
Pte F. .J. Burgess	AIF	2591
Pte J. B. Yate	AIF	4550
Pte A. Smithers	AIF	4244
Pte R. J. McWaters	AIF	4799
Pte M. Bazzina	AAMC	4431
Pte L. H. Edwards	AIF	5087
Pte W. G. Saville	AIF	4182
Pte H. Sievwright	AIF	4768
Pte J. A. Smith	AIF	2256
Pte J. H. Knevitt	AIF	4509
Pte G. B. Bradd	AIF	3385
Pte T. Chinnock	AIF	4622
Pte E. S. McPhee	AIF	1034
Lce-Cpl E. J. Lorentzen	AIF	1737
Pte L.R. Farndon	AIF	1026
Pte A. Jackson	AIF	561
Gnr J. H. Kavanagh	AIF	12736
Cpl C. A. Seymour	AIF	3939
Sgt J. Arbuthnot	Ammn. Col., AFA	6911
Tpr E. H. Combe- Robinson	Yeomanry	992
Tpr J. Lennox	Yeomanry	623
Pte J. P. Davies	R.W.F.	17182

DECEMBER 1916

Pte M. Campbell	AIF	1924
Pte E.J. Brooks	AIF	2787
Pte S. E. Baker	AIF	5059
Pte J. W. Lovett	AIF	1680
Pte F. Jess	AIF	3953
Pte R. C. Hooper	AIF	1779
Pte W. J. Wade	AIF	3602
Lce-Cpl D. Stuart	AIF	682
Pte R. Kay	AIF	2712
Pte F. Flynn	AIF	1185
Pte F.C. Moore	AIF	1867
Pte J. Harrison	AIF	3842
Bombr S. Hulme	AIF	2842
Pte B. F. Baird	AIF	3762
Dvr J. Nisbet	AFA	986
Cpl H. A. Allen	AIF	2340
Pte F. Gray	AIF	2279
Pte T. B. Pole	Aus. Field Amblnce	1828
Pte J. Walters	AIF	754
Pte W. T. Fryer	AIF	3043
Pte F. K. Andersen	AIF	4356
Gnr W. Matthew	AIF	11359
Pte H. W. Love	AIF	1786
Tpr L. Taylor	ALH	1951
Pte J. McNabb	AIF	5412
Pte D. W. Goodall	NZ Inf	6/1855
Pte E. Treloar	AIF	35
Pte F. A. Thomas	AIF	3950
Pte S.A. Ellis	AIF	2458
Gnr E. Hayes	AFA	7385
Pte H. G. Holiday	AIF	1671
Pte H. Fisher	AIF	4422
Cpl F. Lemmon	AFA	4617
Spr E. Stonehouse	Aus. Tun. Company	4789
Pte L. Everett-Norton	AIF	1808
Pte G.E. Rowe	AIF	3206
Pte W. J. Parker	AIF	2510
Pte F. Lawler	AIF	1975
Pte W. A. Clifton	AIF	4391
Pte T. L. Hansen	AIF	1737
Pte D. K. Corderoy	AIF	4763
Pte H. C. Hollingworth	AIF	2382
Pte W. Warrender	AIF	3665
Pte A. Yapp	AMG Company	92
Pte J. Symonds	AIF	1741
Pte J. Caffery	AIF	2607
Pte B. Francis	AAMC	1589
Sgt G. C. Bradshaw	AFA	1956
Pte H. W. Shean	AIF	4202

Cpl J. A. Davis	AIF	1207
Pte J. O. Swift	AIF	2356
Pte F. G. Hull	AIF	4576
Pte W. Rogers	AIF	5485
Pte C. A. Wyndow	AIF	4790
Lce-Cpl C. W. Revell	AIF	2821
Pte H. Hollis	AIF	1551
Pte E. Blundell	AIF	2876
Pte A.O. Neill	AIF	4741
Pte E. Sterch	AIF	4776
Pte C. M. Smith	AIF	5765
Pte C. T. Smith	AIF	5183
Pte W. K. Yeates	AIF	2486
Pte E. A. Plunkett	AIF	4509
Bombr F. Corder	AFA	1736
Pte A. J. C. Frewin	AIF	5393
Pte E. T. Bone	AIF	2294
Pte L. G. Hewitt	AIF	4449
Pte W. P. Price	AIF	1980
Pte F. J. Burgess	AIF	2591
Pte J. B. Yates	AIF	4550
Pte A. Smithers	AIF	4244
Pte R. J. McWaters	AIF	4799
Pte M. Bazzina	AMG Company	4431
Pte G. Saville	AIF	4182
Pte H. Sievwright	AIF	4768
Pte T. A. Smith	AMG Company	2256
Pte J. H. Knevitt	AIF	4509
Pte G. B. Bradd	AIF	3385
Pte T. Chinnock	AIF	4622
Lce-Cpl E. J. Lorentzen	AIF	1736
Pte L. R. Farndon	AIF	1026
Pte A. Jackson	AIF	561
Gnr J. R. Kavanah	AFA	12736
Cpl C. A. Seymour	AIF	3939
Sgt J. Arbuthnot	AFA	6911
Pte H. P. Blake	AIF	2111
Cpl R. D. Alford	AIF	4356
Pte J. Hanley	AIF	1546
Gnr E. P. Owens	AFA	2819
Pte S. Peterson	AIF	3607
Dvr F. Williams	DAC	3507
Pte A. A. Cameron	AIF	3263
Pte F. Barry	AIF	441
Pte G. F. Osborne	AIF	4243
Pte W. A. Johnson	AIF	5128
Cpl G. W. Bayliss	AIF	1946
Sgt H. F. Murray	AIF	238
Pte W. C. Freak	AIF	3696
Cpl T. Barr	AFA	1072
Pte G. F. Brighton	AIF	1220
Pte A. G. Newman	AIF	6056
Pte R. C. Munro	AIF	3586
Pte D. Hay	AIF	264
Pte A. M. Dingwall	AIF	649
Gnr A. H. C. Whitrow	AFA	3529
Pte R. Barnard	AIF	5044
Pte A. W. Williams	AIF	5464
Lce-Cpl W. Bickford	AIF	1716
Gnr A. G. Brisbane	AFA	3479
Pte A. L. Chenhall	AIF	250
Pte F. Berrisford	AIF	1803
Lce-Cpl R. Mills	AIF	30
Pte A. Hogan	AIF	5400
Pte W. Dale	AIF	4216
Cpl J. V. Miers	TMB	3364
Pte J. Cowan	AIF	616a
Sgt V. Powell	Anzac C. Corps	1183
Pte H. M. McCaughey	AIF	1898
Spr E. Rae	Aus Engineers	5193
Pte W. Logan	AIF	5143
Pte J. A. Smith	AAMC	8560
Pte J. E. Edmunds	AIF	3080
Pte W. G. Swan	AIF	3307
Dvr F. C. Smith	AFA	2807
Pte H. V. Barnes	AAMC	6573
Pte J. Lyons	AIF	462
Pte J. Summons	ALF	2004
Dvr J. W. Kent	AASC	11803
Pte F. D. O'Neill	AIF	4241
Pte F. W. Burton	AIF	3479
Pte F. A. Pullen	AAMC	149
Lce-Cpl J. S. Dixon	AIF	2360
Tpr J. Lennox	Yeomanry	623
Pte J. P. Davies	RWF	17182

JANUARY 1917

Pte M. Campbell	AIF	1924
Pte R. C. Hooper	AIF	1779
Pte J. Harrison	AIF	3842
Lce-Cpl D. Stuart	AIF	682
Pte F. Flynn	AIF	1185
Bombr S. Hulme	AIF	2842
Dr J. Nisbet	AFA	986
Corpl H. A. Allen	AFA	2340
Pte H. W. Love	AFA	1768
Tpr L. Taylor	Anzac Mtd Regt	1951
Pte J. McNabb	A.I.F	5412
Pte D. W. Goodall	Canterbury Inf Batt	6/1855
Pte F. A. Thomas	AIF	3950
Pte W. Warrender	AIF	3065
Pte A. Yapp	AMG Co	92

Pte H.W. Shean	AIF	4202
Pte J. O. Swift	AIF	2356
Pte A. J. E. Frewin	AIF	5393
Pte E. T. Bone	AIF	2294
Pte L. G. Hewitt	AIF	4449
Pte W. P. Price	AIF	1980
Pte J. B. Yates	AIF	4550
Pte R. J. McWalters	AIF	4779
Pte M. Bazzina	AMG Co	4431
Pte H. Sievwright	AIF	4768
Pte J. A. Smith	AMG Co	2256
Pte J H. Knevitt	AIF	4509
Pte G.B. Bradd	AIF	3385
Pte T. Climnock	AIF	4622
Lce-Cpl E. J. Lorentzen	AIF	1737
Pte L.R. Farndon	AIF	1026
Pte A. Jackson	AIF	561
Gnr J.R. Kavanagh	AFA	12736
Pte H.P. Blake	AIF	2111
Cpl R.D.Alford	AIF	4356
Pte J. Hanley	AIF	1546
Pte S. Peterson	A. Pioneers	3607
Dvr F. Williams	AFA	3507
Pte A. A. Cameron	AIF	3263
Pte F. Barry	AIF	441
Pte G.F. Osbourne	AIF	4243
Pte W. A. Johnson	AIF	5128
Cpl G. W. Bayliss	AFA	1946
Sgt H. F. Murray	AIF	238
Pte W. C. Freak	AIF	3096
Cpl T. Barr	AFA	1072
Pte G. F. Brighton	AIF	1220
Pte A.G. Newman	AIF	6056
Pte R. C. Munro	AIF	3585
Pte D. Hay	AIF	264
Pte A. M. Dingwall	AIF	640
Pte R. Barnard	AIF	5044
Pte A. W. Williams	AIF	5464
Gnr A. G. Brisbane	AFA	3479
Pte A. L. Chenhall	AIF	250
Pte F. Berrisford	AIF	1803
Lce-Cpl R. Mills	AIF	30
Pte A. Hogan	AIF	5400
Pte W. Dale	AIF	4216
Cpl J. V. Miers	AIF	3364
Pte J. Cowan	AIF	616a
Pte E. J. Brooks	Pioneer Batt	2787
Pte E. S. McPhee	AIF	1034
Sgt V. Powell	Anzac Cycling Batt	1183
Pte H. M. McCaughey	Pioneer Batt	1898
Spr E. Rae	Aust Engineers	5198
Pte W. Logan	AIF	5143
Pte J. A. Smith	AAMC	8560
Pte J. E. Edmunds	AIF	3080
Dvr F. C. Smith	AFA	2807
Pte H. V. Barnes	AAMC	6573
Pte J. Lyons	AIF	462
Pte J. Summons	AIF	2004
Dvr J.W. Kent	AFA	11803
Pte F. D. O'Neill	AIF	4241
Pte F.W. Burton	AIF	3479
Pte F.A. Pullen	AAMC	149
Lce-Cpl J. S. Dixon	AIF	2360
Pte H.G. Streader	AIF	4205
Pte W.J. Sirl	AIF	4195
Pte E. J. Slattery	AIF	4491
Spr F.C. Miller	A. Mining Corps.	2763
Dvr F. C. Lamb	AFA	26927
Pte J. W. Fairclough	AIF	5696
Pte W. H. Palmer	AIF	3282
Pte A. Hutchinson	AIF	2667
Pte G. White	AIF	5475
Pte W. Clarke	AIF	5069
Pte H. V. Mitchell	AIF	3828
Pte H. T. Scott	AIF	1670
Pte J. D. Williams	AIF	4618
Pte W. O. Sleeman	AIF	1325
Pte W. Wray	AIF	5692
Pte H. A. Crotty	AIF	2908
Lce-Cpl W. Bickford	AIF	1716
Pte J. P. Davies	RWF	17182

FEBRUARY 1917

Pte M. Campbell	AIF	1924
Lce-Cpl D. Stuart	AIF	682
Pte F. Flynn	AIF	1185
Cpl H.A. Allen	AIF	2340
Pte H.W. Love	AIF	1768
Pte T. E. Bone	AIF	2294
Pte L.G. Hewitt	AIF	4449
Pte J. B. Yates	AIF	4550
Pte H. Sievwright	AIF	4768
Pte J. H. Knevitt	AIF	4509
Lce-Cpl E. J. Lorentzen	AIF	1737
Pte L. R. Farndon	AIF	1026
Pte E. S. McPhee	AIF	1034
Pte A. Jackson	AIF	561
Sgt H. F. Murray	AIF	238
Pte W. Dale	AIF	4216
Pte J. Cowan	AIF	616a
Pte E. J. Brooks	Pioneer Bn	2787
Pte H. M. McCaughey	Pioneer Bn	1898

Pte J. E. Edmunds	AIF	3080
Pte G. White	AIF	5475
Pte H.V. Mitchell	AIF	3828
Pte J. D. Williams	AIF	4618
Pte W.O. Sleeman	AIF	1325
Pte W. Wray	AIF	5692
Gnr A.H.C. Whitrow	AFA	3529

MARCH 1917

Pte M. Campbell	AIF	1924
Lce-Cpl D. Stuart	AIF	682
Pte F. Flynn	AIF	1185
Cpl H. A. Allen	AIF	2340
Pte H. W. Love	AIF	1768
Pte T. E. Bone	AIF	2294
Pte L. G. Hewitt	AIF	4449
Pte J. B. Yates	AIF	4550
Pte H. Sievwright	AIF	4768
Pte J. H. Knevitt	AIF	4509
Pte E. S. McPhee	AIF	1034
Lce-Cpl E. J. Lorentzen	AIF	1737
Pte L. R. Farndon	AIF	1026
Pte A. Jackson	AIF	561
Sgt H. F. Murray	AIF	238
Gnr A. H. C. Whitrow	AIF	3529
Pte W. Dale	AIF	4216
Pte E. J. Brooks	Pioneer Bn	2787
Pte H. M. McCaughey	Pioneer Bn	1898
Pte J. E. Edmunds	AIF	3080
Pte G. White	AIF	5475
Pte J. D. Williams	AIF	4618
Pte W. O. Sleeman	AIF	1325
Pte W. Wray	AIF	5692
Pte J. Cowan	AIF	616a
Pte H.V. Mitchell	AIF	3828
Pte H.T. Downie	AIF	5011
Pte J. Thompson	AAMC	2078
Pte L. Fox	AIF	3524a
Pte W.J. Cunningham	AIF	3075
Pte B. Nixon	AIF	5730
Pte J. G. Hempshall	AIF	4815
Pte W.E.H. Nicholls	AIF	2757
Pte L.C. Brady	AIF	3023
Pte V.J. Mitchell	AIF	5731
Pte J. Cady	AIF	5060
Cpl G.A. Durrant	AIF	5562
Pte S. McNiven	AIF	378
Pte T.M.M. Morrison	AIF	5735
Pte P.L. Murdock	AIF	2501
Pte W. Hartill	AIF	876
Pte H. Lille	AIF	2177
Gnr L.G. Brownfield	AFA	2184
Pte J. R. Iremonger	AIF	3135
Pte W. H. Fletcher	AIF	1664
Pte T. Mahoney	AIF	5900
Pte T. Fox	AIF	1635a
Pte G. Sherlock	AIF	2801
Cpl D. Wood	AIF	978
Cpl D. Guest	AIF	2383
Pte H. A. Loftus	AIF	4151
Pte M. Milan	AIF	6324
Sgt W. M. Wood	AIF	491
Pte W.C. Craig	Pioneer Bn	2303
RSM J.S. Old	AIF	489
Pte H. S. Gibbons	AIF	5088
Pte S. Mahoney	AIF	2194
Pte E. S. Curnon	AIF	1701
Pte E. L. Bennett	AIF	3074
Pte J. W. Smith	AIF	2454
Pte E. S. Nation	AIF	2201
Spr H. L. Segerbind	A Engineers	7100
Dvr J. Bowell	AASC	7114
Lce-Cpl C. N. Tamlin	AIF	2770
Pte G. Todd	A Cyclist Corps.	4924
Pte J. Cummings	AIF	5356
Pte L. A. Holdoni	AIF	4800
Pte H. Rees	AIF	1075
Pte C. B. Douglas	AAMC	3762
Pte J. A. Thompson	AIF	5934

APRIL 1917

Lce-Cpl D. Stuart	682
Pte F. Flynn	1185
Pte H.W. Love	1768
Pte H. Sievwright	4768
Lce-Cpl E. J. Lorentzen	1737
Pte A. Jackson	561
Pte W. Dale	4216
Pte H. V Mitchell	3828
Pte H. T. Downie	5011
Pte J. Thompson, AMC	2678
Pte L. Fox	3524a
Pte W. J. Cunningham	3075
Pte G. B. Nixon	5730
Pte J. G. Hempsall	4815
Pte W. E. H. Nicholls	2757
Pte L. C. Brady	3023
Pte V. J. Mitchell	5731
Pte J. Cady	5060
Pte G. A. Durrant	5562
Pte S. McNiven	378

Pte T. N. M. Morrison	5735
Pte P. L Murdock	2501
Pte W. Hartill	876
Pte H. Lille, L.M.G.	2177
Gnr L.G. Brownfield, Artillery	2184
Pte J. R. Isemonger	3135
Pte W. H. Fletcher	1664
Cpl D. Guest	2383
Pte M. Nilan	6324
Sgt W. M. Wood	491
Pte W. C. Craig, Pioneers	2303
RSM J. S. Old	489
Pte H. O. S. Gibbons	5088
Pte S. Mahoney	2194
Pte E. L. Bennett, Pioneers	3074
Pte J. W. Smith	2454
Pte E. C. Nation	2201
Dvr J. Bowell A.S.C.	7114
Pte G. Todd, Aust. Cyclist Corps.	4924
Pte J. Cummings	5356
Pte H. Rees, Aust. Cyclist Corps.	1075
Pte C. B. Douglas, A.M.C.	3762
Pte J. A. Thompson	5934
Cpl B. Smith	5196
Pte K. Macrow	4363
Pte J. Couttie	2604
Dvr A. S. Fleming	7316
Pte A. Crowfoot, A.S.C.	2639
Lce-Cpl J. Gartrell, A.M.C.	10253
Temp. Sgt E. Robinson	4886
Cpl F. H. Dowell	1375
Dvr A. V. Shead, A.F.A	7859
Pte W. M. Marshall	5383
Pte H. Bolton	2112
Dvr E. Green, AFA	1365
Pte A. H. Smith-Finkell	5825
Sgt F. R. Dow	5364
Pte A. W. Reid	3622
Lce-Sgt A. C. Julian	28
Pte T. McNamara	1696
Pte W. T. Carey	4149a
Pte P. Seager	2741
Pte W. W. Lillywhite	2712
Cpl W. H. Lenowry	2398
Pte H. Adams	1613
Pte E. Sutton	3639
Pte D. Kingsley	4022
Pte A. E. Hickson	872
Pte W. J. Scott	4916
Sgt N. H. Watson	995
Pte M. D. Townsend	2988a
Pte J. O'Reilly	2196
Pte R. C. Unstead	5107
Lce-Cpl E. R. C. Halliday	2380
Pte A. W. G. Skeates	3887
Pte A. J. Miller	2704
Pte G. W. Julian	2918
Pte W. E. White	2750
Pte J. W. Bankier	972
Pte J. S. Henderson	1670
Pte R. R. Roberts	5427
Pte E. C. Lahey	1933
Pte W. Donnelly	2538
Pte R. H. Hamilton	2606
Pte W. Cunningham	6358
Pte O. O. Upton	6817
Pte W. J. Bradford	2393
Cpl T. N. Harvey	4133
Sgt F. E. Cooper	1372
Cpl J. W. Wilkinson	4948
Pte C. W. Smith	2750
Pte H. M. Martin	2680
Pte W. E. Nairn	1706
Pte D. A. MacPherson	4857
Pte G. G. O'Keefe	6855
Pte A. Angus	2102
Pte L. A. Lapworth, A.M.C.	
Pte J. Weir	724
Lce-Cpl H. Jorgensen	5327
Pte A. Drayshaw, Pioneers	2473
Pte T. Donovan	2647
Pte G. G. Smith	3923
Sgt S. Pleming Machine. Gn. Corps	637
Pte J. C. W. Affleck	282
Pte H. H. Phillips	5136
Pte O. Marron	1958
Pte R. Strange	3469
Pte F. Robinson	2235
Pte J.G. Phillips, Machine Gn. Corps	217
Cpl H. White	2032
Pte J. Jarvis	3494
Lce-Cpl W. Harford, Mchne Gn. Corps	1380
Cpl J. Kelly, Machine Gn. Corps	1612
Pte W. J. Crawford	2158
Pte F. N. Drever	2613
Pte P. S. Newport	4868
Pte N. MacFarlane	5698
Cpl K. McDonald	807
Cpl H. G. Finger	2381
Pte A. Barrow	5042
Pte G. O'Reilly	4582
Pte A. S. Evans	5649
Pte W. Thompson	2265
Pte E. Hobson	6273
Cpl E. B. McLure	2760
Pte J. B. Beyer	994

MAY 1917

Lance-Corporal Douglas Stuart 682
Private H. W. Love 1768
Private H. Sievwright 4768
Private A. Jackson 561
Private V. J. Mitchell 5731
Gunner L. Brownfield, AFA 2184
Corporal Darcy Guest 2383
RSM John S. Old 489
Private T. N.M. Morrison 5735
Private John Cummings 5356
Private Lawson Fox 3524a
Corporal Bert Smith 5196
Private Keith Macrow 4363
Private John Couttte 2604
Driver Alex. Fleming, A.S.C. 7316
Private Arthur Crowfoot 2639
Lance-Corporal James Gartrell, A.M.C. 10253
Temp. Sergeant Edward Robinson 4886
Corporal Frederick H. Dowell 1375
Driver Arthur V. Shead, AFA 7859
Private Wilfred M. Marshall 5383
Private Henry Bolton 2112
Driver Edward Green, AFA 1365
Private Albert H. Smith-Finkell 5825
Sergeant Frank R. Dow 5364
Private Alfred N. Reid 3622
Lance-Sergeant Arthur C. Julian 28
Private Thos. McNamara 1696
Private William T. Carey 4149A
Private Percy Seager 2741
Private William W. Lillywhite 2712
Corporal William H. Lenowry 2398
Private Henry Adams 1613
Private Edward Sutton 3639
Private Daniel Kingsley 4022
Private Albert E. Hickson 872
Private William J. Scott 4196
Sergeant Norman H. Watson 995
Private Mark D. Townsend 2988A
Private James O'Reilly 2196
Private Rupert C. Unstead 510
Lance-Corporal Edwin R. C. Halliday 2380
Private Alfred W. G. Skeates 3887
Private Arthur J. Miller 2704
Private Garnet W. Julian 2918
Private William E. White 2750
Private John W. Bankier 72
Private John S. Henderson 1670
Private Richard H. Roberts 5427
Private Edward C. Lahey 1933
Private William Donnelly 2538
Private Richard H. Hamilton 2666
Private William Cunningham 6358
Private Oswald O. Upton 6718
Private William J. Bradford .2393
Corporal Thomas N. Harvey 4133
Sergeant Frank E. Cooper 1372
Corporal John W. Wilkinson 4948
Private Charles W. Smith 2750
Private Henry M. Martin 2680
Private Walter E. Nairn 1706
Private Dugdale A. Macpherson 4857
Private George G. O'Keefe 6855
Private Archibald Angus 2102
Private Leslie A. Lapworth, A.M.C. 3159
Private Jack Weir 724
Lance-Corporal Henry Jorgensen 5327
Private Albert Brayshaw, Pioneers 2473
Private Timothy Donovan 2647
Private George G. Smith 3923
Sergeant Simon Pleming, Machine-Gun Corps. 637
Private James C. W. Affleck 282
Private Herbert H. Phillips 5136
Private Octavius Marron 1958
Private Richard Strange 3469
Private Frederick Robinson 2253
Private John G. Phillips, Machine-Gun Corps. 217
Corporal Herbert White 2032
Private John Jarvis 3494
Lance-Corporal William Harford, Machine-Gun Corps. 1038
Corporal James Kelly, Machine-Gun Corps.1612
Private William J. Crawford 2158
Private Frederick N. Drever 2610
Private Percy S. Newport 4868
Private Neil McFarlane 5698
Corporal Keith McDonald 807
Corporal Herbert G. Finger 2381
Private Alfred Barrow 5042
Private Gerald O'Reilly 4582
Private Arthur S. Evans 5649
Private William Thompson 2265
Private Edward Hobson 6373
Private Ernest R. McLure 2760
Private John R. Beyer 994
Private Ebb Christianson 36
Private Wilfred Jenner 6280
Private Herbert C. Stevens 3883
Private William Beckett 3239
Private Henry O. Murphy 2190
Corporal James McConnell 886
Private Ernest W. Orchard, Pioneers 2694

Private Hugh J. McAlister 5868
Private David J. McKinley. Machine-Gun Corps 3206
Lance-Corporal Thomas Markham 4194
Private Claude Wilson 4328
Private Eric Turley, T.M.By. 9477
Private Arthur Crossley 2238
Private Percy W. Green 161
Private Phillip Jay 6295
Private Arthur W. Broughton 5299
Private Walter A. Linkins 931B
Private Arthur A. Glasby 1680
Private Herbert Dean 843
Private William Davis 1905
Private James W. Brooks, Pioneers 2130
Private William J. Cooke 6398
Private Vincent W. Smith 2787
Private Maurice H. Hawkins 5101
Lance-Corporal Frank Worley 4561
Private Cecil Mitchell 468
Private Sydney T. Moore 3160
Private Horace Cliff 748
Private William Mullally 6063
Private John Greenwood 4113
Private Alfred Brown 3696
Private Joseph Belson 6460
Private Wilfred Bowden 2236
Private George Brown 4744
Private Norman A. Simpson 320
Gunner Fred Ross, AFA 9970
Gunner James A. Smith, A.F.A 2748
Private Roy Brown 2299
Private George Smith, Pioneers 2447

JUNE 1917

Pte H. W. Love 1768
Pte H. Sievwright 4768
Pte L. Fox 3524
Cpl Alf. Smith 5196
Pte K. Macrow 4363
Pte J. Couttie 2604
Driver A. S. Fleming 7316
Pte A. Crowfoot 2639
Sergt F. R. Dow 5364
Lance-Sergt A. C. Julian 28
Pte Percy Seager 2741
Pte W. W. Lillywhite 2712
Cpl W. H. Lenowry 2398
Pte Hy. Adams 1613
Pte S. Sutton 3639
Pte M. D. Townsend 2988A
Pte A. W. G. Skeates 3887
Pte A. J. Miller 2704
Pte G. W. Julian 2918
Pte Wm. E. White 2750
Pte Rd. H. Hamilton 2666
Pte Wm. Cunningham 6358
Cpl T. N. Harvey 4133
Sergt F. E. Cooper 1372
Lance-Cpl H. Jorgensen 532 7
Pte J. C. W. Affleck 282
Pte O. Marron 1958
Pte Richard Strange 3469
Pte Fredk. Robinson 2235
Pte J. G. Phillips 217
Cpl Herbert White 2032
Pte John Jarvis 3494
Lance-Cpl Wm. Harford 1038
Cpl Jas. Kelly 1612
Pte Wm. J. Crawford 2158
Pte P. S. Newport 4868
Pte Neil McFarlane 5098
Cpl H. Finger 2381
Pte Alf. Barrow 5042
Pte Arthur Evans 5049
Pte Wm. Thompson 2265
Pte John R. Beyer 994
Pte E. Christianson 36
Pte Wm. Beckett 3239
Pte H. J. McAlister 5868
Pte C. L. W. Wilson 4328
Pte Eric Turley 9477
Pte Percy W. Green 161
Pte Philip Jay 6295
Pte A. W. Broughton 5299
Pte W. A. Limkins 931B
Pte A. A. Glasby 1680
Pte Herbert Dean 843
Pte Wm. Davis 1905
Pte Jas. W. Brooks 2130
Pte Wm. J. Cook 6398
Pte V. W. Smith 2787
Pte M. H. Hawkins 5101
Lance-Cpl F. Morley 4561
Pte Cecil Mitchell 468
Pte Sydney Moore 8160
Pte Horace Cliff 748
Pte Wm. Mullally 6063
Pte Jno(sic). Greenwood 4113
Pte Alfred Brown 3696
Pte Joseph Belson 6460
Pte Wilfred Bowden 2236
Pte Geo. Brown 4744
Pte N. Simpson 320

Gunner Fredk. Ross	9970
Gunner James Smith	2748
Pte Roy Brown	2299
Pte Geo. Smith	2447
Cpl Thos. N. Harvey	4133

JULY 1917

Pte H. Sievwright	4678
Cpl Bert Smith	5196
Pte Keith Macrow	4363
Pte John Couttie	2604
Pte Arthur Crowfoot	2639
Pte Percy Seager	2741
Cpl William H. Lenowry	2398
Pte Edward Sutton	3639
Pte Alf. W. Skeater	3887
Pte Arthur J. Miller	2704
Pte Wm. E. White	2750
Pte Fredk. Robinson	2235
Cpl Herbert White	2032
Pte Percy S. Newport	4868
Cpl Herbert J. Finger	2381
Pte Arthur S. Evans	5649
Pte Wm. Thompson	2265
Pte John R. Beyer	994
Pte Walter A. Linkins	931b
Pte Herbert Dean	843
Pte Wm. Davis	1905
Pte Jas. W. Brooks	2130
Pte Horace Cliffs	748
Pte Wm. Mullally	6063
Pte John Greenwood	1255
Pte Joseph Belson	6460
Cpl Thos. N. Harvey	4133
Pte Henry H. Holley	5971
Pte Geo. Fredricksen	4932
Pte Thos. M. Bustin	811
Lce-Cpl Norman Hibbert	2924
Pte Hubt. J. Giblett	3149
Sgt A. J. Sutcliffe	2873
Pte Wm. J. Davis	5683
Pte Alb. V. Coe	2313
Pte Adolph A. Drager	3506
Pte Wm. Hilleard	2704
Pte Felix J. Hamilton	4072
Pte Stanley W. Batten	1036
Pte John A. Gray	3161
Sapper James Bradbury	6872
Pte Stanley Gers	5364
Pte Charles Evans	6183
Pte Richard E. Church	2391
Pte John A. Berry	5794
Pte Wm. R. Kennedy	6377
Pte Reuben Finch	6995
Pte A. W. Fitzpatrick	4490
Lce-Cpl Chas. Smedley	6086
Pte Henry Buchanan	2535
Pte Walter S. Neale	6452
Trooper Geo. Fitzgerald	2884
Pte Peter J. Monahan	3175
Pte Chas. O. Anderson	429
Pte Phillip Brown	2771
Pte R. E. Harrison	2163
Pte Claude Oliver	712
Pte Fredk. C. Randall	6407
Pte Edward N. Stuckey	2386
Lce-Cpl Patrick McLeod	918
Driver Chas. J. Baker	9907
Pte Alb. Geoghegan	2900
Pte Ernest Wells	6845
Pte Terence Wilson	2431
Pte A. D. Simpson	2732
Lce-Cpl Montague Miller	6289
Pte Wm. H. Morrison	2451
Pte W. J. Golley	1133

AUGUST 1917

Pte Keith Macrow	4363
Pte J. Couttie	2604
Pte Percy Seager	2741
Cpl Wm. H. Lenowry	2398
Pte A. W. G. Skeates	3887
Pte Arthur J. Miller	2704
Pte Wm E. White	2750
Pte Fredk. Robinson	2235
Cpl Herbert White	2032
Pte Wm. Thompson	2265
Pte Walter A. Linkins	931b
Pte Herbert Dean	843
Pte Wm. Davis	1905
Pte Horace Cliff	3160
Pte Jos. Belson	6460
Pte Henry H. Holley	5971
Pte Geo. Fredricksen	4932
Pte Thos. M. Bustin	811
Lce-Cpl Norman Hibbert	2924
Pte Hubert J. Giblett	3149
Sergt A. J. Sutcliffe	2873
Pte Wm. J. Davis	5683
Pte Alb. V. Coe	2313
Pte Adolph L. Drager	3506
Pte Wm. Hilleard	2704

Pte Felix J. Hamilton	4072
Pte Stanley W. Batten	1036
Pte Jas. A. Gray	3161
Sapper Jas. Bradbury	6872
Pte Stanley Gers	5364
Pte Chas. Evans	6183
Pte Richard E. Church	2391
Pte J. A. Berry	5794
Pte Wm. B. Kennedy	6377
Pte Reuben Finch	6995
Pte A. W. Fitzpatrick	4490
Lce-Cpl Chas. Smedley	6086
Pte Henry Buchanan	2535
Pte, Walter S. Neale	6452
Trooper Geo. Fitzgerald	2884
Pte Peter J. Monahan	3175
Pte Chas. O. Anderson	429
Pte Phillip Brown	2771
Pte R. E. Harrison	2163
Pte Claude Oliver	712
Pte Fredk. C. Randall	6407
Pte Edwd. N. Stuckey	2386
Lce-Cpl Patrick McLeod	918
Driver Chas. J. Baker	9907
Pte Alb. Geoghegan	2900
Pte Ernest Wells	6485
Pte Terence Wilson	2431
Pte A. D. Simpson	2732
Lce-Cpl Montague Miller	6289
Pte Wm. H. Morrison	2451
Pte Samuel J. Golley	1133
Pte Chas. B. Cass	934
Pte Ernest Allchurch	30
Pte Patrick F. Smith	1101
Sgt Colin T. Mills	2835
Pte Wm. Canneen	2432
Pte Reuben L. Cannon	2928
Gunner Vincent McManus	2373
Gunner Wm. Corfield	9894
Driver Sidney Rosevear	22444
Sgt R. E. Shankland	4271
Trooper Ormond Footit	717
Pte Wm. Bond	1799
Pte Allen Wallace	2910
Pte Andrew Johnson	3239
Pte Percy Smith	731
Pte Jas. McPherson	1908
Pte Geo. Gauntlett	2643
Pte Jno. Knight	462
Pte David Miller	6318
Pte Bert Akers	5029
Pte Clarence King	1660a
Cpl Jas. Bice	2790
Pte Jas. Hembrow	1154
Pte Leslie C. Handel	6107
Pte J. P. Black	2191
Pte Wm. A. Botten	3285a
Pte Leslie Featonby	709
Cpl L. Kenniburgh	4538
Pte Roy Latts	2354
Pte Rudolph Schreiver	378
Bomb Chas. E. Gartrell	26982
Bomb David A. Worland	5406
Pte Reginald Alderson	727
Pte James Hay	3564
Driver Gerald Maling	10444
Gunner Edwd. C. Bostock	1692
Pte Geo. J. Tracy	5349
Sapper Henry N. Hale	3345
Pte Stanley J. Owens	146
Pte Owen O'Keefe	2753
Pte Richard Sams	2727
Pte Geo. Tratt	1792
Pte Henry B. Stewart	6603
Pte Robert Fuhrstrom	1701
Cpl Jas. S. Hasthorpe	1929
Sapper Wm. A. Troughton	14689
Sapper Chas. Walker	14493
Pte J. E. Bennett	402
Pte Walter Smith	2680
Driver Ernest L. Horne	14518
Lce-Cpl Roy Olifent	809
Pte Alb. Rowe	362
Gunner Roy Maher	2228
Pte Fredk. Pendall	3028
Pte Thos. H. Nelson	7055
Pte Fredk. Winkler	4930
Driver Wm. E. Denness	10400

SEPTEMBER 1917

Pte Percy Seager	2741
Cpl Wm. H. Lenowry	2398
Pte A. W. G. Skeates	3887
Pte Wm E. White	2750
Cpl Herbert White	2032
Pte Wm. Thompson	2265
Pte Herbert Dean	843
Pte Horace Cliff	748
Pte Geo. Fredricksen	4932
Pte Thos. M. Bustin	811
Pte Hubert J. Giblett	3149
Pte Alb. V. Coe	2313
Pte Adolph L. Drager	3506
Pte Wm. Hilleard	2704

Pte A. Gray	3161
Sapper Jas. Bradbury	6872
Pte Reuben Finch	6995
Pte Walter S. Neale	6452
Trooper Geo. Fitzgerald	2884
Pte Peter J. Monahan	3175
Pte Chas. O. Anderson	429
Pte Phillip Brown	2771
Pte Fredk. C. Randall	6407
Pte Terence Wilson	2431
Pte Chas. B. Cass	934
Pte Ernest Allchurch	30
Pte Patrick F. Smith	1101
Sgt Colin T. Mills	2835
Pte Reuben L. Cannon	2928
Gunner Wm. Corfield	9894
Sgt R. E. Shankland	4271
Trooper Ormond Footit	717
Pte Percy Smith	731
Pte Jas. McPherson	1908
Pte Geo. Gauntlett	2643
Pte David Miller	6318
Pte Leslie C. Handel	6107
Pte Wm. A. Botten	3285a
Pte Leslie Featonby	709
Cpl L. Kenniburgh	4538
Pte R. Schreiver	378
Bomb Chas. E. Gartrell	26982
Bomb David A. Worland	5406
Pte Reginald Alderson	727
Pte James Hay	3564
Driver Gerald Malling	10444
Pte Geo. J. Tracy	5349
Sapper Henry N. Hale	3345
Pte Stanley J. Owens	146
Pte Owen O'Keefe	2753
Pte Henry B. Stewart	6603
Pte Robert Fuhrstrom	1701
Cpl J. S. Hasthorpe	1629
Sapper Wm. A. Troughton	14689
Pte J.P. Black	2191
Sapper Chas. Walker	14493
Pte J. E. Bennett	402
Pte Walter Smith	2680
Driver Ernest L. Horne	14518
Lce-Cpl Roy Olifent	809
Pte Alb. Rowe	362
Gunner Roy Maher	2228
Pte Thos. H. Nelson	7055
Pte Fredk. Winkler	4930
Driver Wm. E. Denness	10400
Pte Fredk. Saunders	976
Pte Selby Hoddy	2582
Gunner Geo. H. Haywood	643
Pte Fredk. Saunders	976
Pte Alf. Harris	6511
Signaller R. A. Wrightman	6180
Gunner Ray Wortley	2088
Pte Milton Griffin	6983
Pte Alb. T. Duke	6391
Pte Cecil Workman	6412
Lce-Cpl Wm. H. Power	4320
Lce-Cpl Wm. H. Rooney	6034
Lce-Cpl Norman McDonald	5121
Sergt Claude Sewell	1771
Lce-Cpl Alb. Job	3817
Pte Chas. B. Furness	B377a
Cpl Richard W. Williams	1925
Pte Malcolm Melvin	2614a
Pte Robt- Gordon	5582
Pte Henry J. Lewis	6349
Pte Ronald Sloman	6666
Pte Leo. W. Regan	6815
Pte Samuel H. Irwin	3853
Pte Ralph Phillips	1799
Pte Jno. A. Prout	635a
Pte Wm. Haggerty	4135
Pte Chas. H. Wright	14653
Lce-Cpl Chas. R. Perrim	2747
Pte Chas. R. Thompson	1998
Sergt Jno. P. Williams	5465
Pte Arthur Broughton	5299
Lce-Cpl Alb. W. Harvison	6457
Pte Wm. J. Lawrence	6527
Sergt Fredk. Gilbert	852
Pte Tubal (sic) Ph. Bush	5649
Lce-Cpl H. Townsend	2019
Pte Wm. H. Wilson	3000
Pte Jas. Anderson	4012
Gunner G. Ryan	2156
Pte Jno. J. Dunne	2619
Pte Lionel V. Roberts	6178
Pte Thos. W. Morgan	5884
Driver Wm. McElroy	2414
Sapper Alex. Petroff	2360
Sergt Leslie Whiting	1432
Pte Herbert P. Lee	2930
Gunner Eric N. Hewitt	30268
Pte Daniel O'Mara	5446
Pte Alf. E. McEwen	2215
Pte Alec Dawson	2398
Pte Jack Diamond	3138
Lce-Cpl Norman Roberrs	8099
Cpl Alb. O'Dowse	1191
Pte Allan McPherson	2226
Pte Ernest Pennells	6096

Gunner Harry Moss	10276
Sergt Samuel F. Cooling	3261
Pte Wm. H. Carroll	3125
Sergt H. Brakenridge	4738
Pte Jas. H. Gray	813
Pte Alb. Ely	3097
Driver Thos. Sharp	6159
Pte Wm. R. McCartney	2225
Pte Matthew Anderson	3101
Driver Chas. Saunders	1979
Sapper Chas. H. Anderson	3263
Pte Daniel Thornton	3543